OXFORD MONOGRAPHS ON
LABOUR LAW

General Editors: Paul Davies,
Keith Ewing, Mark Freedland

FREEDOM OF SPEECH AND EMPLOYMENT

Oxford Monographs on Labour Law

General Editors: Paul Davies, Cassel Professor of Commercial Law at London School of Economics; Keith Ewing, Professor of Public Law at King's College, London; and Mark Freedland, Fellow of St John's College, and Professor of Law at Oxford University.

This series is the first new development in the literature dealing with labour law for many years. The series recognizes the arrival not only of a renewed interest in labour law generally, but also the need for a fresh approach to the study of labour law following a decade of momentous change in the UK and Europe. The series is concerned with all aspects of labour law, including traditional subjects of study such as industrial relations law and individual employment law, but it will also include books which examine the law and economics of the labour market and the impact of social security law upon patterns of employment and the employment contract.

Titles already published in this series

The Right to Strike
K. D. EWING

Legislating for Conflict
SIMON AUERBACH

Justice in Dismissal
HUGH COLLINS

Pensions, Employment, and the Law
RICHARD NOBLES

Women and the Law
SANDRA FREDMAN

Freedom of Speech and Employment

LUCY VICKERS

OXFORD

UNIVERSITY PRESS

*This book has been printed digitally and produced in a standard specification
in order to ensure its continuing availability*

OXFORD
UNIVERSITY PRESS

Great Clarendon Street, Oxford OX2 6DP

Oxford University Press is a department of the University of Oxford.
It furthers the University's objective of excellence in research, scholarship,
and education by publishing worldwide in

Oxford New York

Auckland Cape Town Dar es Salaam Hong Kong Karachi
Kuala Lumpur Madrid Melbourne Mexico City Nairobi
New Delhi Shanghai Taipei Toronto
With offices in
Argentina Austria Brazil Chile Czech Republic France Greece
Guatemala Hungary Italy Japan South Korea Poland Portugal
Singapore Switzerland Thailand Turkey Ukraine Vietnam

Oxford is a registered trade mark of Oxford University Press
in the UK and in certain other countries

Published in the United States
by Oxford University Press Inc., New York

ISBN 0-19-826830-0

To my husband Dominic, and our children Jonathan, David, and Peter.

Preface

This book has grown out of my PhD thesis on the legal implications for employees who blow the whistle on wrongdoing at work. At the time of completing the PhD, in late 1996, very little employment protection was available for employees in such circumstances, and the PhD concluded with proposals for legislative reform. Shortly after, the Public Interest Disclosure Act 1998 was introduced, with its far-reaching protection for whistleblowers at work, and part of this work is devoted to assessing its effectiveness. The PhD also considered the position of what I termed 'protest whistleblowers', those who use their experience at work to participate in debate on issues of public importance, often using their position inside an organisation to shed new light on issues already being debated in public. I argued that this speech should also be viewed as serving the public interest, and was also worthy of legal protection. The Public Interest Disclosure Act 1998 does not address the issue of protest whistleblowers, nor does it attempt to. My aim in this book has been to set forth the argument that the free speech of employees can serve the public interest in this wider sense, and therefore deserves greater protection in the workplace.

Numerous people have helped me in the process of writing this book, and a few deserve special mention. My thanks go firstly to Brian Napier, who introduced me to the study of labour law as an undergraduate, and supervised my PhD. Thanks are also due to Paul Davies, Keith Ewing and Mark Freedland for their help and guidance during the process of producing this book. Both the Law Department and the School of Social Sciences and Law at Oxford Brookes University have provided invaluable assistance by funding teaching remission to give me time to write and research. Finally, and most importantly, my thanks go to my husband Dominic. This book is dedicated to him and to our children Jonathan, David, and Peter.

L. R. V.
October 2001

General Editors' Preface

The Human Rights Act 1998 has introduced a new dimension to the study of labour law. One of the many questions that it raises is the extent to which workers have a right to freedom of expression in relation to their employment which their employer must respect. This in turn gives rise to a number of other questions about what is meant by freedom of expression in this context, for there are several ways in which the freedom of expression by workers may incur the censure of employers: the worker who expresses personal or political opinions in the workplace which cause offence to other workers or customers; the worker who expresses robust views in the workplace about the way in which the employer conducts his or her business; and the worker who publicly exposes illegal, unethical, or improper practices of the employer in the press.

The Human Rights Act means that these and other matters will have to be re-examined by labour lawyers. Also important is the Public Interest Disclosure Act 1998 which has a bearing on employee free speech. In view of the range of complex philosophical and technical questions which have been raised by these measures, it is particularly timely that they should be addressed by Lucy Vickers in what is the first monograph-length treatment of these issues by a British labour lawyer. As such, *Freedom of Speech and Employment* is a particularly welcome contribution to the Oxford Monographs on Labour Law, and welcome also for straddling the boundaries of labour law and human rights law, in the process of doing so extending the traditional boundaries of both disciplines. It is precisely this type of research and writing which it was intended the series would foster.

The study provides an extensive analysis of the potential impact of the Human Rights Act for labour law, and also deals with other more conventional materials of the labour lawyer. The extent to which freedom of expression is constrained or protected by the common law is considered, as is the role of unfair dismissal law. There is also a valuable treatment of issues arising in the public sector—notably the civil service, local government, and the National Health Service—where a number of high-profile incidents of whistleblowing have arisen. At this point, the study moves into the territory of the public lawyer with treatment of freedom of information, official secrecy, and civil service regulation, other areas where important changes have taken place in recent years. It is clear that this—the seventh volume in the series—will be of great interest to a wide audience.

PLD, KDE, MRF
24 February 2002

Contents

Abbreviations

AC	Law Reports Appeal Cases
All ER	All England Law Reports
BMJ	British Medical Journal
CA	Court of Appeal
Ch.	Chancery Division
Ch.D.	High Court Chancery Division
CLJ	Cambridge Law Journal
COIT	Central Office of Industrial Tribunals
Cr App R	Criminal Appeal Reports
Crim LR	Criminal Law Review
CSMC	Civil Service Management Code
Ct. Sess.	Court of Session
D&R	Decisions and Reports of the European Commission on Human Rights
EAT	Employment Appeal Tribunal
ECHR	European Convention of Human Rights
ECommHR	European Commission on Human Rights
ECR	European Court Reports
ECtHR	European Court of Human Rights
EHRLR	European Human Rights Law Review
EHRR	European Human Rights Reports
ET	Employment Tribunal
GMC	General Medical Council
HL	House of Lords
HRLJ	Human Rights Law Journal
ICR	Industrial Cases Reports
ILJ	Industrial Law Journal
ILO	International Labour Organization
IRLIB	Industrial Relations Legal Information Bulletin
IRLR	Industrial Relations Law Reports
JLS	Journal of Law and Society
KB	Law Reports Kings Bench

LGMB	Local Government Management Board
LQR	Law Quarterly Review
MLR	Modern Law Review
PL	Public Law
QB	Law Reports Queens Bench
RPC	Reports of Patent Cases
UKCC	United Kingdom Central Council for Nursing, Midwifery, and Health Visiting
Web JCLI	Web Journal of Current Legal Issues
WLR	Weekly Law Reports

Table of Cases

Table of Statutes

STATUTORY INSTRUMENTS

CONVENTIONS AND OTHER INSTRUMENTS

1

Introduction: Freedom of Speech and Employment

That freedom of speech is a fundamental human right is well established. The right to free speech or freedom of expression is protected in virtually all international and domestic human rights documents. Yet the scope of the right, and the circumstances in which it can be exercised, have yet to be fully determined. The purpose of this book is to examine the scope of the right to freedom of speech in the specific context of the workplace.

The employment relationship has traditionally been viewed as one of master and servant, with the employer controlling the activities of the employee during the period for which the employee is contracted to work, and sometimes beyond. The control exerted by the employer over the employee can, for the most part, be viewed as a fair exchange for the wages received by the employee. In effect, the employee forfeits personal autonomy in return for financial security. However, it is increasingly recognised that employees do not and should not subordinate their autonomy fully to the employer. Instead, certain fundamental rights are protected at work, regardless of the wage for work bargain. Obvious examples include the rights created in the Sex Discrimination Act 1975, Race Relations Act 1976 and Disability Discrimination Act 1995. The question to be considered here is the extent to which the right to free speech should be added to this growing list.

The right to free speech covers a range of types of speech. One particular form, whistleblowing, has received much publicity in recent years, moving from a pejorative term to one with connotations of public service.[1] The term refers to a person who raises the alarm in public about a wrong being committed in private. Whistleblowing is particularly relevant at work because employees are often the first to know about any wrongdoing. Any discussion of freedom of speech at work is bound to include a consideration of this issue, hence the law as it affects employees who blow the whistle on wrongdoing at work is considered in detail throughout this book as one aspect of the exercise of free speech at work. However, a consideration of the right to freedom of speech as it relates to the workplace requires discussion of more than just whistleblowing. Freedom of speech may also impact on the workplace in more general terms. For example, free speech

---

[1] See J. Bowers, J. Mitchell and J. Lewis, *Whistleblowing: The New Law* (1999) Sweet and Maxwell, London, 12.

issues arise where employees use their experience or expertise at work to participate in debate on issues of general public importance. Such speech can be beneficial to the public interest as employees can use their position inside an organisation to shed new light on issues already being debated in public. Alternatively, an employee may exercise the right to free speech on a matter unrelated to work, for example to engage directly or indirectly in the political process.

Employees who exercise the right to free speech can face many potential difficulties at work. Whatever the type of speech, and regardless of its subject matter, an employer may take advantage of the employment relationship to censure the speech with a work based penalty. This may be because the employee's speech embarrasses or shames the employer, because it interferes with work, or merely because the employer disagrees with the sentiment expressed. A work based penalty does not amount to an outright restriction on speech: the employee remains free to speak, albeit without remaining employed. One might therefore argue that freedom of speech is not affected, or not affected sufficiently to warrant any protective action. Nonetheless, employees faced with the dilemma of whether to speak or to remain in work are likely to be significantly deterred from speaking, and the public interest benefits of freedom of speech will then be lost. In the case of whistleblowing, employees often know about wrongdoing at work, and can act as effective watchdogs and early warning systems to alert management or the public where serious risks arise. Deterring whistleblowing can mean missing the opportunity to avoid such risks. Speech which does not directly disclose wrongdoing can equally benefit the public interest, although more indirectly, by improving accountability at work. Moreover, a healthy democratic system, at local and national level, depends on the participation of as many people as possible in debate on political matters as well as other matters of public interest. If workplace sanctions can deter employees from participating in debate, then the quality of that democratic process is diminished.

Although these various benefits of protecting freedom of speech at work are not generally recognised within the legal system, the argument has been won in the case of whistleblowing at work, with the introduction of the Public Interest Disclosure Act 1998. The introduction of the Act followed a catalogue of cases in which employees' concerns about health and safety, and about other types of wrongdoing, had not been heeded. In some cases concerns had not been raised for fear of retribution; in others, concerns had been ignored. In all cases, the potential for employees to play an active role in preventing disaster, whether physical or financial, had not been fulfilled. Before embarking on an analysis of the legal implications of the exercise of free speech at work, it is worth considering some of these recent cases. They serve as useful examples of the contribution that employees can make to the general public interest if they are allowed to speak more freely. In some of the cases, employees could have prevented physical injury or loss of life; in others, financial disaster or other malpractice could have been averted. Examples also exist of employees being discouraged from participation in wider public debate on matters of public and sometimes political interest, with a consequent impoverishment of that debate.

PREVENTING PHYSICAL INJURY AND LOSS OF LIFE

In a number of high profile disasters, resulting in significant loss of life, employees have either foreseen risks and said nothing, or have raised concerns which have been ignored. In each case, better employment protection for staff might have helped avert the disaster. Those who had concerns about safety could have been encouraged to bring those concerns to the attention of the management, who could then have taken action to avoid the problems. Those who did raise concerns might have been encouraged to take further action to prevent their concerns being ignored. For example, in 1988 the explosion on the Piper Alpha oil platform in the North Sea killed 167 people. In the public inquiry that followed, it emerged that employees had had concerns about dangers to health and safety on the oil rig for some time. But fears about job security among staff, many of whom were employed on short term contracts in an area of high unemployment, meant that they were loath to raise their concerns with management.[2] Had they done so, and had the concerns been acted upon, the lives might not have been lost.[3]

In the case of the capsize of *The Herald of Free Enterprise* ferry at Zeebrugge on 6 March 1987, employees had in fact already reported concerns about the potential safety risks of sailing with open bow doors on roll-on-roll-off ferries. One employee had even suggested a system of warning lights which could alert the captain, before sailing, to the fact that bow doors were not properly closed. The concerns and suggestions were ignored. One hundred and ninety-three people died as a result of the capsize.[4] Similarly, a few months before the train collision that killed 35 people and injured 500 at Clapham Junction in December 1988, a supervisor who was inspecting the wiring noticed that it was faulty. He did not report the problem, for fear of 'rocking the boat'.[5] Although obviously a personal failure by the individual concerned, this also suggests that a culture had built up at that workplace in which staff were disinclined to raise concerns.

---

[2] The Public Inquiry into the Piper Alpha Disaster, November 1990, HMSO Cm 131.

[3] After the public inquiry legislation was introduced to protect employees from victimisation for raising concerns about health and safety on offshore oil rigs. These rights now extend to all workplaces and are contained in Employment Rights Act (ERA) 1996 ss 44 and 100.

[4] Court Inquiry, Department of Transport, Ct No 8074, 1987, HMSO.

[5] Investigation into the Clapham Junction Railway Accident, November 1989, HMSO Cm 820.

FINANCIAL MALPRACTICE

Failure to speak up about concerns at work can also have serious financial consequences as the cases of the BCCI bank and Barings Bank illustrate. The BCCI (Bank of Credit and Commerce International) was wound up in 1991, leaving many small businesses and individual creditors bankrupt. The cause of the BCCI's collapse was a huge level of fraud. One internal auditor had raised concerns about the levels of fraud within the bank, but was chosen for redundancy soon after.[6] At Barings Bank too, the regulator found that a senior manager had failed to raise concerns sufficiently clearly in advance of its collapse.[7]

Another example of blowing the whistle on financial malpractice can be found in the case of Dr Andrew Millar. Rather than keep quiet, in this case the member of staff did raise the concern, but was dismissed for breach of confidence as a result. Dr Millar was the director of clinical research at British Biotech PLC. At the time of Dr Millar's disclosures the company was the largest biotech company in the UK. The company had issued press releases suggesting that they were about to launch two new drugs, including a treatment for cancer. The share prices in the company rose as a result, reflecting the possible financial returns on successful cancer treatment. Dr Millar discovered that one of the drugs was not performing well in trials, and that the cancer drug had only a 40% chance of success. Some months after the press releases, the company announced that no marketing authorisation was to be granted for the drugs, much to the dismay of investors. Dr Millar was contacted by some major investors in the company and asked for his opinion about events. He disclosed the gloomy prospects for the drugs, and also made various critical comments about the management of the company. When the company board learnt of Millar's meetings with investors, they dismissed him for misconduct and sued him for breach of confidence.

Millar's case is complicated by the fact that his discovery that the drugs were not working was made by looking at the results of the trials before they were complete, a practice which is in clear breach of the standard ethical guidelines on the conduct of medical trials. However, despite the fact that he should not have discovered the information in the way that he did, the discovery itself was financially very important. Once he had disclosed internally that the drugs were not working, the company had continued to issue the press releases suggesting that the company was on the brink of a major new advance in the search for a cure for cancer. The case is further complicated by the fact that Millar had started to plan with the company's investors to introduce a new management system with himself at the top. Although

---

[6] Inquiry into the Supervision of The Bank of Credit and Commerce International, 2 October 1992, HMSO Cm 198.

[7] J. Bowers, J. Mitchell and J. Lewis, *Whistleblowing: The New Law* (1999) Sweet & Maxwell, London, 3.

these facts make the rights and wrongs of Dr Millar's case far from clear cut, providing as they do alternative reasons for his dismissal, the fact remains that the company had been involved in suspect financial practice by issuing misleading press releases, and was later formally reprimanded for this by the Stock Exchange. It was Dr Millar who raised the alarm about the company's wrongdoing. After some time engaged in legal battle, British Biotech issued a statement exonerating Dr Millar, withdrew its claims against him, and paid him over £1 million in compensation and costs. Although Dr Millar was financially compensated, the process was not without personal cost. He lost his job, had a period of unemployment and suffered high levels of stress during the proceedings. His case illustrates the personal costs involved in blowing the whistle, even when ultimately successful in raising the concern.[8]

A further example of whistleblowing on financial malpractice is that of Paul Van Buitenen, an assistant auditor who compiled a file detailing fraud and corruption within the European Commission. Mr Van Buitenen passed the file to members of the European Parliament after first raising concerns internally. As a result of the investigation that followed his disclosure, all 20 of the European Commissioners resigned. Dismissal proceedings were brought against Mr Van Buitenen for disclosing the information to unauthorised persons, even though the European Parliament is responsible for checking that European money is used properly. Although not dismissed in the event, Mr Van Buitenen did not return to his former job, but was reassigned to a job auditing furniture in the Commission's offices.[9]

OTHER PUBLIC CONCERNS

The inquiry into patient abuse at Ashworth Special Hospital by Sir Louis Blom-Cooper QC in 1992 concluded that staff who had spoken out about concerns over treatment of patients had been victimised and threatened. This culture had allowed the abuse to continue. The Committee of Inquiry recommended that provision be made for staff to raise concerns about malpractice and abuse.[10] Social worker Sue Machin was one of the staff who had made allegations of cruelty at the hospital. She was later dismissed for gross misconduct. Although she won her claim of unfair dismissal, she claimed that the dismissal was a direct result of the evidence she gave at the inquiry.[11]

Dr Stephen Bolsin, an anaesthetist involved in heart surgery on babies at Bristol Royal Infirmary, raised questions about techniques used by surgeons at the hospital. His questions were not answered, and the surgeons concerned continued to operate on young children and babies, despite mortality rates that were significantly higher than the national average. In Dr Bolsin's view

---

[8] *The Guardian*, 19 June 1999.   [9] *The Guardian*, 5 January 1999 and 24 July 1999.
[10] Report of the Committee of Inquiry into Complaints about Ashworth Special Hospital, August 1992, HMSO Cm 2028-1.
[11] *The Independent*, 3 June 1995.

the high death rates were due to the techniques used by the surgeons involved. His concerns about operating techniques were vindicated at the subsequent inquiry into the conduct of the surgeons concerned, and the surgeons were eventually stopped from carrying out similar surgery.[12] Had Dr Bolsin's concerns been acted on earlier, however, some of the failed operations might have been undertaken by other surgeons with better mortality rates, and some deaths thereby prevented. Dr Bolsin had raised his concerns internally at first, but was warned off raising them further.[13] Although he was not dismissed for raising his concerns, Dr Bolsin's employment was affected. He tried to move to a new job within the UK, but felt shunned by the medical community; eventually he left the NHS and went to work in Australia.[14]

In each of the cases described above, the claims made by the whistleblower have proved correct on subsequent investigation, and serious danger or malpractice has been exposed. In such circumstances, the case for protecting the speech is self evident. If the speech can prevent malpractice or serious risk to health and safety, it clearly should be protected. The issues become more complicated, however, where the speaker discloses concerns that cannot be verified, either because of the current state of scientific knowledge, or because they are matters of personal opinion.

An example of one of these more complicated cases is that of Dr Arpad Pusztai, who was forced to retire after he raised concerns about the potential danger to public health of genetically modified (GM) crops.[15] Again the case illustrates the serious employment consequences for those who raise public interest concerns, and the complexities that can arise in freedom of speech cases in balancing the rights of the employer and the employee. The difficulties arise in Dr Pusztai's case because the concerns he raised have been contested, and unlike the concerns in the examples given above, his claims have not been universally vindicated. Dr Pusztai was the co-ordinator of a government funded research project into the effects on rats of a diet of genetically modified potatoes. His early results showed that the rats suffered various adverse effects from this diet, including changes to the size and weight of bodily organs such as the brain. Dr Pusztai appeared on an ITV World in Action programme to discuss his research. He referred to the damage done to the health of the rats fed the genetically modified potatoes and stated that he would not eat genetically modified food himself. He also criticised the release of genetically modified foodstuffs into the human food chain without adequate trials and tests, and claimed that the public at large were being used as 'guinea pigs' for the new technology. Unsurprisingly these claims attracted huge media interest. At first, his employer, the Rowett Institute in Aberdeen,

[12] Confirmed by the Secretary of State for Health HC Deb, 18 June 1998 cols 529–30.
[13] *The Guardian*, 23 November 1999.   [14] *The Guardian*, 30 May 1998.
[15] For details of Dr Arpad Pusztai's case see *The Guardian*, 12 February 1999, 9 March 1999, 17 October 1999.

backed Dr Pusztai's research, but two days after the broadcast of the World in Action programme he was made to retire, denied access to his research data and ordered not to discuss his findings.

Unlike the other examples given above, Dr Pusztai was not disclosing wrongdoing in order only to prevent its continuation. While no doubt genuinely worried by his findings, he was also actively seeking publicity in order to continue his and his team's research project. Moreover, his research was incomplete, and had not been peer reviewed, a standard process for validating research findings of this type. Once reviewed, the reaction of the scientific community was mixed. An audit report carried out by the Rowett Institute (but which included some independent experts) found no link between the genetically modified crop and health risks: in contrast, an international group of scientists who assessed the data and the Rowett Institute's audit report concluded that at the very least further research was needed, as Pusztai himself had said. Pusztai's research was seized upon by the media as further evidence of the dangers of GM crops, even though the research was in its very early stages and was clearly incomplete. In that climate detailed and objective discussion of the findings was very difficult, and it is arguable that the public disclosure of the findings did not aid balanced public discussion of the issues. However, despite the various factors that may suggest the treatment of Dr Pusztai was deserved, it is hard to see how, on balance, dismissal could be the correct response. Regardless even of the final truth on the safety of the GM potatoes (a fact not knowable for years to come, if ever) it is unlikely to be the case that silencing Pusztai by enforcing retirement and denying him access to his data could ever be the answer to the difficulties his revelations caused his employer. Despite the complexity of some of the issues the case raises, it remains an illustration of the willingness with which employers will 'shoot the messenger' rather than investigate the message.

PERSONAL AND POLITICAL OPINION

The cases discussed so far involve disclosure of dangers to health, safety or financial well being, and can be classified as forms of whistleblowing. However, examples exist of non-whistleblowing speech resulting in similarly severe consequences for the employee. In February 1990, Helen Zeitlin, a consultant haematologist with the Bromsgrove and Redditch health authority, was dismissed for mentioning nursing shortages at a public meeting. She was also known to be critical of the proposals being discussed at the time for the creation of NHS Trusts. Although she was ultimately successful in gaining reinstatement after an appeal to the Secretary of State for Health, she did not return to her original job, and her case acted as a focus for concern about the difficulties faced by staff who speak out about standards at work. According to Zeitlin, before leaving her job, she had been persistently intimidated and undermined by NHS managers, who had, among other things, raised questions about her mental health.[16] A case in a similar vein is that of Graham Pink who was dismissed for gross misconduct after publishing in *The Guardian* a series of letters he had written to hospital managers, his Member of Parliament, the Chief Executive of the NHS, the Secretary of State for Health and the Prime Minister. In these he raised concerns about staffing levels on the geriatrics ward on which he worked.[17] He also spoke to the local press about his concerns.[18] Again, Pink was ultimately successful in his claim for unfair dismissal, but did not return to work in his original job.

In both cases risks to health and safety were involved, in that reduced staffing levels are bound to affect health and safety of staff and patients, and so their speech could be classified as whistleblowing. But it is probably more accurate to say that Zeitlin and Pink were using their positions as employees to protest about developments in the NHS, rather than to alert the public to imminent danger to life or limb. In effect, these employees were using their experience at work and their position inside the organisation to participate in and inform ongoing debate on issues of public importance. A further complicating factor in their cases was the political sensitivity of their speech. As a part of the public sector with key party political significance, criticism from those within the NHS is clearly unpopular with those charged with running it. However, there is a clear public interest in information about how well the service is operating, and informed public debate on the state of the NHS is needed. A clear case can thus be made for protection for such speakers even though no explicit wrongdoing was disclosed.

A final example of the exercise of free speech at work is that of Glen Hoddle, the manager of the England football team, sacked in February 1999 after his views on the causes of disability were made public.[19] In an interview with *The Times*, Hoddle had mentioned that it was his belief that disability is caused by bad *karma*, and was punishment for sins in a former life. His statement caused uproar in the press, and was understandably severely criticised by disabled people's organisations. After a few days of speculation, he was sacked by the Football Association. The reasons for the decision were that Hoddle had shown a serious error of judgement, had offended disabled people, had damaged the Football Association, and threatened to bring the national game into disrepute.[20]

Again the case differs from the whistleblowing cases, and so raises more complex issues than those where wrongdoing is reported by an

---

[16] *The Independent*, 10 September 1993. See also K. Lennane, ' "Whistleblowing": a health issue' (1993) 307 *BMJ* 667.

[17] *The Guardian*, 11 April 1990. See also G. Pink, 'Whistleblowing: for whom the truth hurts' (1992) *The Guardian* and Charter 88, London.

[18] *Stockport Express Advertiser*, 25 July 1990.

[19] For details see *The Guardian*, 30 January 1999 and 3 February 1999, and *The Observer*, 31 January 1999.

[20] *The Guardian*, 3 February 1999.

employee. A number of factors suggest that the decision to dismiss was the right one. Hoddle did not disclose any wrongdoing or threat to health and safety, nor was he contributing to public debate on a matter of political or other public importance. Thus there was no reason based on the content of his speech to protect his employment position. Moreover, he held a very high profile job in an extremely high profile sport, his comments had gained huge adverse publicity for him and for his employer, and his views had in-sulted the disabled community. Yet it is equally arguable that dismissal was the wrong reaction. His views on the causes of disability had no impact on his ability to carry out his job as a football manager, and he had expressed a purely personal point of view. To that extent his conduct was a private matter with no connection to work, and should not have been subject to a work based penalty. Moreover, his views reflected his religious beliefs, and so his dismissal could be said to have interfered not only with his right to free speech but also with his freedom of religion or belief.

THE MAINSTREAMING OF WHISTLEBLOWING AND FREEDOM OF SPEECH AT WORK

The catalogue of cases described above demonstrates the range of ways in which employees' freedom of speech may serve the public interest, by dis-closing wrongdoing, averting disaster, uncovering financial malpractice and by contributing to important public debate. The contribution that employees may make to the public interest has gradually achieved recognition since the early 1990s. Following the Piper Alpha disaster, the Offshore Safety (Protec-tion Against Victimisation) Act 1992 was introduced. This was later replaced with general protection against victimisation for raising health and safety concerns at work.[21] Early recognition of the contribution staff can make to the good governance of an institution came from the National Health Service, due in part to the publicity surrounding the cases of Helen Zeitlin and Graham Pink. In 1993 guidance was published by the NHS Executive confirming that employees' free speech should be encouraged because of its role in improving the health service. The guidance required management to create internal systems to encourage staff to report concerns.[22] 1993 also saw the launch of Public Concern At Work, a charity set up to help employees raise, and employers address, concerns about malpractice at work. The char-ity provides legal advice and assistance to employees who may face dismissal

---

[21] ERA 1996 ss 44 and 100, introduced following the adoption of the EC Framework Directive 89/391.
[22] 'Guidance for Staff on Relations with the Public and the Media' (1993) NHS Executive. This was updated in August 1999 to reflect the entry into force of the Public Interest Disclosure Act 1998, 'The Public Interest Disclosure Act 1998: Whistleblowing in the NHS', NHS Executive, HSC 1999/198, 27 August 1999.

or discipline for raising concerns, and also advises employees on how best to raise concerns internally. In addition, it provides training and consultancy to employers on how to deal with concerns raised by employees. In 1995, the first report of the Nolan Committee on Standards in Public Life made recommendations for the introduction of whistleblowing procedures for employees of several public bodies, including the NHS.[23] These proposals were accepted by the government.[24] In 1998, Richard Shepherd MP used his place in the Private Members ballot to bring forward the Public Interest Disclosure Act 1998. The Act received government support, and was passed virtually without opposition. The level of support for the Act, following two earlier attempts which had failed,[25] demonstrates that consensus had finally been reached on the need to protect staff who raise concerns about malpractice at work.

Although the issue of whistleblowing has achieved recognition and some legal protection, other types of speech have not achieved the same level of recognition. Employers are able to impose work based penalties on employees who exercise the right to free speech in more general terms, whether the right is exercised at work or outside of work, in work time or in their own time. The law on unfair dismissal does provide generalised employment protection, but often the speech can be shown to involve a breach of contract or other misconduct on the part of the employee. For example, if speech is critical of the employer's practices or policies, damages its reputation, involves disclosure of confidential information, or causes any other loss to the employer, this may give grounds for a potentially fair dismissal for misconduct or may provide some other substantial reason for the dismissal, again potentially fair.[26] Unless the speech is covered by the Public Interest Disclosure Act 1998 (PIDA), there is currently no additional protection from work based penalties for employees exercising the right to free speech. Of the examples given above, Helen Zeitlin, Graham Pink and Glen Hoddle would not find any protection against dismissal in the PIDA, even though Zeitlin and Pink's speech arguably served the democratic process by contributing to legitimate public debate on the current state and future of the NHS. Dr Arpad Pusztai too may have found himself unprotected by the PIDA as he made his claims on television to a national audience. This is despite the fact that his claims were scientifically based and suggested significant health dangers to the general public as a result of current agriculture and food production policies, policies that were already the subject of significant public and political debate.

---

[23] First Report of the Committee on Standards in Public Life, 1995, HMSO Cm 2850 I–II.

[24] Government Response to the First Report of the Committee on Standards in Public Life, 1995, HMSO Cm 2931.

[25] A ten minute rule bill, The Whistleblower Protection Bill, sponsored by Tony Wright in 1995, and a private members bill, the Public Interest Disclosure Bill, sponsored by Don Touhig in 1996.

[26] Discussed further in Chapter 5.

The view taken throughout this book is that the right to free speech should be given greater protection in the workplace than has traditionally been the case. This is not to say that employees should necessarily have a right to speak whilst at work, or in work time, nor even that they should have an absolute right to speak about work matters outside of work. It is merely that employees should not have work based penalties imposed upon them for exercising their right to free speech in an appropriate manner and at an appropriate time. Exactly what amounts to an appropriate time and manner will depend on many circumstances, and is the subject of much of what follows.

The next chapter examines the right to free speech, its philosophical basis and its interaction with the rights of the employer. From this, a model for free speech protection at work is developed. It seeks to establish a principled basis upon which the scope of the employee's right to free speech can fairly be determined, taking into account the rights of both employers and employees. This model for free speech protection is then used as a measure of the adequacy of the current employment protection available for free speech. The third chapter assesses international standards on the protection for free speech at work. Particular focus is on the impact of the Human Rights Act 1998 in implementing the ECHR. The jurisprudence of the European Court on Human Rights in Strasbourg is examined, in particular the right under Article 10 of the ECHR guaranteeing freedom of expression. Subsequent chapters consider the current workplace protection under English law for freedom of speech, firstly in the law on the contract of employment and the public interest, and secondly in the law on unfair dismissal and the Public Interest Disclosure Act 1998. The final full chapter considers some of the specific restrictions on the right to free speech found in the public sector areas of the civil service, local government and the NHS. The potential for the Human Rights Act 1998 to improve employment protection for free speech is discussed throughout.

2

The Scope of Free Speech at Work

In the last 50 years significant progress has been made towards the legal regulation of the workplace and the protection of basic human rights. These advances have, to a large extent, been made in parallel to each other: they have occurred during the same time period but have not really come into contact with each other, leaving the protection of human rights within the workplace itself relatively undeveloped.[1] With the exception of the right to freedom of association which is included in many of the human rights documents and also protected via employment legislation, most other basic human rights such as the rights to privacy and rights to freedom of thought and conscience are not explicitly protected at work. This chapter considers the extent to which one human right in particular, the right to freedom of expression, should be given protection within the sphere of work. It seeks to create a model for determining what the ideal protection for freedom of expression in the workplace should be. The issue is complex because of the competing interests that can arise, the different types of speech, and varied circumstances that can be involved. The various justifications for allowing free speech and their interaction with a number of different variables that can impact on the decision to protect speech will be examined. The argument is made that, in order for freedom of expression to be given the protection it deserves, those who exercise the right to free speech should be able to enjoy a degree of job security through the creation of a new ground of employment protection.

THE PARALLEL DEVELOPMENT OF HUMAN RIGHTS AND EMPLOYMENT PROTECTION

Until the relatively recent introduction of individual employment rights, the workplace was viewed as a private forum in which the rights of the employer and employee to enjoy privacy in their contractual arrangements had taken precedence over other individual or personal rights. Protection of workers' rights was, by and large, provided by agreement between employer and

[1] V. A. Leary, 'The Paradox of Workers' Rights as Human Rights', in L. A. Compa and S. F. Diamond (eds), *Human Rights, Labor Rights and International Trade* (1996) University of Pennsylvania Press, Pennsylvania.

employee. Where general workers' interests were protected, this was likely to be on a collective level, by agreement between employer and union. These agreements were reached outside of the legal framework, with little judicial or legislative intervention. Statutory regulation had existed for centuries, regulations such as the Statutes of Artificers 1563, the Truck Act of 1831 and various Factory Acts in the 1800s. However, this regulation existed against the backdrop of a *laissez-faire* approach to regulating workplace relationships.[2]

Since the 1960s, external supervision of the workplace has accelerated, and by the start of the new century includes such varied rights as the right not to be discriminated against on grounds of sex and race,[3] the right to join, and not to join, a trade union,[4] rights relating to working time,[5] parental leave,[6] a minimum wage,[7] and rights relating to disability discrimination.[8] The workplace can certainly no longer be viewed as a private forum lacking in legislative intervention, if it ever was. In addition to the extensive statutory regime that now exists, the common law has also developed a range of duties which are imposed on employers to protect their employees' interests. Employers are now required to take reasonable steps to safeguard their employees' financial interests,[9] to treat staff with dignity and respect[10] and to maintain the general relationship of trust and confidence between themselves and their employees.[11] It is evident that the employment relationship cannot be viewed purely as a private matter for negotiation between the parties, or for voluntary collective agreement. The amount of legal regulation that applies in the work context provides clear recognition that workers have individual and personal workplace rights.

As well as an acceleration in the provision of employment rights, the last 50 years has also seen the development in the jurisprudence of human rights, with the adoption of the Universal Declaration of Human Rights (UDHR) in 1948, the creation of the European Convention on Human Rights (ECHR) in 1950 and the International Covenant on Civil and Political Rights (ICCPR) in 1966. The right to freedom of speech is universally acknowledged as a primary human right of fundamental importance; it is protected by all the major treaties on human rights[12] and is contained in most

---

[2] For a history of the development of labour law in the second half of the twentieth century, see P. Davies and M. Freedland, *Labour Legislation and Public Policy* (1993) Clarendon Press, Oxford.

[3] The Sex Discrimination Act 1975 and Race Relations Act 1976. The Race Relations Act 1976 replaced earlier, more piecemeal legislation passed in the 1960s.

[4] Trade Union and Labour Relations (Consolidation) Act 1992.

[5] Working Time Regulations (1998) SI 1998/1833.

[6] The Maternity and Parental Leave etc. Regulations (1999) SI 1999/3312.

[7] National Minimum Wage Act 1998.   [8] Disability Discrimination Act 1995.

[9] *Scally v Southern Health and Social Services Board* [1992] 1 AC 294.

[10] *Woods v WM Car Services (Peterborough) Ltd* [1981] IRLR 347.

[11] *Malik v BCCI SA* [1997] IRLR 462.

[12] Including Article 19 UDHR, Article 10 ECHR, Article 19 International Covenant on Civil and Political Rights and Article 13 American Convention on Human Rights.

written constitutions.[13] Human rights have not, however, been widely recognised as being applicable in the workplace. Where particular human rights
appear to be protected at work, for example non-discrimination rights and
maternity rights, these have been treated as separate employment rights,
rather than extensions of human rights such as the right to respect for family
life which is protected in many human rights documents.[14] This general failure to protect human rights in the workplace means that employees can be
vulnerable to work based sanctions such as disciplinary action or dismissal
when their actions displease their employers, even though in taking those
actions the employees may be legitimately exercising their human rights.
Human rights can only be comprehensively protected where individuals who
exercise their rights are protected against work based sanctions and guaranteed security of employment.

However, a major difficulty in extending protection for the right to freedom of expression into the workplace is that in none of the conventions or
constitutions is freedom of expression protected absolutely.[15] Well established as it is, it has to compete with the rights of others, for example to
privacy, to security, to confidence, and to the enjoyment of a good reputation.
The fact that the right to freedom of speech is never applied in an absolute
manner allows an assumption to be made that the right cannot be guaranteed
when exercised in relation to the workplace; an employer's right to freedom
of contract (or more precisely, freedom to terminate the contract) can easily
be presumed to prevail over the right of the employee to freedom of expression. This is especially the case when one bears in mind the traditionally
private nature of the workplace.

Nonetheless, the importance of freedom of speech as a fundamental
human right is such that it should be afforded some level of protection at
work. The need for employment protection arises, potentially, whenever an
employment sanction is used against a worker for exercising the right to free
speech. This is the case whether the employee speaks about work related matters or matters unconnected with work, whether the speech takes place in the
workplace or outside, and whether or not the speech occurs in work time. If
the limitation on free speech is experienced in the sphere of work, then this is
the sphere in which protection is needed. Thus in what follows, the argument
is made that some form of employment protection is required for employees
who suffer work based sanctions for the exercise of their freedom of speech.
Protection may be needed at work, regardless of whether the speech itself
took place at work.

That a degree of employment protection is needed to fully protect free
speech is fairly simple to establish. Determining the proper scope of that protection is far more complex, as a large number of factors are involved. In the

---

[13] For example, First Amendment to the US Constitution, Article 19 Constitution of India.
[14] For example, Article 8 ECHR.
[15] Except Article 19 of the UDHR, which is not directly enforceable.

first place, there is the wide range of conduct that can be classed as expression, for example artistic or dramatic expression; commercial speech and advertising; personal expression by way of dress codes; obscene speech and pornography; political demonstrations; and political speech.[16] The second variable is the subject matter of any speech. This can range from disclosure by an employee of serious wrongdoing at work, to comment about company policy in public which embarrasses the employer. Clearly, the arguments for protecting the former type of speech will differ from those, if any, in favour of the latter. Thirdly, the circumstances of the speech can vary widely. Speech may be motivated by malice, or by an interest in protecting the public; speech may refer to matters that are true, false, or a matter of conjecture; the speech may take place during work time, or outside of work; comments may be made by an office junior, or by a senior manager; may be made internally or to the national press, and may or may not cause financial loss to the employer. The exact circumstances of the speech will impact on the extent to which the speaker should be given legal redress for any work based sanctions received. Finally, underlying any debate on the scope of any proposed employment protection for free speech are various philosophical arguments for upholding a right to freedom of speech at all: freedom of speech as a personal right to autonomy, contrasted with the right of the public to hear what the speaker has to say.

In order to determine the scope of any potential workplace protection for the exercise of free speech, all these issues and their interrelationships need to be considered. The last variable, the philosophical basis for protecting free speech, will be considered first, as an appreciation of the underlying reason for protecting the right to freedom of speech is vital for determining the proper scope of the right itself, and in particular, the extent to which it should be protected from work based sanctions. The chapter then moves on to consider the strength of the employer's interests which compete with the right to free speech, and shows why a presumption should be made in favour of freedom of speech being protected in the workplace. It will then look at various factors that may confirm or rebut that presumption in individual cases, and the circumstances in which they will do so.

THE PHILOSOPHICAL BASIS FOR THE PROTECTION OF FREEDOM OF SPEECH

The starting point for the consideration of the scope of any protection for the right to enjoy free speech has to be to establish the philosophical basis for that protection.[17] Two fundamental interests are served by the protection of free-

---

[16] For discussion of what can be classed as speech, see E. Barendt, *Freedom of Speech* (1985) Clarendon Press, Oxford and F. Schauer, *Free Speech: A Philosophical Enquiry* (1982) Cambridge University Press, Cambridge.

[17] See further, Barendt and Schauer, n 16 above.

dom of speech: the individual speaker's personal interest in autonomy; and the interests of those who hear what is said. The extent to which the free speech of employees should be protected will be influenced by which of these interests is recognised, and why. If the basis for protecting free speech is that it is an individual, personal right, it will be relatively easy to argue for its limitation in the context of work, on the basis that it interferes with other individuals' rights, such as the right of employers to run their businesses as they choose. However, the argument advanced below is that the right to free speech serves many interests beyond those of the speaker. This strengthens the case for providing protection against work based sanctions for those who exercise their right of free speech.

ARGUMENTS FROM AUTONOMY

Personal Autonomy

The most basic justification for protecting free speech at work, as elsewhere, is that it protects the personal autonomy of the speaker. The ability to hold opinions and beliefs, and to communicate them to others, is what makes us fully human. In order for individuals to be able to develop their ideas on moral or political issues, they need to have access to a wide range of views and opinions. The right to speak, write, and discuss freely is therefore fundamental to individual development, autonomy and human dignity. The protection of the right to communicate is thus essential in a civilised society.

The argument from autonomy gives strength to the view that free speech should be granted employment protection, as human dignity and autonomy need protection in the workplace as in any other sphere, so that workers can enjoy freedom to express opinions and discuss ideas in every aspect of their lives. Rights of autonomy which only operate in the world outside work are very limited in practice. A counter argument might be that employees give up much of their personal autonomy when entering the workplace. The 'wage for work bargain' entered into by employees provides that the greater part of each day is assigned to do the employer's bidding, the consequence being an inevitable decrease in individual autonomy during that time. However, it is clearly recognised that the employee retains autonomy over the rest of his or her life. After all, since the abolition of slavery, employees have not been required to sign over the whole of their lives to their employer. Moreover, it is increasingly recognised that employee autonomy does not just mean that hours outside work are free for employees to use as they wish, but involves the way in which the workplace itself operates. Even whilst at work, employees retain a high level of autonomy over their persons, including enjoying the right not to be discriminated against on unlawful grounds and the right not to be unfairly dismissed. In fact, it has been suggested by Collins that much of the legal protection for employees at work can be understood to be based on the need to protect the dignity and autonomy of employees in the workplace.[18] Limits on working time, the allowance of maternity leave and time off for parental leave and urgent domestic matters all recognise the dignity of the worker and the existence of an autonomous life beyond work.

The increasing recognition of the autonomy of employees is demonstrated by recent developments in the common law on the duty of the employer to respect the trust and confidence of the employee. For example, the duty of trust and confidence owed by the employer goes beyond the treatment of employees during working hours. It now provides a duty to compensate where the employer's conduct has damaged the employee's future career prospects,[19] and a general duty to safeguard the employee's economic interests.[20] This more extensive protection reflects a more holistic view of the employee, who is viewed not only as an employee or worker, but as a person with financial and other needs that extend beyond the current job into life outside. This forms part of a general trend towards recognition of a right on the part of employees to dignity, respect and autonomy both at work and beyond. Indeed, Collins argues that the main value of work to the employee is as an aid to the achievement of such autonomy.[21] It follows from this that, along with other rights that impact on individual autonomy, the right to free speech should not be left at the factory gate or office door. If it is a necessary condition for the enjoyment of individual autonomy, then free speech should extend into the workplace.

Whilst very attractive, an approach based on individual autonomy has several limitations as a justification for granting protection for freedom of speech in the context of the workplace. The main difficulty is that employee autonomy may be counterbalanced by the competing need for autonomy for the employer. The employing organisation also enjoys a right to autonomy, which may be served by the right to freedom of expression too. This could well involve dismissal of an employee because the employer does not agree with the sentiments expressed by the employee, or wishes to distance himself from the view expressed for reasons of expediency. If the employee's right to autonomy is offset by the employer's right to autonomy, then the two rights will cancel each other out. The status quo of freedom of contract will then prevail, leaving the employee vulnerable to dismissal.

This limitation, in its simple form, should not present too much difficulty for the philosophical case in favour of employment protection, where the employer is a company. There is good reason to suggest that the autonomy of the individual employee should prevail over the rival autonomy interest of a company. Corporate rights to self expression will not fare well in competition

---

[18]   H. Collins, *Justice in Dismissal* (1992) Clarendon Press, Oxford, at 16.
[19]   *Malik v BCCI SA* [1997] IRLR 462 and *Spring v Guardian Assurance plc* [1994] 3 All ER 129.
[20]   *Scally v Southern Health and Social Services Board* [1992] 1 AC 294.
[21]   Collins, n 18 above, Chap 1.

with the rights of human persons to express themselves. There is no reason, based on principles of individual personal autonomy, to give companies human rights: they are unable to become fully human no matter how much dignity they are given. In any competition the right of the employee to enjoy freedom of expression should not be overridden by a corresponding right of a company.[22]

However, employers will not always have corporate personality. They may be partnerships or private individuals. In such cases, the non-corporate employer's autonomy rights may indeed cancel out the right to individual autonomy of the employee. Moreover, more complex difficulties also exist for the argument that free speech at work can be justified on the basis of individual autonomy. First, there are other rights that may be necessary to the full development of human dignity and autonomy. Most obvious is that personal autonomy will be served by continued employment. This means that if the exercise of free speech could jeopardise the continued existence of the employing organisation, by causing significant economic loss, the right to free speech could be legitimately curtailed. In addition, it is not clear why the right to freedom of speech should prevail over any other individual autonomy rights, such as rights to privacy, and an interest in enjoying the confidence of friends, colleagues or employees. There are also other rights that may be just as beneficial to humankind, and equally necessary for the full development of autonomy, such as rights to education or housing. It is not clear why free speech should enjoy precedence over these other aids to human autonomy by being given positive employment protection, except on the purely practical ground that it is easier to prevent encroachments on a right to free speech, than to require the positive action necessary to ensure that, for example, a right to education or housing is available to all. However, this is a very negative basis for requiring protection for freedom of speech, and it reduces the moral imperative to put individual speech above the rights of others, such as employers, to restrict speech.

A more particular problem is that an argument based on autonomy essentially seems to place value on the personal act of expression rather than any inherent value in what is spoken, thereby raising questions about how the right to free speech should fare in competition with other aspects of human dignity, such as a right to confidentiality, and a right to enjoy a good reputation. Nor is it clear how rights based on autonomy should fare in competition with other rights such as proprietary or economic rights of employers and shareholders. Yet despite these weaknesses, the argument for employment protection for freedom of expression, based on individual autonomy, does

---

[22] Note, however, that corporations are entitled to protection under the ECHR; and under the First Amendment to the American Constitution, *First National Bank of Boston v Bellotti* 435 US 765 (1978).

still have some credence. In particular, the fact that there are other rights that may be deserving of employment protection does not remove the case for protecting freedom of expression. The main weakness of the argument based on the individual autonomy of the speaker is the ease with which, as an individual right, it can be outweighed by other individual or collective interests. The argument from individual autonomy remains a valid reason for protecting a basic right to free speech, but it will need extra weight if it is to form the theoretical basis for protecting free speech in the context of the workplace.

Audience Autonomy

Strength can be added to the argument for the protection of free speech by considering the autonomy of the audience, that is, the right of the audience to hear what is said. Free speech supports the human dignity of the audience as well as the speaker, as beliefs are developed by hearing the ideas and opinions of others.[23] This idea has been used to argue for special protection for political speech (considered below), but even at the level of general, non-political speech, such a view gives a stronger reason for upholding the right of one person to speak over the rights of another to confidence, loyalty or privacy. Once the interests of the audience are taken into account, one employee's right to speak is no longer weighed against one employer's right to loyalty, with the danger that one personal right is cancelled out by another. Instead, the right of the employer is weighed against the rights of the employee and the audience, with the result that the right to speak is much more likely to prevail.

Despite the extra strength that the case for employment protection may gain from the introduction of audience interests into the equation, the approach does have a weakness. It provides, in its simple form, a purely utilitarian basis for protecting speech. Free speech is protected as the means of satisfying the interests of the greatest number. It is not based on anything inherent in the right to speech itself. Consequently, it only takes the interests of the employer in restricting speech to be augmented, in turn, by the interests of others, for the right to free speech to become extremely vulnerable. For example, if the exercise of free speech by an employee were to put in jeopardy the profits to which shareholders are entitled, the fact that a wider interest of the audience was served by the speech could be cancelled out by the fact that a large number of shareholders' rights were damaged. Employee protection for free speech justified only by arguments of utility is unlikely to survive for long.[24]

---

[23] T. Scanlon, 'A Theory of Freedom of Expression' in R. M. Dworkin (ed), *The Philosophy of Law* (1977) Oxford University Press, Oxford.

[24] See N. Rongine, 'Toward a coherent legal response to the public policy dilemma posed by whistleblowing' (1985) 23 American Business Law Journal 281 at 287.

The concept of individual and audience autonomy may thus provide a good basis for recognising the right to free speech as a fundamental human right, but it is not sufficient by itself to justify the provision of specific protection for the right in the workplace. It is too easy for it to be outweighed by other interests that operate in the work context, not least the right of the employer to freedom to operate autonomously and to run the enterprise without external restraint. To justify anything other than token employment protection for free speech, something stronger is needed.

Arguments Based on the Content of Speech

The extra factor that can justify protection for the right to free speech at work can be found if value is placed on the content of the speech. The argument here is not that the availability of free speech protection should be determined by the content of speech. The basic premise that content restrictions should not be imposed on the right to freedom of speech must be correct, as that way censorship lies. Yet even those most committed to speech protection agree that some restrictions on speech are acceptable, such as restrictions on the time, place and manner of expression, rather than its content.[25] The difficulty for the employee is that restrictions on speech imposed at work may be regarded as acceptable because they are not absolute restrictions. The speech itself is not barred: the employee retains the right to leave his employment and then freely exercise the right to speak. Additional argument is therefore needed to reach the conclusion that employees should be allowed protection *at work*, so that they can exercise the right to free speech and remain employed. This protection is needed whether or not the speech takes place at work. It is in this context that content becomes relevant.

Arguments Based on Truth

The simplest and oldest argument in favour of protecting speech based on its content is that freedom of speech leads to the discovery of the truth. This view can be traced most famously to Milton. In *Areopagitica*, his defence of the freedom to publish without state censorship, he claimed that without the freedom to debate new ideas there is no health in intellectual or moral life, and that truth, when contrasted with error, will always win the day.[26] This argument was developed by Mill, who argued in 'On Liberty'[27] that freedom

---

[25] See C. Edwin Baker, *Human Liberty and Freedom of Speech* (1989) Oxford University Press, Oxford, and T. Emerson, *The System of Freedom of Expression* (1970) Random House, New York.

[26] 'Let [truth] and falsehood grapple; whoever knew Truth put to the worse, in a free and open encounter? Her confuting is the best and surest suppressing.' *Areopagitica* (1644) in J. Milton, *Areopagitica and Other Prose Works* (1927) Dent and Sons, London.

[27] J. S. Mill, 'On Liberty' in S. Collini (ed), *On Liberty and Other Writings* (1989), Cambridge University Press, Cambridge.

of speech is essential if the truth on any matter is to be discovered. An opinion that is silenced may in fact be true and by silencing it, one will have prevented the truth from being established. Moreover, he believed that even if the silenced opinion turns out to be in error overall, it may contain an element of truth that will be lost in the silencing of the whole. Furthermore, even if the opinion is totally in error, the truth will be strengthened by the debate. In fact, he goes as far as to say that truth is enfeebled if not fully and regularly debated.[28]

Although this approach has led to extensive protection for many types of speech,[29] it has a number of limitations which restrict its usefulness as a basis for general protection of speech at work. First, it makes the presumption that there is an objective truth that can be known. This is not always the case.[30] In some instances, of course, factual information can be said to be true without the need for wide public debate. For example, allowing employees to speak about regular breaches of health and safety standards by an employer will help establish the fact that such breaches have occurred. In fact the input of employees into any discussion on the issue could be key to uncovering the truth, as they will be the ones who know what happens in the place of employment on a day-to-day basis. Protecting this form of speech could well be justified on the basis that it aids the discovery of the truth on important matters.

In many other situations, however, the argument based on truth will not be so helpful. Wide debate may lead to an increased understanding on some issues but not to the discovery of an objective truth. For example, public discussion of the merits of genetic modification of food may aid decision makers in deciding whether to license the growing of genetically modified crops, but the absolute truth on the matter may be elusive at this point in time. Moreover, on many issues there may be no truth, however long discussion continues. Debate on issues such as surrogacy, abortion and animal or human cloning, or the merits of using private funding in the provision of public health care, or the benefits of comprehensive over selective or specialised education, are unlikely to be resolved by extensive discussion, however many people are allowed to participate, and no matter where the debate takes place. It will be impossible to justify protection of speech on the basis that it helps discover the truth where the issues spoken about are, in effect, matters of political opinion or personal conscience.

---

[28] 'If the opinion is right, [people] are deprived of the opportunity of exchanging error for truth: if wrong, they lose, what is almost as great a benefit, the clearer perception and livelier impression of truth, produced by its collision with error.' J. S. Mill, ibid, at 20.

[29] See E. Barendt, *Freedom of Speech* (1985) Clarendon Press, Oxford and F. Schauer, *Free Speech: A Philosophical Enquiry* (1982) Cambridge University Press, Cambridge.

[30] Some would assert that truth is always a subjective concept; however, that view is not taken here.

Moreover, whilst suppression of views may prevent the emergence of truth, the causal link between wide and public debate and the emergence of truth has not been established: society does not necessarily recognise the truth when presented with it. The only way round this difficulty is to redefine truth, from an objective concept to a relative one in which the 'truth' is that which is generally accepted by society. Thus, in the USA it has been said that 'the ultimate good desired is better reached by free trade in ideas . . . the best test of truth is the power of the thought to get itself accepted in the competition of the market'.[31] The suggestion on the face of it appears to be that the truth is that which most people believe.[32] If such a weak model of truth is accepted, it becomes unclear why 'truth' must emerge only from public debate and not from any other source recognised by society, such as myth or tradition. Truth effectively becomes a relative concept and there is then no reason for granting free speech special protection, or for ranking the need to protect speech above the need to protect privacy and confidence, and the freedom to hire and fire employees at will.

Apart from the difficulties inherent in establishing the truth of any matter, perhaps the greatest weakness in the simple argument based on truth is that it takes as its starting point the presumption that the only reason for suppressing speech is that it is false. In fact there are many occasions where people wish to restrict free speech, not because it is incorrect but because it conflicts with some other interest. An employer in the agro-chemical industry may want to prevent an employee from discussing the merits of genetic modification of crops not because the employee may be mistaking the truth, but because the speech harms the economic interests of the employer. A health trust may wish to prevent an employee from disclosing poor staffing levels on a ward not because they believe the levels are adequate, but because patient confidentiality or even commercial interests may thereby be put at risk. The proposed introduction of private funding for public health care could make such concerns even more real. The government may want to prevent civil servants from discussing defence procurement contracts for reasons of national security. It is not, after all, the fear of falsity that usually leads to the suppression of speech, but a fear of the consequences of the truth being widely known and discussed. It is this view that has led to the development of a more refined argument based on the content of speech. The theory is based on Meiklejohn's argument from democracy but gains strength from Mill's truth argument.

---

[31] *Abrams v United States*, 250 US 616, 630 (per Holmes, dissenting).

[32] However, this often quoted short comment is taken slightly out of context. In the original dissenting judgment, it forms part of a strong defence of a broad right to freedom of speech.

Arguments Based on Democracy

The argument that free speech upholds democracy is mainly associated with the work of Alexander Meiklejohn.[33] He argues that for a democratic system of self government to work properly, the electorate must be well informed on political issues. The process of running a democracy requires that the electorate participates, by stating its preferences on various issues via the ballot box. If the electorate is ill informed, the statement of preferences will not be accurate. Members of the public therefore need all relevant information before them when playing their part in the democratic process, and for this reason, freedom of speech must be maintained. In particular, any false statements made by a party in the political process must be able to be corrected. The interests served by freedom of speech, according to this view, are still those of the audience rather than the speaker. The emphasis remains again on the content of speech, but it is basically an argument in favour of protection for political speech.

The theory in its pure form has a number of criticisms, the main one being that it is based on the idea that the electorate is sovereign: government's role is to serve the people, thus people need information in order to be able to judge whether the government has done what they want it to do. However, if the justification of free speech is the need to do the sovereign will of the electorate, this does not in fact automatically guarantee free speech. After all, the electorate could choose a government which does not uphold free speech; and there is no reason why a majority of the electorate may not choose to suppress the speech of a minority.

This limitation can only be overcome by refining the approach with insights gained from Mill's arguments from truth considered above. Schauer argues that it is in conjunction with the argument from truth that the argument from democracy gets its strength as a rationale for giving special protection to political speech.[34] Since governments have enormous power, they have the potential to make errors of great size and import, greater than most decision makers. Because the issues surrounding the decisions in which governments are involved are rarely clear cut, it is vital that they are debated and discussed widely so that the possibility of error is minimised. Speech which informs public debate on matters that relate in any way to government policy should be given the widest possible protection. This should therefore extend to protection in the sphere of work. Information about how a government policy is working, how government funding policies will affect parts of the public sector or about how a public utility is being run may all be necessary to enable the electorate to participate knowledgeably in the political process.

---

[33] A. Meiklejohn, *Free Speech and its Relation to Self Government* (1972) Kennikat Press, New York.

[34] F. Schauer, *Free Speech: A Philosophical Enquiry* (1982) Cambridge University Press, Cambridge.

The refined argument based on democracy is further strengthened by considering the reasons for suppression of speech. Free speech is often suppressed not because it is false, but from a fear of what the truth may lead to in public hands. The argument takes into account the tendency of governments to restrict information that is harmful to them. As Schauer puts it: 'Freedom to criticise the government is a check on the survival instincts of self-perpetuating governmental organisations.'[35] Thus free speech is not merely necessary because the electorate needs certain information: it is also necessary to act as a check on governments' tendency to be economical with the truth when it is in their interests to be so. Governments can be notoriously partisan and unreliable where political issues are concerned. Political speech is therefore distinctively important, deserving particular protection to prevent governments from determining when speech should be allowed.[36] In effect, the right to freedom of speech in relation to government actions and policies acts as a form of accountability on the state.

This argument cannot apply directly to purely private or commercial information, and so cannot justify universal workplace protection for any speech. But a recognition of the scope of information to enrich public debate may mean that it is of wider import than at first appears. Although at its most powerful in the context of political speech, the recognition of audience interests in hearing speech as well as the speaker's interest in speaking can provide additional reasons for protecting speech even where the subject matter is not overtly political. This is particularly the case if the power of many major employers is recognised. The assumption behind the original free speech rights was that the state represented the primary threat to individual rights. The First Amendment to the American constitution creates a right exercisable against the state, and the ECHR too creates rights exercisable only against the state unless the individual state incorporates it more widely. It has been recognised in recent years, however, that the state is not the only threat to individual freedom.[37] Indeed, it is increasingly the case that the state protects individuals from encroachments on their freedom from other private bodies, in particular, the power of large corporations.[38] The state, via legislation, protects employees from discrimination and arbitrary dismissal by both private and public employers; it regulates working time and provides health and safety standards in the public and private sector. Outside of the employment context the state regulates business to a huge degree, including

---

[35] Ibid.

[36] See T. Scanlon, 'Freedom of Expression and Categories of Expression' (1979) 40 University of Pittsburgh LR 519.

[37] O. Fiss, *Liberalism Divided: Freedom of Speech and the Many Uses of State Power* (1996) Westview Press, Boulder, Colorado; Oxford.

[38] L. Blades, 'Employment At Will vs. Individual Freedom: On Limiting the Abusive Exercise of Employer Power' (1967) Columbia Law Review 1404.

safety regulation of products, environmental and financial regulation, and the regulation of competition. Recognition of the potential dangers for the public interest of the power exercised by big business explains the very existence of the Competition Commission (and before that the Monopolies and Mergers Commission) whose aim is to protect the public interest where too great a market share in one area of business is held by any one enterprise, creating a near monopoly situation, and to investigate complaints about abuses of market power.[39]

Large private enterprises wield enormous power in our society, and it is therefore quite arguable that the type of accountability that freedom of expression provides for the state should be extended to the private sector. In particular, many functions that were previously carried out by the state are now carried out by private companies: provision of pensions, transport, essential utilities, some prison services, and telephone, postal and other communication services including the broadcast media. The change to privatised provision of essential public services creates a renewed public interest in extending accountability to the enterprises involved. The fact that the public interest is served by improving accountability within parts of the private sector is demonstrated by the inclusion in the Freedom of Information Act 2000 of a facility for the Secretary of State to designate some private bodies to be public authorities for the purposes of allowing access to information.[40]

This is not to say that the rights to freedom of expression as regards the state should be identical to those in relation to private business; but in assessing the value of protecting free speech, the extensive power of many employers needs to be taken into account.[41] If this is not done, it may be too easy to argue that the rights of the employee are outweighed by the rights of the employer; they can be viewed as two individual rights, one corporate and one human, which cancel each other out. Once the relative strength of the parties is established, the case for allowing a degree of accountability becomes stronger. Allowing greater public discussion of the affairs of such enterprises is one way to achieve that greater accountability.

Arguments from Democracy, Accountability, and Freedom of Information

Returning to the public sector, the argument from democracy and for improved accountability has also been used to favour the introduction of free-

---

[39] Competition Act 1998.

[40] Private bodies can be designated public authorities under s 5 of the Freedom of Information Act 2000 where they exercise functions of a public nature, or provide, under contract with a public authority, any service whose provision is a function of that authority.

[41] The public interest in information about the running of large businesses was accepted by the European Court of Human Rights in *Fayed v UK* (1994) 18 EHRR 393.

dom of information legislation.[42] The argument from democracy suggests that greater availability of information to the public can bring improvements to the democratic process by creating a better informed electorate. The provision of more information about public institutions can also help in holding those institutions to account for their actions. It might be thought that greater freedom of information would diminish the need for free speech protection, as the electorate would no longer be dependent on insiders for information, but could instead ask for and be provided with information directly. However, easier availability of information does not reduce the need for freedom of speech. The audience interest in greater access to information can be served both by allowing those inside an organisation to talk to those outside (freedom of speech), and by allowing public access to formerly inside information (freedom of information). To this extent the two mechanisms are complementary, and both can be seen as necessary for maintaining a properly informed electorate.

Furthermore, a right of access to information will only aid accountability and the democratic process if the public know the significance of the information or indeed that the relevant information even exists. In some cases the public will not be aware of the existence of information and so will be unable to make a request, unless an employee alerts them to the fact. In other cases it will be the experience and additional information known by the employee that reveals the significance of the information. Thus, the advent of the freedom of information legislation in 2000, granting access to the public to information regarding the public sector, does not change the arguments in favour of protecting free speech against work based sanctions.

Moreover, although the Freedom of Information Act 2000 provides individuals with a right of access to information held by public authorities, it contains a large number of exemptions,[43] and where those exemptions exist, there is no right even to be told that the information exists, let alone be provided with the information itself. Thus, even with a Freedom of Information Act in existence, a significant role still exists for employees to serve audience interests by exercising the right to freedom of speech.[44]

CONCLUSION

Arguments based on truth and autonomy give good grounds for strong protection for freedom of expression both outside the workplace and within it.

---

[42] P. Birkinshaw, *Freedom Of Information: The Law, the Practice and the Ideal* (2001) Butterworths, London. Full discussion of the Freedom of Information Act 2000 is beyond the scope of this book, although it is discussed in brief in Chapter 6 below, at p 202.

[43] Part II Freedom of Information Act 2000.

[44] For an assessment of the Freedom of Information Act 2000 see T. Cornford, 'The Freedom of Information Act 2000: Genuine or Sham?' [2001] 3 Web Journal of Current Legal Issues.

However, these are not the only interests that would be protected by the creation of employment protection for the exercise of free speech. There is also legitimate public interest in many types of information being discussed publicly, both in relation to government and the public sector, and in relation to some private enterprises. Adequate protection for such speech can only be provided by granting strong protection against work based sanctions for those who speak. The vast majority of workers are economically dependent on their employers. If the exercise of freedom of speech threatens job security, then freedom of speech will not be exercised very often. As Mill points out in 'On Liberty', 'Men are not more zealous for truth than they are for error, and a sufficient application of legal or even of social penalties will generally succeed in stopping the propagation of either . . . men might as well be imprisoned, as excluded from the means of earning their bread.' [45] This observation is no less true today than it was in Mill's time, despite the improved safety net of social security benefits that exists for those out of work. The fact that threats of dismissal will act as a significant deterrent to freedom of expression makes the need for employment protection imperative where a wider public interest is served by the speech. Personal autonomy and the dignity of the speaker may not provide a sufficient basis for the creation of employment protection for the exercise of free speech, because of the existence of countervailing employer interests in curtailing speech. However, where speech serves the public interest, particularly by improving accountability and the operation of the democratic process, the right to free speech should surely prevail.

INTERESTS IN RESTRICTING FREEDOM OF SPEECH

Establishing a strong human rights basis for the provision of employment protection for those who exercise the right to freedom of expression is only a beginning. The legitimate parameters of that right also need to be determined. In order to do this, the arguments with which the right to free speech competes and which favour employer freedom to dismiss need to be assessed. The strength of each argument and its application to the circumstances of any given case will be important variables to consider when judging whether free expression should be protected. There are a number of factors that support an employer's freedom to impose limits on his employees' speech. The extent to which any of them can provide a principled basis for overriding the strong arguments in favour of allowing free speech protection is discussed below.

---

[45] J. S. Mill, 'On Liberty' in S. Collini (ed), *On Liberty and Other Writings* (1989) Cambridge University Press, Cambridge, 31 and 34.

THE PUBLIC INTEREST IN EFFICIENCY

The clearest reason for allowing free speech to be restricted at work is where the right to freedom of speech conflicts with the interests of the enterprise for which the speaker works. That conflict may arise in a number of ways, the most obvious being the economic interests of the business, considered further below, but other interests include an interest in good management and in the efficient running of the enterprise. These interests can be framed as private interests of the employer, as to an extent, good management and efficiency are both ways of maximising the economic purposes of the employer in making a profit. However, there is also a public interest dimension to the need for good management and efficiency in a business. There are obvious public interests in a strong economy and good levels of employment, both of which are dependent on the existence of profitable businesses. Moreover, many businesses serve the public interest via the services which they provide. Most obvious are the public services some of which are provided by the public sector and some by private sector companies, such as health care, education, prison services, parks and leisure services, environmental health services, provision of newspapers and other news media, essential utilities, etc. The public interest is served not only by ensuring that such enterprises continue to act as employers of the population, but by ensuring that they provide as good a level of service as possible.

Given that there is a public interest as well as a private interest in the efficient running of an enterprise, the question is whether these interests are ever served by limiting the right to freedom of speech. To the extent that they are, this will provide a counterweight to the arguments advanced above in favour of providing employment protection for freedom of speech.

THE EMPLOYER'S ECONOMIC RIGHTS

An additional and obvious basis for restricting an employee's speech is where that speech interferes with the economic rights of the employer. After all, the aim of any commercial enterprise must be to make a profit. Moreover, as mentioned above, these basic economic interests of the employer coincide with a public interest in encouraging successful businesses for the good of the economy as a whole. Where the profitability of an enterprise is put at risk by the conduct of an employee, deliberately or not, there may be a legitimate case for restricting the employee's rights to job security. Not only are the economic interests of the employer jeopardised in such a situation, but so too are the economic interests of other workers. If economic loss caused by the exercise of free speech puts the business at risk, the livelihoods of all workers will be affected. Of course, the economic loss will not always be so serious as to jeopardise the very future of the business, and may not even be directly caused by the speech itself. But where the exercise of free speech by an employee creates some level of economic cost to the business, this may give grounds for restricting the protection provided.

Although the right of an employer to enjoy the fruits of the business is clearly deserving of some protection, this is not, nor should it be, an absolute right. Indeed the existence of a large number of employment rights in the UK demonstrates that current law does not give absolute priority to the employer's right to maximise profit. In particular, the provisions of the Employment Rights Act (ERA) 1996 provide that any dismissal must be carried out fairly, usually in procedural terms,[46] and numerous rules prevent profit coming before health and safety.[47] However, despite these and other restrictions on employer power, economic loss caused to an employer can give reason to restrict an employee's rights. If the employee has caused the employer significant financial loss this would give grounds for a potentially fair dismissal on grounds of misconduct or some other substantial reason. Likewise, significant financial loss to the business can give grounds for other fundamental rights in employment to be justifiably restricted, such as the right to equal pay and the right to be free from indirect discrimination.[48]

It may therefore be the case that where the exercise of free speech by an employee causes economic loss to an employer, comprehensive employment protection will not be justified. Moreover, it cannot be denied that the exercise of freedom of speech by employees does have the potential to cause such loss. Although compliance costs in the case of a right to freedom of speech may be non-existent, requiring only a forbearance from dismissing or disciplining an employee for speaking where that speech is carried out in an appropriate manner, other costs may arise. Most directly, the employee could disclose commercially sensitive information, resulting in reduced profits. Or the employee may criticise the quality of the employer's product resulting in a loss of sales. Alternatively, an employee could bring the employer into disrepute, for example, by making statements that outrage public sensitivities such that they eschew the employer's business, again resulting in loss of profit. Or an employee's opinions and views, expressed either at work or outside, could upset colleagues to the extent that the efficiency of the workplace is reduced. In such situations, a case can easily be made for restricting the employment protection available for freedom of speech. The strength of that case overall may well be determined by other factors arising in the particular case, including the type, manner and subject matter of the speech, the motive of the employee, and level of loss, but nonetheless the economic interests of the employer, and the corresponding public interest, should be recognised as legitimate interests which can provide a principled basis for restricting employment protection for free speech.

---

[46] ERA 1996 s 98.   [47] e.g. The Health and Safety at Work Act 1974.

[48] See *Rainey v Glasgow Health Board* [1987] IRLR 26 and Disability Discrimination Act s 6(4) which allows the cost of any adjustment to be considered in deciding if reasonable adjustment has been made.

THE RIGHT TO MANAGE

A further employer right that can be upheld by restricting speech is the right of the employer to run his business as he sees fit, exercising a degree of managerial prerogative. This right is well established in employment law, albeit subject to some major restrictions, such as the duty not to dismiss staff unfairly. There are a number of arguments in favour of retaining as much employer freedom as possible. If these are given credence, then protection of free speech at work could be given very short shrift. The simplest and most extreme case for maximum employer prerogative is clearly put by Epstein,[49] and is based on the primacy of freedom of contract, a freedom that is said to be mutual as between employer and employee. The benefits of such freedom are said to be two-fold: freedom of contract upholds the autonomy of the parties, and it contributes to the efficiency of the business. In terms of autonomy, the employer's freedom to employ and dismiss is balanced by the employee's freedom to take up or leave employment. The financial and organisational efficiency of the workplace is maximised, as the employer can dismiss inefficient or ineffectual workers without cost to the business. The threat of dismissal which is constantly with employees is also said to improve performance. Furthermore, the employer can reduce staffing levels to suit demand, without incurring the costs that would arise if it were necessary to compensate the staff lost.

Whilst it is not immediately apparent that this is the case, this model of employment relations does recognise the interests of employees in its own way. Employees' interests are served by the ability to leave employment without notice, enhancing job mobility and freedom of choice of employer. This freedom acts as a check on the employer's superior economic power. The ability of the employer to abuse his freedom is restricted by the need to maintain the reputation of the business as a good employer in order to attract good quality staff. If the employer's power is abused, staff will leave, and extra costs will be incurred for recruitment and retraining of new staff. Moreover, the freedom of the employer to dismiss employees is likely to encourage more imaginative recruitment, and the introduction of new systems of work. The increased viability of businesses allowed to operate in this way will, Epstein argues, allow high levels of employment to be sustained.

Whilst it is no doubt the case that management prerogative is still extremely strong, and given broad support in terms of the operation of the rules on unfair dismissal,[50] this argument in its pure form has certainly been lost in the UK, as demonstrated by the raft of employment protection introduced over the last three decades. The flaw in Epstein's argument is his refusal to acknowledge the extent to which inequality of bargaining power

---

[49] R. Epstein, 'In defense of the contract at will' (1984) 51 University of Chicago LR 947.

[50] See Collins on the operation of the 'range of reasonable responses test' in H. Collins, *Justice in Dismissal* (1992) Clarendon Press, Oxford, Chapter 1.

exists between employer and employee. He asserts that there is no real inequality of bargaining power as the employee's freedom to leave employment acts as a counterbalance to the employer's freedom to fire.[51] Yet it is usually recognised that there is significant inequality in bargaining power between the parties in the employment relationship.[52] The freedom to leave employment, with all the financial, social and emotional consequences of such a step, cannot be equated with the freedom of the employer to dismiss. As for the inherent check on abuse of employer power, the constant stream of cases being brought to employment tribunals suggests that the long term consequences for businesses of treating employees unfairly are not recognised by most managers. Arguments based on the need to uphold employer prerogative, for its own sake, are thus insufficient to refute the case for allowing human rights protection to permeate the workplace.[53]

By considering the case in its most simple and extreme form, the employer's interest in the maintenance of managerial prerogative may, however, be disposed of too readily. A need for total freedom of contract and pure, unrestrained managerial prerogative clearly does not provide a strong enough reason to outweigh a right to free speech, especially when that right is viewed as a fundamental human right. Yet it must be recognised that a degree of managerial prerogative does serve a legitimate purpose in the running of any enterprise. As established above, the public interest is served by efficiently run businesses, both in terms of the economic strength of such businesses and in terms of the public interest in services being well run. However much discussion and debate is allowed about the policy to be pursued by businesses and service providers, in the end a policy will need to be implemented, even if some do not agree with it. If this is to occur, managers need a certain level of discretion to run the business as they see fit. The public interest in good management and the efficient running of the enterprise thus requires that a reasonable level of managerial prerogative and discretion over how to manage the business is maintained. These are legitimate public interests that need to be balanced against the public interest in upholding free speech rights at work.

The remaining arguments in favour of restricting freedom of speech are of a more private nature than the two already discussed. The interests served by

---

[51] R. Epstein, 'In defense of the contract at will' (1984) 51 University of Chicago LR 947 at 973.

[52] See H. Collins, *Justice in Dismissal* (1992) Clarendon Press, Oxford, 1 and 2, and G. Pitt, *Employment Law* (4th edn, 2000) Sweet and Maxwell, London, 2.

[53] For further discussion of the benefits to business of providing employee protection, see P. Blumberg, 'Corporate Responsibility and the Employee's Duty of Loyalty and Obedience: A Preliminary Inquiry' (1971) 24 Oklahoma Law Review 279, and N. Pasman, 'The Public Interest Exception to the Employment at Will Doctrine: From crime victims to whistleblowers, will the real public policy please stand up?' (1993) 70 University of Detroit Mercy LR 559.

encouraging profitable, efficient, and well run organisations can be viewed as both private economic interests and public interests. The following employer interests, in autonomy, in a good reputation, and in trust and confidence, are more clearly private in nature. Nonetheless these interests are of some value, and further counterbalance the interests served by protecting free speech at work.

THE EMPLOYER'S RIGHT TO LOYALTY AND CONFIDENCE

Employees need to accord the employer a reasonable level of loyalty in order for an enterprise to function smoothly. The right of the employer to enjoy the loyalty and trust of employees in this way is well established.[54] An interference with this right may give rise once again to a legitimate reason to restrict the protection available to freedom of speech. The duty of loyalty will at least require that the exercise of freedom of speech should be practised to cause minimum disruption for the employer. External disclosure should therefore be avoided where possible, particularly if the aims of the employee, to prevent wrongdoing for example, can be achieved without it.

However, as with each of the employer's rights, the duty on employees to be loyal to the employer is not absolute, and will certainly not give grounds to restrict employee speech in all circumstances. First, employees of different levels of seniority may owe different levels of loyalty.[55] A senior employee, especially one whose views are likely to be equated with those of the employer, will owe a considerable duty of loyalty; more junior staff will owe a lesser one.[56] Second, the scope of the duty of loyalty will also be affected by the type of speech involved, and other circumstances such as the motive of the employee, and the extent to which the speech is made publicly. Whether or not the speech is made at work may be relevant. The duty of loyalty may extend to speech outside the workplace, but it will be more limited. In cases where external speech has caused significant embarrassment or financial loss to the employer, a breach of the duty of loyalty may, however, be established. Finally, and most importantly, the employee owes more than one duty of loyalty. Apart from a duty to be loyal to the employer, the employee also owes loyalty to the outside world. Well established as the duty of loyalty to the employer may be, it is not owed where it is undeserved, and disclosure of wrongdoing by the employer should not therefore be restricted.[57] Even where there is no wrongdoing by the employer, the right to loyalty will become secondary where a wider public interest is served by the exercise of freedom of speech.

[54] *Malik v BCCI SA* [1997] IRLR 462, and *Ticehurst v British Telecommunications plc* [1992] IRLR 219.
[55] V. Sims, 'Is Employment a Fiduciary Relationship?' [2001] ILJ 101.
[56] This is examined in more detail under the heading 'The status of the employee' below.
[57] *Initial Services v Putterill* [1968] 1 QB 396.

EMPLOYER AUTONOMY

A further reason that might be put forward for limiting employee speech in the workplace is based on the autonomy of the employer. This can apply whether the employer is a corporate or human person, as it is well established in both the US and in the European system that companies can enjoy the same rights as human persons, including the right to freedom of speech.[58] The full enjoyment of employer autonomy may involve freedom to dismiss employees who exercise their rights to freedom of speech in the workplace. If an employee expresses an opinion with which the employer disagrees, recognition of employer autonomy could mean that the employer can dismiss.

However, the need to protect employer autonomy does not provide much weight in favour of the right to dismiss. Where the employer is a corporation, it is not human and so cannot find fulfilment through self expression. In a straight competition between the right of a human being to autonomy and the same right for a commercial enterprise, the right of the human being should prevail. Even where the employer is another person, his or her rights will not necessarily outweigh the right to freedom of speech, particularly if one adds audience autonomy into the equation. If the good served by the right to speech is that members of the public have a greater pool of information on which to base their ideas and opinions (in the pursuit of their own personal autonomy) then this can be achieved just as well by the views of employers as of other persons. This argument has been supported in the US jurisdiction in terms of a company's right to express itself by taking part in lobbying and political campaigns,[59] but it does not extend to freedom to express oneself via employment policies. Employers may be free to contribute to a debate (in the pursuit of their own autonomy and that of the audience), but this does not entail a freedom to prevent others, including their employees, from doing the same.

It may be that in some circumstances, discussed below, the position of the employee who contributes to debate is such that it is reasonable, in the name of autonomy, for the employer to distance itself from the expression of opinion of an employee, even by going as far as to dismiss that employee. But in most cases, the employee who wishes to contribute to public debate should not be prevented from doing so on the basis only of employer autonomy.

THE EMPLOYER'S INTEREST IN A GOOD REPUTATION

At times, the exercise of free speech by an employee may cause embarrassment to the employer. This could arise if an employee uncovers wrongdoing by the employer, or exposes a practice which may not be illegal, but which does not present the employer in a good light, for example participation in animal experimentation, or links with oppressive regimes. Such disclosures have potential to cause significant embarrassment to the employer and may

---

[58] *First National Bank of Boston v Bellotti* 435 US 765 (1978).   [59] Ibid.

damage its commercial reputation. The employer has a legitimate interest in safeguarding its reputation and this is infringed by such speech. Employers, corporate or otherwise, can protect their reputations via the law of libel,[60] but in many cases such action will not be appropriate. Instead, an employer may wish to dismiss or take other action against an employee because of the embarrassment caused to the enterprise by the exercise of free speech.

If personal embarrassment is caused to an individual as a result of a disclosure, as opposed to embarrassment at the level of the general enterprise, then this may give rise to a legitimate reason to restrict the speech of the employee. Here a personal harm has been caused, which infringes that individual's human dignity. This may cancel out the interest in personal dignity served by allowing the speaker to speak. In such a case, the question of whether protection is deserved will turn on whether other interests, such as those of the audience, operate in favour of protecting the speech. Protection will thus depend on the subject matter of what is said.

However, at the level of the general enterprise, an interest in safeguarding reputation and avoiding embarrassment is not strong enough to overcome strong individual and audience interests in protecting speech at work. As in the case of employer autonomy, arguments based on the feelings of the employer do not stand up to close scrutiny. Where the employer is a company, it is not human. It is a legal construct, a financial device for running business enterprises. It has no personal feelings to be hurt, and cannot actually suffer embarrassment. Although not all employers are corporate entities, the same arguments will apply to partnerships, and quasi corporate bodies. The success or failure of business enterprises is judged in financial terms. Embarrassment or other harm to the reputation of an employing enterprise should thus not of itself count against protecting employee speech. If the 'embarrassment' caused to the enterprise has financial implications, then this may be a separate legitimate interest to weigh against the interest of individual and audience autonomy served by the speech: and if the speech causes embarrassment to any individual, possibly by association with the employer, then this too may be set against the individual right to free speech. Even then, the financial interests of the employer and the individual right to a reputation will not necessarily prevail over the right to free speech.

In relation to a public sector employer the interests in reputation are even weaker. In this sector, the creation of a good or bad reputation may well have political implications. Restricting freedom of speech on the basis that it may damage the reputation of a public institution is not justifiable. The audience interests in having an informed opinion on the reputation of a public service provider is extremely strong, because of the direct impact that this may have on the democratic process. The democratic importance of free political speech has been discussed above; the point being made at

---

[60] *South Hetton Coal Co v N.E. News Association* [1894] 1 QB 133.

this stage is that, as with employer autonomy, there is no principled case for restricting free speech at work based on the right of the employer to maintain its reputation and avoid embarrassment alone, particularly in the case of a public sector employer. Where financial loss is incurred, or personal embarrassment is caused, this may give a separate basis for restrictions on speech.

Conclusion

In the preceding discussion, a number of employer interests in restricting freedom of speech have been identified, in particular the public and private interest in ensuring the good management and efficiency of businesses, and in maintaining their profitability. To a greater or lesser extent, these interests, and the others identified above, can give rise to a principled basis for limiting the employment protection available for the right to free speech. However, it is also established that employer interests will not always prevail. Instead some balance needs to be struck between the legitimate interests of employers and employees. How that balance might be achieved, and the various factors that will influence its outcome, are discussed below.

ACHIEVING A FAIR BALANCE: THE PARAMETERS OF THE RIGHT TO FREE SPEECH AT WORK

There is a convincing philosophical and practical case for providing protection against work based sanctions for the exercise of free speech. Employees who seek protection may do so both on the basis that it will uphold their human dignity, and that it will serve the public interest by enriching the pool of ideas from which opinions may be drawn, and hence improve the level of public debate. The strength of these interests requires the broadest possible protection for the right to free speech. The fact that work plays a central role in many people's lives means that the personal autonomy of employees should be upheld by supporting free expression in the workplace. Equally, the control which employers have over the lives of their employees means that any failure to protect free speech at work thoroughly undermines the operation of the freedom, harming both the personal autonomy of the worker and the interests of the audience to hear what is said. A right to speak, without a corresponding right to remain in one's job whilst one does so, is, in practice, a very weak right indeed.

Despite the force of these arguments, the fact remains that a valid case can be made for restricting the protection of employees, based on the legitimate economic interests of the employer, freedom to manage staff, and a right to enjoy a degree of loyalty from staff. If both sets of interests are to be given adequate protection in law, then a fair balance needs to be struck between them. The outcome will depend on the individual circumstances of the case (discussed below): for example, whether audience interests are served by the speech, the motive of the employee and the extent of any economic loss to the employer.

BALANCING COMPETING INTERESTS

One way in which a fair balance can be struck between these two competing interests is to weigh the various interests against each other, with the stronger interests winning. Balancing exercises of this nature are a common method of resolving the competition between different interests, particularly in human rights cases, and it is tempting to resolve the difficulty in the context of workplace protection for free speech in the same way. However, there are a number of problems with such an approach.

First, some free speech theorists[61] have argued that a balancing of interests test can never produce sufficient protection for free speech, because it is bound to produce conservative decisions. The final decision on the outcome of the balancing exercise is made by members of the establishment, such as judges, the police (or in this context, tribunal members), who have an interest in protecting the established order, by virtue of their training and position in society. They are thus ill-placed to assess the full weight of the competing interests, tending to side with the interests of business. They argue that the balancing of interests approach is unlikely to achieve much by way of protection for individual rights.

Even if the view that the decision makers are inherently biased is overstated (particularly given the tripartite nature of the employment tribunals which are likely to hear free speech cases in the employment context), it is hard to deny that there are problems with the idea of balancing competing interests. Such an approach tends to favour the stronger party, particularly when the interests appear finely balanced, because in the absence of a clear result the balance is bound to favour the status quo. This point is made by Collins[62] in the context of employment protection against unfair dismissal. The test of fairness of dismissal takes a balancing approach, fairness being weighed by the tribunal from an officially neutral starting point. This tends to result in more findings of fairness than of unfairness, as the common law presumption of management prerogative prevails unless there is sufficient evidence of unfairness to show that the dismissal is unfair. In relation to the protection of free speech at work, a balancing of interests test may lead to a position where protection does not extend to the workplace *unless* the interest in speech outweighs the common law presumption of managerial prerogative.

One way to avoid such a result is to introduce an alternative bias into the system, and have a presumption in favour of protection for free speech. This

---

[61] For example, C. Edwin Baker, *Human Liberty and Freedom of Speech* (1989) Oxford University Press, Oxford.
[62] H. Collins, *Justice in Dismissal* (1992) Clarendon Press, Oxford, Chapter 1.

can then only be outweighed by strong interests to the contrary. Using the balancing terminology, the scales are weighted in favour of protecting the speech. Unless the interests in favour of restricting the right to free speech are strong, then the presumption will be in favour of its protection.[63] According to this view, the right to free speech would be presumed to apply within the workplace, unless there are strong reasons to the contrary. A 'tilted' balance of this type overcomes many of the objections to the use of balancing tests in reconciling competing interests.

However, more fundamental problems with using a balancing approach remain. Although the metaphor of balancing rights in a weighing scale is often used to decide between conflicting rights, at a theoretical level the method is flawed.[64] The basic premise of using a balance to weigh competing interests is that it allows a level of objectivity into the decision making process. The balancing test also allows the judge to be seen to consider all factors relevant to the question: any extra factor that impacts on the issue can just be added to the scales. Yet the assumptions inherent in this approach are false. The problem is that a balancing test attempts to subject to a common measure ('weight') a number of factors that are not commensurate.[65] Apples and pears can be weighed in scales to decide which is heavier, but this does not mean that rights and interests can be weighed against each other to determine which is worthier of protection. Indeed, apples and pears can only sensibly be weighed against each other if weight in pounds and ounces is being measured. If one has to decide which tastes better, or which is more beautiful, weighing scales will not help. Similarly, it is impossible to measure by metaphorical scales which is more worthy of protection, human autonomy as upheld by free speech, or human dignity as served by the ability to make profit. Even if it can be identified that one interest is a strong one and the other a weak one, the effect that those interests will have on the 'scales' is no clearer. For example, the right to free speech is a strong interest, strong enough to tilt the metaphorical scale clearly in favour of protection. The right of the employer to autonomy may be weaker, and so not tip the scales back. But how many weak interests will it take to outweigh a strong one? It may be known that eight apples will outweigh two pears, but on what basis can it be decided that the right to free speech is outweighed by two competing interests, such as employer autonomy and the employer's economic interests? Even if the fact that the employee was motivated by spite is added to the equation, it is not clear when the (tilted) scales will tip. Ultimately that decision is

    [63] F. Schauer, *Free Speech: A Philosophical Enquiry* (1982) Cambridge University Press, Cambridge.
    [64] See T. Aleinikoff, 'Constitutional Law in the Age of Balancing' (1987) 96 Yale LJ 943 and M. Tushnet, 'Anti-Formalism in Recent Constitutional Theory' (1985) 83 Michigan LR 1502.
    [65] On incommensurability, see J. Raz, *The Morality of Freedom* (1986) Clarendon Press, Oxford.

one for a human judge to make; no amount of metaphorical weighing and measuring can really help. The aura of objectivity provided by the idea of balancing interests is, in the end, deceptive.

The only way to produce even a semblance of objectivity is to use a utilitarian measure, weighing up how many people can benefit on each side of the equation. Such a measure is not really objective, as it takes as its initial premise that no right is inherently more valuable than another, the only relevant measure being the number of people affected by any decision. A utilitarian weighing scale would be unlikely to lead to much protection for any fundamental human rights, and in any event, one of the perceived advantages of balancing is that it allows all relevant factors to be considered, not just issues of utility.

Apart from the theoretical problems, there are also practical difficulties with using a balancing test. The approach is very flexible, and allows all factors relevant to the decision to be taken into account. But a corollary of that flexibility is that it is difficult to find any certainty of outcome. If every relevant factor is considered in every case, then each case will turn on its own unique facts, and precedent will be hard to establish. Anticipating whether there will be protection in advance of exercising the right to free speech then becomes very difficult, and there is likely to be a consequent reduction in the numbers exercising the right. Lack of certainty in the scope of any employment protection for free speech would significantly reduce its effectiveness.

Although there are serious problems with using a balancing test to arbitrate between competing rights, finding an alternative can prove problematic. Any model for protection of free speech is likely to be based on the international obligations on human rights, each of which calls for protection for freedom of speech but which also sets out restrictions on the right.[66] Given the validity of the different interests at stake, it will be impossible to avoid comparing the relative strength of different interests altogether. However, the choice is not between an absolute right to free speech and a straight balancing approach. A third option exists, which involves the introduction of a staged test for determining when free speech should be protected at work. Although ultimately competing interests will still need to be considered and compared, such an approach involves a move away from the balancing metaphor, towards the creation of a more settled right, albeit one with some restrictions and limitations.

The right to equal pay can provide a useful example of a system which arbitrates between different rights without direct recourse to a balancing test. The right is well established in domestic and international law,[67] but is subject to a defence for the employer where there is a genuine material factor that

---

[66] Except Article 19 of the UDHR, which is not directly enforceable.
[67] ILO Convention 100, Article 119 Treaty of Rome 1957, Equal Pay Act 1970.

justifies an incursion into the right, one of these being commercial or market forces.[68] It could be claimed that this, in effect, amounts to no more than a balancing of the right to equal pay against the economic rights of the employer, and to an extent this is the case. But the symbolism of the framework of the protection is important. The right to equal pay is framed as a clear right for the employee. The employer's interests form a defence to any claim that the right has been infringed. If there is uncertainty, or using balancing terminology, if the rights are evenly balanced, then a presumption would be in favour of allowing equal pay, because the employer would not have made out the defence. This avoids the difficulties of a neutral test which can in effect uphold the status quo.[69] Although it does not fully overcome the difficulties of a balancing test, the rights based model avoids the false objectivity of the balancing metaphor. Competing interests are given recognition, but no implicit assumption is made that the different interests are all relative. A clear statement is made that the right to equal pay is the primary right.

Improved employment protection for free speech could be based on a similar model, with a clear statement of principle that the right to free speech extends to the workplace.[70] The legitimate interests served by restricting employee speech can then be met by framing a defence or limiting clause on the free speech right. The concept of proportionality, used in the jurisprudence of the ECHR, could provide a second useful model here in framing the limitations on free speech. Under the ECHR, the basic right to free speech is protected, with legitimate exceptions. Those exceptions can only restrict speech where they do not disproportionately interfere with the basic right. Applied in the context of a right to free speech at work, this would mean that courts should accept a basic position that freedom of speech is protected against work based sanctions. Any such sanctions would only be allowed where they aim to achieve a legitimate objective. The legitimate objectives which courts might recognise in this context have been explored above, and include the need to maintain business efficiency, the avoidance of significant harm to the economic interests of the employer, the protection of the employer's managerial prerogative and autonomy, and the maintenance of employee confidence and loyalty. Even where sanctions imposed on speech aim to achieve one of these objectives, they should be unlawful when they disproportionately interfere with the basic right to freedom of speech of the individual.

To an extent this model only avoids the difficulties in the balancing approach by choosing to give priority to the right to free speech over other

---

[68] Equal Pay Act 1970 s 1(3). See *Rainey v Greater Glasgow Health Board* [1987] IRLR 26.

[69] See Collins, discussed above, n 62.

[70] This would overcome the difficulty discussed in relation to the ECHR below, where it has not been clear that Convention rights, including the right to free speech, extend to the workplace.

competing rights. It might be argued that there is no justification for granting this priority to free speech over other competing interests. However, the justification for such an approach can be found in the arguments in favour of protecting the right to freedom of speech as a fundamental right. The public interest in protecting human dignity and individual autonomy, and the audience interests served by encouraging free speech, have been set out extensively above.[71] In the equal pay example, a clear message is created that the right to equal pay is the primary right, albeit subject to exceptions where other interests outweigh it. In the same way, the interests in protecting free speech justify the creation of a clear right to free speech at work. The many competing rights would be protected under this model by the creation of the exception where there is a legitimate need to restrict speech and the need for any restriction to be proportionate to that aim.

The creation of such an exception to the right to free speech when exercised at work may seem to give with one hand and take with the other, and to an extent it does reintroduce an element of balancing, but this is inevitable if any recognition of the rights of the employer is to be allowed. Given that the right to free speech is never absolute in any event, such a compromise must be made. But a rights and proportionality approach still represents an improvement over a simple balancing test, or even tilted balance test, because it sets out the primary right much more clearly. As with the right to equal pay, the symbolism of the approach is important. Obviously there will be many cases in relation to both equal pay and free speech where these rights will not prevail over other interests. But the use of a rights based model for protection provides clear recognition of the status of free speech as a fundamental human right.

The final task in ascertaining the proper scope of any right to free speech to be exercised at work now becomes the determination of the question of when a restriction on speech will be proportionate. The remainder of this chapter will consider the various circumstances and other factors that should be considered in answering this question.

THE PROPORTIONALITY OF WORK-BASED RESTRICTIONS ON FREE SPEECH

Even though the individual right to free speech is strong, the interests of the employer in maintaining a degree of loyalty from staff, and in safeguarding the economic interests of the enterprise, mean that the right to freedom of expression as enjoyed at work will not be exactly consonant with the right as enjoyed in the outside world. In some circumstances, therefore, the employer will be able to show that disciplinary action or dismissal is proportionate even

---

[71] See the discussion at the start of this chapter.

though it has infringed an employee's free speech. It is not the purpose of this chapter to establish with precision exactly when an interference with the right to free speech will be proportionate. Instead, the factors that will influence the decision are considered. A number of factors have been touched on already, such as the status of the employee and the subject matter of the speech. How these issues should affect the scope of protection for the right to free speech at work, and how they should influence the issue of the proportionality of any restrictions, is the subject of the next section.

The factors that will influence the issue of proportionality fall into three main categories: the philosophical basis of the protection; the type of speech; and the individual circumstances of the speech. The philosophical basis on which speech is protected has already been considered above in some detail, but will continue to be of relevance as it interacts with the other factors to be considered below.

TYPE OF SPEECH

There is a close interaction between the philosophical basis for protecting speech at work and the type of speech that should be protected. If the primary philosophical basis for extending protection to the workplace had been individual autonomy, then the scope of the right would be wide, covering any type of speech in any circumstances.[72] But, as discussed earlier, individual autonomy is not strong enough in itself to justify the extension of protection to the workplace as it can too easily be overridden by the interests of an enterprise in autonomy in the way that it runs its business. Instead, the basis for extending protection to the workplace was the additional weight of the audience interests served by speech. Where the type of speech is one that serves clear audience interests, it will be much more difficult for an employer to establish that any restriction on free speech is proportionate. There are three main types of employee speech that may be said to serve audience interests: whistleblowing; political speech; and individual comment or dissent on corporate policy or other matters. These will be considered in turn.

Whistleblowing

'Whistleblowing' refers to raising the alarm in public about a wrong being committed in private. Where employees act as whistleblowers, they disclose work related information that can be used to prevent harm or loss to the public. An employee might disclose a safety risk to other employees at work, an environmental or health hazard for members of the public, serious fraud, or gross waste of public funds. In each case, the employee can be termed a whistleblower. By definition, whistleblowing cases involve the

---

[72] For discussion of different types of expression, see E. Barendt, *Freedom of Speech* (1985) Clarendon Press, Oxford and F. Schauer, *Free Speech: A Philosophical Enquiry* (1982) Cambridge University Press, Cambridge.

disclosure of wrongdoing or malpractice that is taking place at work, and so the audience interests in the speech are strong. Moreover, in most cases whistleblowing involves employees revealing work related information. Protection is therefore needed *in the context of work*. If employment protection is not granted to whistleblowers, the whistleblowing may well not take place, and wrongdoing and dangers will not be uncovered. This will clearly harm the interests of the public at large.

It is difficult to argue that the rights of employees to be protected from dismissal for engaging in whistleblowing speech should be restricted. The only such argument is based on managerial prerogative to run a business without interference by way of employee rights. Where the employee is disclosing wrongdoing *by the employer*, this argument is easily overcome. The strength of any rights based argument in favour of freedom to manage the enterprise without outside interference is totally undermined if the employing enterprise is trying thereby to cover up its own wrongdoing. Even if the wrong reported by the whistleblower is not the fault of the employer, such as a previously unknown environmental hazard, the public interest in knowing the information is so strong that it overcomes any interest of the employer to manage free from interference. The benefits that may be gained in terms of efficiency from unfettered managerial prerogative are undermined where that prerogative is used to hide wrongdoing. In most cases of whistleblowing, where the information disclosed relates to wrongdoing by the employer, or a serious danger to the public, the employer will find it difficult to make a case for imposing penalties on the exercise of free speech.

However, the fact that the type of speech involved in cases of whistleblowing justifies its protection in the workplace does not mean that restrictions imposed on speech by an employer can never be defended. Depending on the circumstances, the employer could argue that a restriction on the right to speak is proportionate. For example, speech may not be justified if it is broadcast to a wide audience via the media, or if it causes financial loss to the employer, unless the content of the speech relates to very serious issues. In such cases, the particular circumstances of the whistleblowing would mean that restrictions could be proportionate and the speaker could lose the protection.[73]

Political Speech

The right of individuals to take part in the political process serves both personal autonomy goals and those of the audience. Although the personal fulfilment achieved by those who express their political opinions may not be strong enough alone, the additional audience interests in political speech are enough to warrant some specific employment protection for such

---

[73] The limits on employment protection for whistleblowers under the Public Interest Disclosure Act are discussed in Chapter 5.

speech. As already discussed, for the democratic process to work properly, the electorate needs to be well informed. This requires full participation in public debate by those with something to say of relevance to the democratic process. Employees wishing to take part in public debate on matters of political significance should therefore be protected from work based penalties imposed for doing so, even if this interferes with the rights of the employer to manage the enterprise free from intervention. On this basis employment protection should be extensive in respect of political speech.

The scope of protection under this heading will depend on the extent to which different types of speech are classified as political. Some political speech will relate to the workplace specifically, other speech may be political in nature but wholly unconnected to the enterprise for which the employee works. Employment protection already exists for workplace speech that amounts to trade union activity.[74] This can be justified on the basis that the speech is a form of political activity *and* it relates to the workplace: special employment protection is therefore appropriate. In order to further the democratic process, speech relating to party politics and the governmental process, both national and local, should also be given strong employment protection. This will apply whether the speech relates to the work environment or not. An employee should not be dismissed or subjected to other detriment purely because the employer disagrees with his or her political views. Failure to protect such an employee would represent a failure to uphold the democratic process. The interests served by protecting employee political speech are powerful and any competing interests should be correspondingly strong if an enterprise is to be able to show that restrictions on such speech are proportionate.[75] Clearly there may be times when the public interest is in fact served by curbing even political speech. For example, if a policy is formulated via a legitimate democratic process, then those who disagree should not be indefinitely protected if their critical speech interferes with the employer's ability to implement the policy.

The additional audience interests in protecting political speech mean that classification of speech as political is important. Yet this classification has given rise to difficulty for the courts in the past.[76] Public discussion of a political party's policy is overtly political, but the expression of satisfaction or disappointment with the impact of the implementation of government

---

[74] Trade Union and Labour Relations (Consolidation) Act (TULR(C)A) 1992 s 146.

[75] The extent to which the Local Government and Housing Act (LGHA) restrictions and civil service restrictions on political activity are compatible with this standard will be discussed later.

[76] In contexts such as the political activities of charities and trade unions, campaigning for a change in the law or in government policy is classed as political. In the trade union context see *Mercury Communications Ltd v Scott-Garner and the POEU* [1983] IRLR 494, *Associated British Ports v TGWU* [1989] IRLR 291 and *London Borough of Wandsworth v NAS/UWT* [1993] IRLR 344. For charities, see *National Anti-Vivisection Society v IRC* [1948] AC 31, *Baldry v Feintuck* [1972] 1 WLR 552 and *McGovern v A-G* [1982] Ch 321.

policy may have a more ambiguous status. Yet an employee who engages in public debate about policy changes on matters such as health or education could well be said to engage in political speech.[77] The interests of the public are probably best served by allowing full public debate on matters that relate to government policy and its implementation, and so political speech should be given a wide definition in this context. Moreover, the difficulties over precise classifications could be largely avoided by concentrating instead on the content of the speech itself. In effect, speech that aids the democratic process should be readily protected, because it serves such strong audience interests. Where speech is less overtly political, or is even interfering with the democratic process, and where the audience interests are correspondingly weaker, it becomes more likely that the restrictions on speech will be proportionate.

Principled Dissent

The employee's position at work does more than give access to information about wrongdoing or malpractice, the disclosure of which can be termed whistleblowing. Employees also develop an area of expertise relating to the workplace which can be used to make a valuable contribution to public debate on matters of public importance. Allowing those with specialised knowledge to participate will enrich that debate, serving the audience interests in autonomy. Where an employee agrees with company policy on any issue of public interest, his freedom to express that opinion is unlikely to be curtailed by the employer; indeed it is likely to be encouraged. The threat to freedom of expression occurs where the employee does not agree with an employer's policy: hence the term *principled dissent*.[78] There are strong audience interests to be served by allowing that dissent to be voiced.

The arguments for protecting principled dissent are strongest in relation to the public sector, where the political significance of dissent is clear.[79] For instance, the state education system has seen huge organisational change over recent years with the introduction of local management of schools, a national curriculum, attainment testing, league tables, changes to the system of schools inspection, introduction of specialisms, etc. Shortcomings in the education service are likely to be seen to be the result of these changes and therefore the responsibility of the governments that have implemented them. Debate about the state of the education system is therefore of political significance. The argument can be applied in any part of the public sector which

---

[77] See also *R v Radio Authority ex parte Bull* [1997] 2 All ER 561, 'Campaigning against a government in order to persuade it to change its law or its policies is unquestionably a political activity in the natural and ordinary meaning of the word "political"' per Brooke LJ.

[78] The phrase comes from M. Miceli and J. Near, *Blowing the Whistle: The Organisational and Legal Implications for Companies and Employees* (1992) Lexington Books; Maxwell Macmillan International, New York and Oxford.

[79] The difficulties in determining the status of bodies as public or private are discussed below at pp 48–50.

is the subject of public debate, whether because of organisational change, the level of funding available or simply the standards of service provided. It is of political importance that the public sector is understood to be working successfully by the voting public, and it is therefore essential that public opinion on these issues be well informed. In order to ensure that the public will be able to obtain sufficient information to participate fully in the electoral process, the rights of those who work within the service, and therefore have first hand experience of them, to speak publicly need to be assured. The same argument can be applied to justify the protection of principled dissent in the recently privatised sector; again, the question of whether these industries operate effectively is politically sensitive, and should be the subject of fully informed debate.

The extent to which protection should be extended to employees who engage in principled dissent within the private sector depends on the extent to which audience interests in their concerns are recognised. In the main, these industries and companies operate to serve the private interests of shareholders and consumers. Where these might be harmed by the voicing of dissent, it is arguable that those voices should be restricted. However, there may well be times when the audience interest in speech relating to private companies may justify its protection even in the private sector. Concerns about the policies adopted by the agro-chemical industry in the development of genetically modified foods can be said to be of public interest, even though they are not overtly party political questions. The tendency of fast food manufacturers to market their products to children may be a similar issue that is of public, but not political, interest. In both these cases, principled dissent voiced by employees would be worthy of protection because of the audience interest in hearing the speech. However, the protection would not be absolute. Whether or not a restriction would be proportionate would be influenced by the other circumstances of the speech, such as the extent to which the speech interferes with the effective running of the enterprise, the identity of the employee voicing the dissent, and any economic loss that ensued.

Personal Views

The starting point in any conflict between the right to speak and the right to dismiss is that freedom of expression should be protected at work unless there is good reason to restrict it. Where speech is of a purely personal type, it will only be proportionate for an employer to justify imposing restrictions on speech where some interest of the employer is infringed. The expression of unpopular views should not of itself be grounds for dismissal. The dismissal of Glen Hoddle, former manager of the English football team, is an obvious example.[80] His expressed belief that disability is caused by bad *karma* was

---

[80]   *The Guardian*, 3 February 1999.

offensive to many, but that did not of itself give grounds for dismissal from his job as a football manager. For his dismissal to be justified, it is necessary to consider the other factors, discussed below, that were at work in his case, such as his seniority in a job with a high public profile.

Non-Verbal Forms of Expression

The emphasis in this book is on freedom of speech or verbal expression. However, it may be that employees choose to express themselves through non-verbal forms of expression such as mode of dress or the wearing of badges.[81] In such cases, the issues for a court or tribunal to consider in determining whether to protect the freedom of expression will be similar to those considered in other free speech cases. The interests in upholding personal autonomy would suggest protection for any form of free expression, including forms of dress,[82] but as has been argued above, the interest in personal autonomy for employees is easily outweighed by the interests of the employer. Thus the desire on the part of the employer to present a certain image to the public will usually outweigh the right of employees to express themselves via an individualised dress code.

In most cases where an individual does not wish to comply with an employer's dress code it will not be because he or she is expressing a particular opinion or idea via the chosen clothes.[83] If, however, the employee is expressing a view via clothing and can assert additional audience interests in this form of expression, it may be possible to argue that it should be protected at work. Using this argument it could be argued that an employee who wishes to wear a badge bearing a political slogan should be protected from any work based sanction. This may well be the case if the badge is worn outside of work, but it would be unlikely to apply to the wearing of political insignia in a workplace, particularly if the workplace involved contact with the public, as the employer's own autonomy interest may be served by presenting a politically neutral stance to the public. Moreover, the strength of the audience autonomy which is needed to add weight to the individual autonomy interest of the employee is at its greatest where the employee's speech involves the dissemination of information that can help improve the quality of the democratic process. The wearing of a badge or clothing that signals a personal political allegiance does not help inform the public about matters of public interest. It is thus unlikely that it would aid the democratic process sufficiently to warrant protection at work.[84]

---

[81] See for example *Boychuk v Symons* [1977] IRLR 395.

[82] The right to free expression was recognised as including the right to express oneself through the way one dresses by the European Commission on Human Rights in *Stevens v UK* (1986) 46 D&R 245.

[83] In *Stevens v UK* expulsion from school was not in breach of the ECHR in part because the student was not expressing an opinion or idea through his refusal to wear a school tie.

[84] See further G. Clayton and G. Pitt, 'Dress Codes and Freedom of Expression' [1997] European Human Rights Law Review (EHRLR) 54.

However, the fact that dress codes or other forms of non-verbal expression are unlikely to be granted protection against workplace sanctions is not based on the form of speech involved. Rather, it is the nature of the content of the speech which militates against its protection at work. If the content of non-verbal expression warrants protection, because it involves politically relevant information, or the disclosure of wrongdoing, then its non-verbal nature would not prevent its protection. Thus the content of the expression, as with verbal speech, remains the key factor.

Conclusion

The nature of the speech is the key factor in determining the scope of any free speech protection at work. If protection for speech were based mainly on individual autonomy, then the content and nature of the speech would be less important. But as the argument for employment protection for the exercise of free speech is predicated on the interests of the audience to hear what is said, the nature of the speech becomes paramount. The scope of the protection and of any limitation on it will therefore be determined by the extent to which the speech serves the interests of the audience.

Where audience interests are served by the speech it will be difficult for the employer to show that there are good reasons to allow a restriction on the right to free speech. Some types of speech should clearly be protected virtually regardless of any other factors; after all, it is hard to find any reason not to grant protection to an employee who discloses an imminent and serious physical danger to the public. Protection from retribution at work in such circumstances cannot really be gainsaid. In other circumstances, other factors, discussed below, could combine to mean that the employer can establish a case for restricting the right to free speech at work, even if protection of the right to speak itself remains.

The Status of the Employer and the Public/Private Divide

The exact dividing line between public and private sector employers is acknowledged to be difficult to draw with any certainty.[85] It may well be that, in any event, the distinction has only limited relevance in assessing the extent to which freedom of speech should be protected at work, and the consequent breadth of any restrictions placed on it. Deciding whether a body is public or private in nature is vital in areas such as judicial review, as the status of the body determines whether the remedy is available at all. The distinction is less important in relation to the extent to which freedom of speech should be protected in the workplace. As with the argument for special protection for

---

[85] G. Morris, 'The Human Rights Act and the Public/Private Divide in Employment Law' [1998] ILJ 293, G. Morris and S. Fredman, 'Public or Private? State Employees and Judicial Review' (1991) 107 LQR 298, D. Oliver, 'Common Values in Public and Private Law and the Public/Private Divide' [1997] PL 630.

political speech, the emphasis is better placed on the subject matter of the speech than on the legal form of the employer.

There is an extent to which the interests of public and private sector employers differ. The economic interests of the public sector employer are more limited, as the state provides services to the public not to make a profit, but because of a need for the services. This is not to say that public sector employers have no financial interests, but in the public sector in particular, financial considerations alone will not give rise to strong grounds for restricting employee speech. Instead the requirements of the audience are likely to take precedence, because the arguments in favour of freedom of speech based on the democratic value of speech are particularly strong in the case of public sector employment. There is a clear interest in allowing the workings of government, national or local, to be open and subject to scrutiny by the people who form the electorate to whom it is accountable.[86] This interest extends beyond the workings of central or local government and covers information on what occurs within industries and services funded by the public. The significant public interest in the workings of the state and its emanations means that greater rights to free speech at work are warranted in relation to the public sector and the private providers of essential services than for the rest of the private sector.

Because of the different audience interests at stake, the distinction between the public and private sector may therefore be of some relevance in determining the extent to which freedom of speech should be allowed in the workplace. However, its relevance is limited, not least because of the difficulty in deciding exactly which enterprises are public sector and which are not. This question has become increasingly complex in recent years after the privatisation of numerous public utilities, the contracting out of some parts of state run enterprises such as cleaning and catering in hospitals to private contractors, and the move of parts of the public sector, such as individual prisons, to the private sector.[87] Moreover, it is notable that many businesses which provide important public services, and in which the public have a legitimate interest, such as newspapers and other parts of the media, have always been firmly in the private sector.

As with the question of classifying what amounts to political speech, exact classification of employer status will not always be helpful. The focus should rather be on the importance of the information spoken about. Strong audience interests in speech are more likely where the employer is in the core of the public sector because of the potential political implications of what is said; but it is the political significance of the speech rather than the status of the employer which determines its importance. There will be times when the

---

[86] As recognised by the introduction of the Freedom of Information Act 2000.

[87] See G. Morris, 'The Human Rights Act and the Public/Private Divide in Employment Law' [1998] ILJ 293.

status of the employer defines the status and significance of the information. Take the example of an employer's costs in extravagantly redecorating the workplace. Public discussion of the matter is of little public interest if the employer is clearly in the private sector. If it is clearly in the public sector, on the other hand, it may be a legitimate subject for discussion, as it will involve the use, and possible misuse, of public money. If the employer is of mixed status, for example a catering company with contracts for catering in hospitals, among many others, the information may also not be of much public interest, assuming the contract with the hospital is provided at a competitive rate, so that there can be no allegation that the redecoration is to the detriment of levels of service provided by public money. In contrast, if the subject for discussion was poor standards of work, this would be of public interest in the case of both the public sector employer and the catering company, as both are providing a service used and funded by the public. The legitimacy of any restrictions on speech will usually depend more on the type of information discussed than on the precise legal status of the employer, but at times the identity of the employer will determine the public importance of the information.

THE STATUS OF THE EMPLOYEE

Unlike protection for free speech in any other context, the question of whether to provide employment protection for freedom of speech may depend to a degree on the status of the speaker. The status of the employee can be relevant in two contrasting ways. First, although, in terms of its contribution to personal autonomy and dignity, the status of the speaker is irrelevant to the value of the speech, once audience interests in the speech are considered the position changes. In some contexts, the higher the status of the employee, the greater the value to the audience of what is said. Of course the extent to which status is relevant does depend on the type of information. Where speech relates to an imminent danger to health or safety, or some other urgent matter, the identity of the speaker is not of importance. But in respect of other types of speech, the status of the employee may be relevant, as the views of those with seniority may be understood to be more authoritative than those of more junior employees. An allegation of fraud against a senior manager in a company may be more credible if it comes from another senior manager than from a junior employee, if the more senior person is likely to have had access to a greater range of information about the allegation. Similarly, in cases of personal comment or principled dissent, seniority may be relevant. An assertion that government policy is not working to achieve its objectives, made by a senior employee within a part of the public sector such as education, may well be seen as of high value because the seniority or status of the speaker impacts on the audience interests in the speech. This is the case, even though at the level of personal autonomy the speech is of equal value whoever the speaker.

Set against this are a number of reasons why the speech of senior employees should be subject to greater restrictions. It has been argued in relation to the US jurisdiction that senior employees owe a greater duty of loyalty to the employer than their juniors,[88] particularly where an employee's performance is assessed partly on the basis of loyalty to the employer. In many employment sectors the performance of more junior staff is readily assessed in terms of either input or output, hours worked or goods produced. Where staff are involved in management level tasks, performance becomes more difficult to measure. At this level, employees act as representatives of the employer, both in the eyes of the outside world, and internally, and so may owe a more extensive duty of confidence to the employer.

Moreover, senior staff are likely to be identified more readily as representing the employer, and this may give a further reason to restrict their speech. The employer does enjoy some rights to autonomy, albeit not as strong as those of the employee, and these rights are infringed if an employee can appear to speak on behalf of the company, and yet not represent company policy. If a senior employee at an agro-chemical company expresses doubts over the safety of genetically modified crops, this is likely to give rise to significant publicity and public comment, potentially leading to economic loss for the employer. Such a comment from a more junior, or less specialised employee, such as a member of the secretarial staff, is unlikely to have the same impact. Employees with a sufficiently high level of seniority to be taken to represent the views of the company may, legitimately, have their rights to free expression restricted in the workplace, subject always to the paramount consideration of the subject matter of the speech. Any employee, however senior, should be protected from retaliation for raising matters of a serious and urgent nature, particularly matters impacting on health and safety.

An employee, even though not particularly senior, may have the duty to represent the employer as part of the job. A press spokesperson may not be senior enough to represent the company in any other context (such as to bind the company in terms of criminal liability),[89] yet the nature of the job means that such an employee will have the right to freedom of speech legitimately curtailed to the extent that that right may not be exercised at work. For instance, the dismissal of an employee whose job is to act as a spokesperson for a defence manufacturer could be proportionate if the individual has been speaking publicly in favour of reduced arms spending.[90] The individual may have a right to voice such an opinion, but the right does not extend to a right to remain in that particular job whilst doing so.

---

[88] C. Glick, 'Free Speech, the Private Employee and State Constitutions' (1982) 91 Yale LJ 522.

[89] *Tesco Supermarkets Ltd v Natrass* [1972] AC 153.

[90] See *Korb v Raythorn* 574 NE 2d 370 (Mass 1991) where dismissal in such circumstances was not in breach of public policy.

The fact that an employee represents the employer in the eyes of the public gives rise to one of the stronger reasons for restricting employment protection for exercising freedom of speech. In the case of Glen Hoddle, the manager of the England football team sacked for expressing his views on the causes of disability,[91] his status in a very public job must have played a large role in the decision to dismiss him. His was probably the most high profile job in the most popular sport in the country. The attention of the whole country and beyond were drawn to his comments, and to allow him to stay on without a clear retraction of his views, or at least a fuller explanation and apology for any offence caused, could bring the whole sport into disrepute. In order to dissociate the Football Association from his comments, dismissal was perhaps inevitable. There were many factors that suggest that protection should have been available: the subject matter of the speech was a personal view or opinion; and the opinion bore no relation to his conduct in the job. Moreover, it is arguable that dismissal interfered with his right to freedom of religion. However, the high status of the employee in that case gave rise to a justification for the employer to restrict his right to remain in that particular job.

FINANCIAL LOSS TO EMPLOYER

It is arguable that financial implications should not be a relevant consideration. Freedom of speech, being an important part of personal autonomy and human dignity, cannot have financial value attached to it. The consequences for the employee of speaking up at work can be serious, involving significant financial and social loss, loss of security, of identity, and of the autonomy that can be found through a job. Where audience interests to hear what is said are added to the personal interest in speech, it becomes more difficult to argue for restrictions on speech on purely financial grounds. However, the restrictions considered here are not absolute restrictions on the right to speak, but restrictions on the extent to which the right extends to the sphere of work. The financial interests of employers do therefore have a place in the equation. Indeed, when considering the interests of employers above, the need for the enterprise to make a profit was identified as a legitimate interest of the employer and of the other employees in the enterprise, one which had the potential to justify restricting freedom of speech in the workplace.

Whether or not the employer suffers economic loss as a result of an employee's speech is therefore a relevant circumstance to consider in assessing the proportionality of any restrictions on the right to free speech. In some circumstances, employee speech will have no financial impact on the employer. For instance, participation by teachers in any public debate on the merits of selective or specialist education would be unlikely to have financial implications for a state school. At the other end of the scale, a public declaration that

---

[91] *The Guardian*, 3 February 1999.

goods produced by the employer were of low quality, or constituted a safety hazard, would have a significant impact on profit margins. Dr Andrew Millar's case is a good example of significant financial loss caused by the exercise of freedom of speech. Before his disclosure to shareholders that press releases reporting the imminent launch of a major new cancer drug were misleading, shares in his employer, British Biotech, were worth £3; by the time the case was settled, they had slumped to around 15p.[92] As with the other factors considered here, the question of financial loss is subsidiary to the issue of the subject matter of speech, but where a concern raised does not relate to immediate danger to the public, the financial implications of the speech for the employer will be a legitimate consideration in determining whether a restriction on speech is proportionate. Moreover, if the financial loss caused is of a degree that risks the viability of the enterprise altogether, so that the interests of other employees are also harmed, it will be very hard to justify protection of the right to free speech. In cases of significant financial loss, protection will only be necessary where clear audience interests are served by the speech, such that the individual rights of the workforce are overridden by the interests of the general public in the information disclosed. In Dr Millar's case, the disclosure was justified as it revealed serious financial malpractice by the company. Moreover, although the financial success of the company was jeopardised, that success had been maintained by issuing misleading press releases. British Biotech was later formally reprimanded for this behaviour by the Stock Exchange.

In assessing the relevance of financial issues to the scope of employment protection for free speech, it is of course necessary to consider the actual level of financial loss caused. In some cases, financial loss could be large, even involving job losses. However, in many cases the level of financial loss will not be large. Of more concern to the employer can be the embarrassment caused by the speech. To have a member of staff criticise a corporate policy in public often just causes the employer loss of face rather than loss of profit. Any claim of financial loss pleaded by an employer as a relevant circumstance to be taken into account in assessing whether speech warrants protection should be considered carefully. There should be no assumption that public embarrassment of the employer will actually cause financial losses. In many cases, embarrassing an enterprise does not have a great financial impact: attempts by anti-apartheid campaigners to embarrass companies operating in South Africa in recent decades did not lead the targeted companies to go out of business; the leaflet circulated by the defendants in the 'McLibel' case[93] which was critical of many of the practices of McDonalds does not seem to have reduced consumption at their fast food outlets despite the publicity for the trial. Taking a hypothetical example of speech affecting the public sector,

[92] *The Guardian*, 19 June 1999.
[93] *McDonalds Corporation v Steel and another* [1995] 3 All ER 615.

speech critical of staffing levels at a hospital, aimed at the wider public, may not have a dramatic effect on use of the hospital by commissioning GPs, who are likely already to be aware of standards in their locality.

Financial loss caused to the employer may thus be a relevant consideration in assessing the proportionality of any workplace restrictions on free speech, but it should not be given undue weight. Other considerations, such as the subject matter of the speech, are more important. Moreover, a claim of financial loss by an employer should be considered carefully to check the extent of the loss. Causing embarrassment or humiliation should not be equated with financial loss. Given the importance of the right to freedom of speech as a right that upholds personal autonomy, it should not be overridden, in effect, by an employer's wish to avoid embarrassment.

CHANNEL OF COMMUNICATION

After the subject matter of the speech, the channel of communication used by the employee to speak, with which it is closely connected, is probably the most important factor involved in assessing whether a restriction on the right to speak at work is justified. This is because the interests of the employer that are harmed by speech vary considerably depending on whether the speech is made internally within the organisation or externally, either to a regulatory body or on a wider basis such as to the press.

Where disclosure is made internally to the business very few employer interests are harmed. The interests that are threatened when employees speak were identified above as the employer's economic interests, interests in autonomy, interests in loyalty and confidence, and the interest in freedom to run the business as the employer chooses, or to enjoy managerial prerogative. These interests will not usually be harmed by speech that remains internal to the enterprise. In particular, there is no breach of confidence or loyalty if the matter is raised internally. If employer interests are harmed by internal speech then this may give initial grounds for restricting free speech, but other factors, such as the subject matter of speech, may still mean that any such restrictions would be disproportionate.

Harm could be caused to an employer's interests even if speech remains internal, particularly if the disclosure leads to disruption at the workplace. For example, an employee who discloses wrongdoing by a colleague may well be viewed with disfavour by the rest of the workforce for supposed disloyalty, and this could be very disruptive. In such a case the subject matter of the speech could be critical in deciding whether speech should be protected. If the matter revealed relates to wrongdoing, protection should still be allowed despite the interference with employer interests. If no wrongdoing is involved, employment protection would not be automatic and may depend on other factors such as the level of disruption caused, any financial loss, and the motive of the employee. However, in most cases, internal disclosure should be given employment protection on a fairly automatic basis: few employer interests are harmed by the speech, the speech can serve strong personal interests of the employee and, where wrongdoing is disclosed, it can serve the public interest by discovering and then preventing wrongdoing.

More complicated is the case of speech made in a public forum. Here the interests of the employer are more obviously infringed. Except where the information has no quality of confidence at all, for example because it relates to the disclosure of serious wrongdoing,[94] the right to enjoy confidentiality from staff is immediately breached in cases of external speech, as is the right to a degree of loyalty from staff. If the disclosure results in adverse publicity for the employer, it may also cause financial loss and loss of reputation for the employer. In such cases it is likely that restrictions on the right to free speech will be proportionate, unless there are extremely strong reasons for protecting the speech. Again, the different types of speech need to be distinguished. Whistleblowing speech, which involves the disclosure of wrongdoing in the enterprise, may warrant different protection from political speech, which again may warrant different treatment from speech which amounts to more general comment; and different forms of external disclosure can be distinguished.

Whistleblowing

It will be hard to argue against allowing external disclosure of wrongdoing, as the public interest is most obviously served by disclosure of the information. In fact, in some cases in the USA, the view has been taken that if wrongdoing is disclosed, then *only* external disclosure should be protected. The theory is that internal disclosure should not be encouraged as it allows wrongs to be covered up by the employer.[95] However, such an extreme stance is unnecessary. Internal whistleblowing can also allow a good employer to put right the wrong reported with the minimum of loss and disruption. But in cases where the wrong is not put right after an internal disclosure, wider disclosure will be justified. External disclosure of serious and imminent threats, such as to health and safety, will also be justified without prior attempts to minimise disruption by internal reporting. The deciding factor in such cases will be the exact nature of the speech and therefore the scope of the audience or public interest served by the speech.

A further factor of relevance in such cases is the extent of the external reporting. Reporting outside the enterprise to a regulatory body charged with investigating the subject matter of the report (disclosure of tax fraud to the Inland Revenue, for instance) will be easier to justify and protect than disclosure of such a matter to the press. Disclosure to regulatory bodies, although technically external to the enterprise, can really be viewed in the

---

[94] *Initial Services v Putterill* [1968] 1 QB 396, discussed in more detail in Chapter 4 below.
[95] *Zaniecki v P. A. Bergner & Co* 493 NE 2d 419 (1986), *Wiltsie v Baby Grand Corp* 774 P 2d 432 (1989), *House v Carter-Wallace Inc* 556 A 2d 353 (1989).

same light as internal disclosure. If the allegation of wrongdoing is well founded, then any loss to the employer will be justifiable. If it is unfounded, there is unlikely to be much loss to the employer as the matter should remain confidential. The only cost will be the cost of complying with any investigation undertaken by the regulatory body. However, the risk of wasted costs is outweighed by the public interest in allowing regulators to do their work of uncovering wrongdoing and maintaining safety. Moreover, the costs are unlikely to occur repeatedly to the same employer, unless an employee is being vindictive. In such a case employment protection for the speaker would not be warranted; the bad motive of the employee, the inaccuracy of the information and the financial loss caused mean that the employer's restriction on the right to free speech would be proportionate.

External disclosure can also be made on a much wider basis, such as to the press. In these circumstances, the employer's interest will be much more severely infringed, and again this may give reasonable grounds for a restriction on speech. If the subject matter is such that it demands immediate and widespread publication, then restrictions on speech may not be proportionate. Otherwise, if the same result (the ending of the wrongdoing) could have been achieved by internal disclosure, then employment protection may not be justified: the implied duty of loyalty owed by employees to the employer will require that they find the least harmful way to achieve their ends. If internal disclosure could equally well achieve the ending of wrongdoing, external disclosure will not be warranted, and sanctions imposed by an employer for making such disclosures may well be proportionate. Conversely, internal disclosure may be inappropriate because of the seriousness of the issue or because of fear of retaliation, or internal disclosure may have been tried already but without success. In such circumstances, the extension of protection to external disclosure will usually be justified.

Political Speech

Where the employee's speech relates to a political matter, the public and audience interest in hearing the speech is likely to provide strong grounds for protection. In order to serve its purpose of contributing to the democratic process such speech requires publicity, and so the only suitable channel for communication of the ideas will be external to the employer. With such strong audience interests adding to the personal autonomy interests of the speaker, any interests of the employer in restricting the speech will need to be very strong if they are to be upheld. Perhaps the only case where employer interests will be strong enough will be where the expression prevents the employee from fulfilling key aspects of the job. An example of such a situation can be found in the case of *Van Der Heijden v the Netherlands*[96] heard by the

---

[96] (1985) D&R 101.

European Commission on Human Rights, but whose facts could arise in any jurisdiction. Here a regional director of a welfare service for immigrants was dismissed for being a member of an extreme political party which was publicly hostile to the presence of immigrant workers in the country. The work of the employing foundation would have been hampered by the continued employment of Van Der Heijden. The decision of the European Commission on Human Rights that his right to freedom of expression was not breached by the dismissal fits the suggestions made above on how political speech should be treated. Van Der Heijden's speech was incompatible with his senior post and his freedom of speech was not totally curtailed: he remained free to express his political views via membership of the political party, but his employment status could not be simultaneously protected.

General Comment and Principled Dissent

Where the employee wants to exercise the right to freedom of speech in a more general way, the issue of the channel of communication causes more difficulty. Employment protection may not be warranted in cases where general comment (presumably critical) is made in public, in particular because the philosophical basis for protecting such speech is much more limited than in the case of whistleblowing or political speech. Where the speech is of a general nature, such as adverse comment on corporate policy, the audience interests are not as clear as in cases of whistleblowing or political speech. The employer is thus more likely to show that restrictions on free speech are proportionate, especially if the speech causes financial loss or disruption at work. Yet it should not be assumed that employment protection should be restricted in all cases of external comment. In assessing the proportionality of any restrictions on speech, it should be borne in mind that as with political speech, general comment can serve audience interests (as discussed above) and that such speech by its nature usually requires publicity if it is to be of any value. Once these facts are taken into account, it may again be harder for the employer to show that restrictions are proportionate in the circumstances.

Accuracy of Information Disclosed

Where speech is viewed as an aspect of personal autonomy, the accuracy or otherwise of the statements made is not particularly important, as the value of speech as an aspect of individual expression does not depend on it being accurate. But for the interests of the audience to be served by speech, the content of the speech does need to be reasonably accurate. Where the speech consists of opinion, personal views, political or other comment, it may be appropriate to consider accuracy, but it cannot be given much weight, as opinion, by its nature, cannot always be 'accurate'. In cases of whistleblowing, however, accuracy becomes important. There is obviously no inherent value in being informed about a non-existent danger or risk. Indeed, disclosure of inaccurate information can create its own dangers.

Yet, to refuse protection to an employee in a whistleblowing case because the claim turns out to be inaccurate will militate against any disclosures being made, accurate or not. If an employee is granted protection in cases of accuracy and inaccuracy, the wrongdoing can be uncovered; if protection depends on being right, then many employees will not raise a concern unless they can guarantee its truth, for fear of being dismissed if they turn out, with hindsight, to be wrong. Mill's argument for freedom of speech based on the discovery of truth[97] applies in such a case. The freedom to disclose suspicions of wrongdoing will enable the true wrongdoing to be discovered. If in the process some false claims are made, this is an acceptable price to pay for the discovery of the truth in the other cases.

Again, the accuracy of information is a factor that can be of relevance to the question of whether restrictions on speech are proportionate. Its exact relevance will depend to a large extent on the channel used to raise the concern. Disclosure of an unfounded suspicion in a national newspaper is unlikely to warrant employment protection. In contrast, the raising of a concern informally within the organisation should be protected, whether or not the concern is well founded. Moreover, the motive of the employee may well be relevant. Malicious spreading of rumour is unlikely to be protected: an attempt to avoid losses being caused to the employer (for example by disclosing suspected fraud) may be viewed very differently.

MOTIVE

The question of motive, both of employee and employer, is closely bound to other circumstances already discussed. The motive of the employer in restricting speech clearly needs consideration. If the employer's motivation in dismissing an employee who has exercised the right to free speech is to increase profits, or to avoid embarrassment, it will be unlikely that restricting free speech will be proportionate. The right to free speech is too fundamental to be easily displaced by a profit motive or a desire for an undeserved untarnished reputation. On the other hand, as discussed above, if financial loss is to result from the speech, then an employer motivated to avoid such loss may well find that it is proportionate to restrict the speech of an employee.

The motive of the employee may also be a relevant factor in establishing whether a restriction is proportionate. Where the speech is justified only on the basis of personal autonomy, a malicious motive on the part of the speaker may seriously undermine the right to speak. The right to self expression does not extend to a right to criticise another for purely malicious purposes. However, if the speech serves audience interests as well, then a malicious

---

[97]   J. S. Mill, 'On Liberty' in S. Collini (ed), *On Liberty and Other Writings* (1989) Cambridge University Press, Cambridge.

motive on the part of the employee will not necessarily prevent protection of that speech.

A contrast has to be drawn here between banning the speech altogether and allowing employment protection to the speaker. An employee, regardless of motive, should not be prevented from reporting serious fraud by the employer, or a severe safety risk. The nature of the information means that the speech needs to be heard. Whether or not that employee deserves employment protection is a different question altogether, and may depend on the other circumstances of the case. Vindictive disclosure to a wide audience, timed to cause maximum embarrassment to the employer, will not warrant employment protection, and in such circumstances an employer should be able to establish that any resulting dismissal was a proportionate response to the damage caused to the enterprise. The employer's case will be strengthened further if the information is inaccurate, but even if the information is accurate, the malicious motive will mean that the employer's actions in dismissing will be likely to be reasonable. Even though the actual speech should be allowed to be made, the employee's vindictive conduct will have indicated too low a level of loyalty towards the employer to warrant continued employment. Yet again, the subject matter of the disclosure is relevant here. Disclosure of a serious risk to an appropriate person, even with malicious motives, may be regarded as warranting protection. Although the actual disclosure may have been prompted by malice, it may be sufficiently important for the information to be disclosed for some reward to be deserved by the employee; continued employment may well be seen to be an appropriate reward. Maliciously disclosing false information, on the other hand, clearly does not warrant protection.

DISRUPTION AT WORK

The exercise of free speech by an employee may cause significant disruption at the workplace. For example, time may be spent dealing with the repercussions of the speech, or dealing with the media reaction where controversial views are aired. Moreover, other employees may be upset by the disclosures made or views expressed, making them unwilling to work with the speaker and severely interfering with the smooth running of the enterprise. Clearly in such circumstances, even if no large scale financial loss is involved, the disruption caused may be a relevant circumstance to consider in deciding whether to extend employment protection to the speaker. One of the reasons for recognising an employer's right to loyalty from the employee is that it allows for the workplace to be run as smoothly as possible. Where this is disrupted, an interest of the employer is infringed, and this may give grounds to the employer to restrict the employee's right to speak.[98]

---

[98] *Camelot Group plc v Centaur Communications Ltd* [1998] 1 All ER 251 CA. 'Clearly there is unease and suspicion amongst the employees of the company which inhibits good working relationships', per Schiemann LJ at 261.

More important, perhaps, than a recognition of the right of the employer to avoid disruption of the workplace, is the converse: that where no disruption is caused, speech should be allowed. In assessing whether an employer's actions in restricting speech are proportionate, it should not be assumed that disruption will be caused to the workplace by the exercise of free speech. Even if other staff are upset by a view expressed, this should not be relevant to the assessment of proportionality unless it affects working practice in a significant way. Any claim that the speech has caused disruption at work should be examined carefully and only taken into account if the disruption is significant, for example it causes financial loss, or is prolonged over time so that the morale of staff is severely affected. In this way, the importance of free speech as a fundamental right is recognised, whilst allowing adequate recognition of the employer's interests when they are significantly interfered with.

THE INTERACTION OF DIFFERENT FACTORS

Where a workplace sanction is imposed on an employee for the exercise of his freedom of speech, a number of the factors discussed above will impact on the proportionality of that sanction. The case of Dr Arpad Pusztai, discussed in the introduction, illustrates the complexity that can arise, and can serve as a useful example of how the many different factors interact. Dr Pusztai used the national media to raise his concerns about the potential health hazard of genetically modified potato crops. He was then forced to take early retirement, and was prevented from discussing his research data further. The concern he raised was one about public health and safety, and arguably therefore needed the widest possible discussion, suggesting that widespread external discussion was reasonable. However, a number of factors could suggest the opposite. His claims related to preliminary findings of incomplete research. Although a definitive answer on the health effects of GM crops may not be possible at this stage of the research process, his research had not even been peer reviewed, a recognised verification process in this type of research. The potential lack of accuracy of the claims could affect the reasonableness of his external speech. Moreover, Dr Pusztai was seeking publicity primarily to attract research funding, so that his motive was not merely to alert the public to potential health risks. Had the concerns been raised with the Department of Health, the Scottish Office (the sponsor of the research), the House of Lords committee that was looking at European regulation of GM crops at the time, or with any other interested party, the matter might be viewed differently, and it would then be very hard to argue that any restrictions on his speech were reasonable. On the other hand, despite these factors suggesting that the restrictions were proportionate, the overall outcome may still be that restrictions were a disproportionate response by the employer. The nature of the health risk, if Dr Pusztai's fears are correct, is huge. As GM crops are used in many foodstuffs, there is the potential for most of the population to be affected. It is quite arguable therefore that the nature of the information is such that an early and widespread warning, via national media, is appropriate. Moreover, the discussion did not cause financial loss to the employing institution, it might even have attracted more funding, as Dr Pusztai hoped. Given these circumstances, a warning about premature discussion of preliminary research findings might have been appropriate, but it is hard to argue that enforced retirement and a ban on discussion of the research was a proportionate response to Dr Pusztai's conduct.

CONCLUSION

The aim of this chapter has been to create a model for determining what the ideal protection for freedom of expression in the workplace would be. The large number of factors considered in the chapter demonstrates the complexity of formulating optimal protection for free speech at work. The consideration of each factor and its interaction with all the others indicates that in any individual case there will be such a variety of different circumstances that impact on a decision that it is difficult to predict in the abstract when employment protection ought to be provided. However, the discussion of the numerous circumstances that may impact on that decision have highlighted some key issues.

First, identification of the various philosophical underpinnings of the right to free speech is necessary if the real importance of the right is to be recognised, such that it can prevail over the traditional view that the autonomy of the employer is paramount. The fact that the right to freedom of speech does more than uphold the human dignity and autonomy of the speaker, and also promotes the interests of those who hear what is said, explains not only why protection is needed, but why it needs to extend to the workplace. Without a sufficient understanding of this aspect of free speech theory, the right to freedom of expression can too easily be viewed as a personal right to dignity and autonomy which the employee chooses to forfeit when he or she enters the workplace.

Secondly, the content of the speech is of greatest significance in determining whether the speaker warrants employment protection where that speech offends the employer. It is only when the subject matter of the speech can be shown to serve the interests of the audience that the right to free speech will be sufficient to prevail over the interests of the employer. The third issue leads on from the second and is this: protection of free speech will only be adequately protected if a sufficiently broad notion of audience interest is espoused. Use of the term 'public interest', with the connotations the term has of relating only to specific information that the world *needs* to know, may be too narrow a term. Audience interest suggests something wider; a recognition that the population as a whole benefits from wide debate and free access to information. The protection of an individual right to free speech in the otherwise private sphere of the employment relationship is justified because of the support it gives to the wider public to enhance their dignity and autonomy through hearing the well informed views of others. A full understanding of the scope of the audience interest in information will explain why an assumption should be made in favour of protecting a right to free speech at work.

The final key point here is the question of where this leaves the interests of the employer who may be offended or harmed by the speech. The answer is that employer interests do have some validity, and that this should be recognised by allowing proportionate restrictions to the right to free speech. Where the speech relates to serious wrongdoing by the employer, restrictions will rarely be proportionate, particularly if an appropriate medium of communication is used. In other cases, such as cases of general comment on corporate policy, the issues are more complex, and the full circumstances will need to be considered. Although it is impossible to avoid any form of balancing of interests, the creation of a clear right, with restrictions allowed where they are proportionate to serve legitimate employer interests, should create the right tone for the protection. The emphasis is put on the right to free speech, but the rights of employers are given protection where such protection is deserved.

Later chapters will consider the extent to which the arguments explored in this chapter are recognised within the law as it currently stands.

3

Freedom of Expression and Human Rights: The European Convention on Human Rights

The right to freedom of expression is well recognised in international law. Articles protecting free speech are contained in, among others, the Universal Declaration of Human Rights, the European Convention on Human Rights and the International Covenant on Civil and Political Rights.[1] As well as protection in human rights documents, international standards relating to freedom of speech and work can be found in the Conventions and Recommendations of the International Labour Organisation (ILO). The main focus of this chapter is on the law of the European Convention on Human Rights, and its implementation in the United Kingdom through the Human Rights Act 1998. Before turning to the law under Article 10 of the ECHR, the standards set by the ILO for workplace protection of rights of freedom of expression will be discussed.

INTERNATIONAL LABOUR STANDARDS AND FREE SPEECH

The International Labour Organisation was founded in 1919 by the peace treaties concluded at the end of the First World War. The aims of the ILO were to improve the chances of lasting peace by the establishment of social justice, via improved employment standards on an international scale.[2] The ILO now forms part of the United Nations, and the United Kingdom is bound under international law to comply with conventions which it ratifies. The ILO is a tripartite organisation, having representatives from governments, and employers' and workers' representatives in each part of its organisation. The ILO has three limbs: it is made up of a governing body; a permanent secretariat, the International Labour Office; and the International Labour Conference which meets on an annual basis.

---

[1] Article 19 UDHR, Article 10 ECHR, Article 19 International Covenant on Civil and Political Rights. Free speech is also protected by Article 13 American Convention on Human Rights.

[2] See A. Alcock, *A History of the ILO* (1971) Macmillan, London.

To date, the ILO has passed 183 conventions covering a huge range of issues such as maternity rights, health and safety, night working rules and freedom of association. States that ratify conventions are required to take measures to put the standards enunciated in the convention into practice. The effectiveness of these measures is monitored on a regular basis by expert committees of the Labour Conference. Mention of a state's failure to comply can be made in a special paragraph of the Committee of Experts' report, but no stronger or more direct sanctions are available to the ILO if a state does not comply with a convention. In addition to the regular monitoring of compliance, individual states can make complaints about non-compliance. However, there is no individual right of petition regarding the interpretation of standards or failures of implementation. Moreover, many conventions have very low rates of ratification and states can denounce conventions after ratification if they no longer comply with their terms. The enforcement mechanisms available to the ILO are therefore very weak, relying mainly on embarrassment and diplomatic pressure to compel states to comply. Nonetheless, the conventions of the ILO can be used as models against which domestic law can be measured. Where employment protection in the UK falls below the international standards, the ILO conventions can be used as an aid to interpreting domestic law, or to add pressure for its reform. With the introduction of the Human Rights Act 1998 courts will increasingly need to consider the law of other jurisdictions when interpreting domestic law, and it is possible that this may lead to increased use of international comparisons and standards.

Two conventions are of relevance to the issue of freedom of expression and the workplace. The first is Convention No 158 on Termination of Employment. This Convention requires states to protect staff from dismissal without good cause. A number of causes are listed[3] as prohibited grounds for dismissal, such as membership of or activities in trade unions and absence on maternity leave. Other prohibited reasons for dismissal are 'the filing of a complaint or the participation in proceedings against an employer involving alleged violation of laws or regulations or recourse to competent administrative authorities'; and 'race, colour, sex, marital status, family responsibilities, pregnancy, religion, political opinion, national extraction or social origin'. Where an employee is dismissed for disclosing that an employer has broken the law it may be that dismissal would contravene Convention No 158. So might dismissal for voicing political opinion. Compliance with the Convention by the UK would require that protection be granted to employees against such dismissals. With the introduction of the Public Interest Disclosure Act 1998, it may be that staff are granted protection for disclosing wrongdoing, although protection against dismissal on grounds of political opinion is less specific. However, Convention No 158 is

---

[3] Convention 158 Article 5.

not ratified by the UK, and so non-compliance cannot leave us open to sanction.

The second relevant convention was ratified by the UK in 1999. The 1958 Discrimination (Employment and Occupation) Convention No 111 obliges the UK government to ensure that measures are in place to protect workers against discrimination at work on a number of grounds including political opinion. This may have some relevance in cases where the views expressed by staff exercising the right to freedom of speech can be classed as political. If employees are not protected against work based sanctions for the expression of political views, it could be argued that the UK is in breach of its treaty obligations under Convention No 111. The Convention cannot be relied on directly by individuals, but the fact that under the Convention such speech should be protected could add weight to the other arguments explored in Chapter 2 in favour of protecting political speech against workplace sanctions.

Guidance on the scope of the non-discrimination rule can be found in the reports of the Committee of Experts on the Application of Conventions and Recommendations.[4] Guidance can also be found in the findings of the Committees of Experts that have considered referrals regarding discrimination on grounds of political opinion in a number of countries in recent years, such as the bans on certain types of work in Germany and the Czech and Slovak Republics for members of particular political parties.[5] From these reports, it is clear that the protection against discrimination on grounds of political opinion applies not only to the holding of political opinions, but also to the expression and communication of those opinions.[6] Staff dismissed or disciplined for expressing views that are seen as political could therefore be said to be discriminated against on grounds of political opinion. According to the Convention, staff should also be protected if they are not offered employment on grounds of their political opinion.[7]

However, the prohibition against discrimination in employment on grounds of political opinion is not absolute and a number of exceptions

---

[4] Report III, Equality in Employment and Occupation, General Survey of the Reports on the Discrimination (Employment and Occupation) Convention (No 111) and Recommendation (No 111) 1958, International Labour Conference 1988, ILO, Geneva; Report III, Special Survey on Equality in Employment and Occupation in respect of Convention No 111, International Labour Conference 1996, ILO, Geneva.

[5] Report of the Commission of Inquiry appointed under Art. 26 of the ILO Constitution to examine the observance by the Federal Republic of Germany of Convention No 111 (1987) LXX ILO Official Bulletin, Series B, Supplement 1; Report of the Committee set up to examine the representations made by the Trade Union Association of Bohemia, Moravia and Slovakia and by the Czech and Slovak Confederation of Trade Unions under Art. 24 of the ILO Constitution alleging non-observance by the Czech and Slovak Federal Republics of Convention No 111 (1992) LXXV ILO Official Bulletin, Series B.

[6] Report III, Special Survey on Equality in Employment and Occupation in respect of Convention No 111, International Labour Conference 1996, ILO, Geneva, para 45.

[7] Convention No 111, Article 1(3).

apply. If those exceptional circumstances are present, any lack of protection in domestic law against the imposition of penalties at work for the expression of political views would not be subject to adverse comparison with the international standards. Exceptions are allowed when they are based on the inherent requirements of the job.[8] For example, it has been accepted that some jobs, especially in parts of the public service, require political neutrality from staff. This is particularly so in the case of jobs with a high degree of responsibility or trust involved. Such exceptions are only accepted when they are based on detailed examination of the job involved: they cannot apply to whole sectors of work.[9] This requirement was discussed in detail in the report on the German work ban case, which considered the duty of faithfulness to constitutional principles required of all German civil servants, including teachers. The impact of this duty was that members of extreme right wing or left wing political parties could be dismissed or denied employment because their political parties were anti-democratic.[10] The Commission of Inquiry in the case found that the practice in Germany was incompatible with the terms of Convention No 111.[11] Whilst the need to maintain neutrality in the public service was accepted, it was being applied too indiscriminately. In many cases the ban on working was imposed even though the individual had never expressed anything but support for democratic principles. It was suggested that a blanket ban on working in the absence of any abuse by the individual was too broad an exception to the basic non-discrimination right.

Any exception should thus be construed narrowly, and should not be applied indiscriminately to whole sectors of work. Allowing discrimination against categories of staff, such as teachers, on the basis of political opinion is unnecessary. Closer regard has to be had to the particular aspects of the job, and the behaviour of individual members of staff. Teachers can be prevented from using their position to indoctrinate students, but those who do not take advantage of their position should not be discriminated against purely because their job gives them the potential to do so. This is not to say that some posts may not require staff to be politically neutral. For example, restrictions on grounds of political opinion would probably be justified for jobs which involve high levels of responsibility for policy making. However, individual jobs need to be classified for this purpose, in terms of the actual performance of the job or of particular tasks, rather than relying on restrictions applied to all staff in a particular area of public service. As in the German work ban case, a blanket ban on membership of certain political parties for all teachers is too

---

[8] Convention No 111, Article 1(3).

[9] Report III, Special Survey on Equality in Employment and Occupation in respect of Convention No 111, International Labour Conference 1996, ILO, Geneva, para 119.

[10] See further the cases of *Kosiek*, *Glasenapp* and *Vogt* discussed below at pp 78–81.

[11] Report of the Commission of Inquiry appointed under Art. 26 of the ILO Constitution to examine the observance by the Federal Republic of Germany of Convention No 111 (1987) LXX ILO.

indiscriminate to be a valid exception under the Convention. Moreover, where a particular job justifies restrictions on political opinion, those restrictions need to be proportionate. Thus for a number of public service jobs it may be justifiable to prevent staff from campaigning for political parties, but only in very sensitive posts will it be necessary to prohibit simple membership.

The standard of the ILO in Convention No 111 largely matches the model for protection against work based sanctions for political speech at work suggested in Chapter 2. Dismissal or other detriment imposed for exercising the right to freedom of expression on matters of a political nature would amount to discrimination at work on grounds of political opinion, unless there is an exception based on the inherent requirements of the job. Such action would clearly be in breach of Convention No 111. Likewise, in Chapter 2, it was suggested that staff should enjoy a right to free speech, particularly in relation to political speech, unless the employer could show that a restriction on the right would be proportionate, because the speech harmed other legitimate interests of the employer. To the extent that domestic law fails to protect employees against such discrimination, it may be that the UK is in breach of its treaty obligations. As suggested above, such a finding would not have huge practical significance for the employee. However, it may be of some persuasive value in formulating an individual challenge against the imposition of a work based sanction for exercising the right to free speech. Of more direct value, however, is the case law and jurisprudence on the European Convention on Human Rights.

THE HUMAN RIGHTS ACT 1998 AND THE EUROPEAN CONVENTION ON HUMAN RIGHTS

The implementation of the Human Rights Act 1998 opens up significant new avenues to explore when looking at the rights of those who exercise the right to free expression at work. It came into force on 2 October 2000 and partially incorporates the European Convention on Human Rights into domestic law. As a result, the ECHR contrasts strongly with other international standards such as those of the ILO, which cannot be enforced by individuals. The Human Rights Act 1998 (HRA) is arguably one of the most radical pieces of legislation in recent times. It changes the way in which the legal process will work, and transfers significant political power from parliament to the judiciary.[12] This shift is achieved by the Act's requirement that all UK statutes be interpreted to comply with the Convention, and that the common law be developed in harmony with Convention jurisprudence. The full impact of the

---

[12] See K. Ewing, 'The Human Rights Act and Parliamentary Democracy' (1999) 62 MLR 79, and C. Gearty, 'The Human Rights Act 1998: An Overview' in K. Ewing (ed), *Human Rights at Work* (2000) Institute of Employment Rights, London.

Act on the English legal system can only be guessed at at this stage, as judges adjust to making their decisions comply with European-wide standards of human rights protection. Moreover, unlike the system of judicial precedent and statutory interpretation to which the courts are used, the standards of the European Convention are often expressed as statements of principle rather than clear rules, and this will, in turn, change the way in which fundamental rights are protected in English law in future.

Whatever the full impact of the Act turns out to be, the presence in the Convention of a right to freedom of expression must have significant implications for workers who exercise that right. The remainder of this chapter will consider the working of the Human Rights Act 1998 and the various ways in which, through its operation, the jurisprudence of the ECHR will impact upon the employment relationship.

THE LEGAL POSITION PRIOR TO
THE HUMAN RIGHTS ACT 1998

The process of incorporation of the European Convention on Human Rights has been slow. Drafted in the aftermath of the Second World War, the Convention was ratified by the UK in 1951,[13] but operated only as an international treaty, binding the government in international law. It was not until 1966 that British citizens were granted an individual right of petition to the European Court of Human Rights in Strasbourg. Between 1966 and 2000, individual claims could be taken to the European Court of Human Rights, but its jurisprudence could not be relied on directly in British courts, and breaches of the Convention could not found a claim. The introduction of the Human Rights Act 1998 (HRA) allows individuals for the first time to bring human rights claims under the Convention directly before UK courts and tribunals.

Despite the lack of direct enforceability prior to 2000, courts in the UK have been using the jurisprudence of the Convention indirectly for some time to aid the interpretation and development of the common law, as well as to help interpret domestic primary and secondary legislation in cases of uncertainty or ambiguity.[14] However, this use of the Convention has been strictly limited to cases of ambiguity.[15] In *R v Secretary of State for the Home Department, ex p Brind*[16] it was held that ministers could not be required by law to exercise the discretion granted by legislation in accordance with the Con-

---

[13] The UK was the first state to ratify the Convention. The Convention came into force in 1953. For a full history of the ECHR see A. W. B. Simpson, *Human Rights and the End of Empire* (2001) Oxford University Press, Oxford.

[14] The extent to which the Convention was relied upon is reflected in the fact that some argued that full incorporation of the Convention might have become unnecessary; see Lord Browne-Wilkinson, 'The Infiltration of a Bill of Rights' (1992) PL 397.

[15] *Waddington v Miah* [1974] 1 WLR 683.   [16] [1991] 1 AC 696.

vention. This was confirmed in *R v Ministry of Defence, ex p Smith*[17] in which the Court of Appeal held that a failure to take account of the Convention was not of itself grounds for impugning the exercise of discretion of a minister. The Convention could only provide background to a complaint of irrationality in a claim for judicial review. The Convention has also been used by courts (as opposed to ministers) in considering whether or not to grant discretionary remedies such as injunctions. In *Attorney-General v Guardian Newspapers Ltd*[18] the House of Lords considered the Convention in deciding to uphold the injunctions against publication of the book *Spycatcher* on grounds of national security.[19]

A further way in which Convention law has been able to be used in domestic courts is via the law of the European Union. Article 6(2) of the new Treaty of European Union requires the EU to respect fundamental rights under the ECHR, and the ECJ has accepted that EC law is to be interpreted so as to conform with the Convention.[20] Since the UK courts must interpret domestic legislation to comply with EU law, there are therefore areas of national law, such as discrimination law, that should be interpreted by UK courts to comply with the Convention independently of the Human Rights Act.[21] However, apart from these fairly limited areas, and particularly where there has been no inherent ambiguity in the law, the jurisprudence of the Convention has been, until the introduction of the HRA, of limited direct use domestically.

THE OPERATION OF THE HUMAN RIGHTS ACT 1998

The Human Rights Act introduces a crucial change in the role of the Convention in domestic law, significantly enhancing its influence, particularly in the introduction of individual rights of action against public authorities for breach of Convention rights. However, it should be noted this is not achieved by directly incorporating the European Convention on Human Rights into UK law. Instead, the doctrine of parliamentary sovereignty is preserved.[22] Where domestic law and the law of the Convention conflict, courts are to interpret statute and delegated legislation to comply with the Convention

---

[17] [1996] 1 All ER 257.   [18] [1987] 1 WLR 1248.

[19] For a thorough account of the development of the use of the Convention in domestic law see M. Hunt, *Using Human Rights Law in English Courts* (1997) Hart Publishing, Oxford.

[20] Case 130/75 *Prais v Council* [1976] ECR 1589. See also more recently *P v S and Cornwall CC* [1996] IRLR 347 and *Grant v South West Trains* [1998] IRLR 206. More generally, see N. Grief, 'The Domestic Impact of the European Convention on Human Rights as Mediated Through Community Law' [1991] PL 555.

[21] Moreover, as the European Union moves towards greater unity the areas covered will expand. Given that EU law is fully incorporated into UK law, this point will remain significant, even after the introduction of the HRA, limited as it is to partial incorporation.

[22] A. Dicey, *Introduction to the Law of the Constitution* (10th edn, 1959) Macmillan, London.

where possible,[23] but are not given the power to set aside national legislation in favour of Convention rights. Where a statute cannot be interpreted to comply, the courts can only make a declaration of incompatibility.[24] It is then for Parliament to introduce amending legislation under a fast track procedure set out in the Act.[25] The speed with which they do so may depend on a number of factors both political and practical. If large numbers of declarations are made, even a fast track procedure may not be able to keep up. Furthermore, a failure to implement the fast track procedure is not of itself reviewable under the Act as Parliament is exempt from the process.[26]

Section 6 of the HRA creates a new cause of action against public authorities when their actions are incompatible with the Convention. Where a public authority is involved, the Act allows direct claims of breach of the Convention. In contrast to the position prior to the HRA, a breach of a Convention right can now form the basis upon which the use of ministerial discretion is open to challenge. In cases which do not involve a public authority, the Convention will apply less directly to shape the interpretation of statutes and the development of the common law. In addition, of course, the rights of individuals to bring a case against the state to the European Court of Human Rights (ECtHR) in Strasbourg remain.

When presented to Parliament, the HRA was said to 'bring rights home'[27] in that for the first time individuals were to be able to enforce Convention rights in domestic courts. However, this description of the effect of the Act is far too simplistic to describe the way in which the HRA will affect the development of domestic law. Closer examination reveals some limitations on the power of courts to protect human rights, and which challenge the idea that rights have been brought home in any meaningful way. However, even closer examination reveals that these limitations may not be as severe as first appears, and suggests that the Act may provide a way for the Convention to be used even in relation to private relationships.[28]

The most obvious limitation on the power of the HRA to protect human rights is the fact that the Convention is not fully incorporated. The retention of parliamentary sovereignty means that courts can only interpret domestic law to comply, or make a declaration of incompatibility and leave it to Parliament to amend the law. The second major limitation of the HRA is that, on the face of it, the Act cannot be used as the basis of claims between private individuals. Instead, only the acts of public authorities are directly

---

[23] HRA s 3.
[24] HRA s 4. Only the High Court (excluding the EAT) and superior courts can make such a declaration.
[25] HRA s 10.   [26] HRA s 6(3).
[27] The title of the Government White Paper introducing the Bill in October 1997 was 'Rights Brought Home'.
[28] See G. Marshall, 'Interpreting Interpretation in the Human Rights Bill' [1998] PL 167 for an example of those who fear that the restrictions on the scope of the HRA will render it virtually powerless.

actionable.[29] These restrictions on the scope of the HRA appear at first sight to be severely limiting. However, for a number of reasons, they may not be as significant in practice as they first appear.

First, although courts are not able to set aside incompatible legislation, they are, nonetheless, given wide powers of interpretation, in order to avoid a finding of incompatibility in the first place. Section 3(1) of the Act states: '*So far as it is possible* to do so, primary legislation and subordinate legislation *must* be read and given effect in a way which is compatible with the Convention rights' (emphasis added). Thus the Act requires that a new approach to statutory interpretation be developed, away from the clear meaning of words, the intention of Parliament, literal, golden and mischief rules[30] towards purposive interpretation and beyond. The Act can even be taken to allow courts to make strained interpretations of statutory language in order to find compatibility. In relation to legislation passed after the HRA the responsible minister will be required to make a statement about compatibility with the Convention.[31] Although the minister can state that it is incompatible it is very unlikely that governments will be ready to make such a statement (except where a recognised derogation applies). In practice, then, it should be easy with respect to future legislation for courts to find that even a strained interpretation which achieves compatibility accords with the intentions of Parliament, since the ministerial statement could be referred to by a court under the rule in *Pepper v Hart*.[32]

The HRA requires courts to interpret statutes to comply with the Convention 'so far as it is possible'.[33] The ability of courts to make even strained interpretations of statutory provisions in order to comply with the Convention could prove one of the strongest aspects of the HRA. The obligation on government to introduce amending legislation in cases of incompatibility may in practice be met by the most minimal change necessary. In contrast, it is open to the courts to make more radical and generous interpretations in order to ensure compliance. For example, in *R v DPP, ex p Kebiline*,[34] a case decided before the HRA came into force, but in which its impact was taken into account, the House of Lords suggested that a statutory provision putting the burden on the defendant to prove his innocence in a criminal trial might be interpreted, after the HRA, as requiring him merely to bring evidence to support his defence, in order to accord with the Article 6 Convention right to a fair trial. This interpretation means that a declaration of incompatibility was avoided.

A second example of the use of the new powers of interpretation given to the courts is *R v Offen*,[35] decided soon after the HRA came into force. Here the Court of Appeal gave the term 'exceptional circumstances' in the Crime

---

[29] HRA s 6.
[30] See R. Cross, *Statutory Interpretation* (3rd edn, 1995) Butterworths, London.
[31] HRA s 19.   [32] [1993] AC 593.   [33] HRA s 3(1).
[34] [2000] 2 AC 326.   [35] [2001] 1 WLR 253.

(Sentences) Act 2000 an interpretation that is virtually the opposite to its usual meaning. The case arose out of the 'three strikes and you're out' legislation, whereby courts are bound to order a life sentence after a third serious offence unless there are exceptional circumstances. In cases prior to the coming into force of the HRA the word 'exceptional' had been interpreted to mean out of the ordinary, unusual or uncommon.[36] Adopting a purposive approach to the interpretation (the purpose being to protect the public) and having regard to the need to comply with Article 3 of the ECHR (protecting against inhuman and degrading punishments, and respecting the right to liberty) Lord Woolf CJ decided that the word exceptional meant 'where there are circumstances that mean there is an exception from the norm'. Thus whenever a lesser sentence than life was suitable, because of the nature of the third offence, or because the defendant posed no significant risk to the public, the circumstances were in this new sense 'exceptional', even though they may be quite common. In this way, the usual meaning of the word was ignored, in order to give effect to the 'possible' interpretation that could comply with the demands of the ECHR. In this case, as with *Kebiline*, above, it is not clear that, had a declaration of incompatibility been made instead, any required government amendment to the legislation would have gone so far to protect the rights of the defendant.

The removal of the need for ambiguity before a statute can be interpreted to comply with the Convention is potentially highly significant. Prior to the introduction of the HRA, courts first had to consider the wording of the provision, without regard to the ECHR, and only if it was ambiguous on its face could the ECHR be brought into play to aid interpretation. However, consideration of the ECHR from the start of the process may reveal an ambiguity not otherwise evident, a meaning which would otherwise be ignored in the court's deliberations. As Murray Hunt puts it, once ambiguity is removed as a precondition of the consideration of the Convention, as is the case under the HRA, the Convention and its jurisprudence then 'forms part of the very context in which the court decides on what the possible meanings of the relevant provision are, rather than being artificially kept out of sight until the court has decided whether there is an ambiguity which the [Convention] could help to resolve'.[37] Any ambiguity revealed by considering the Convention is then resolved in favour of the interpretation complying with its requirements. Only where the domestic legislation is *unambiguously* in breach of the Convention will a declaration of incompatibility be necessary.

The effect of this change in the role of ambiguity in statutory interpretation can be illustrated by the decision of the EAT in Scotland in *MacDonald v Ministry of Defence*,[38] decided only days before the entry into force of the

---

[36]   [1999] 2 Cr App R (S) 178.

[37]   M. Hunt, *Using Human Rights Law in English Courts* (1997) Hart Publishing, Oxford, at 40.

[38]   [2000] IRLR 748.

HRA. The decision was subsequently overruled by the Court of Session,[39] who felt that the meaning of the Sex Discrimination Act was not ambiguous. However, the EAT decision remains an interesting illustration of the role of ambiguity in interpreting statutes using the HRA. The EAT in *MacDonald* decided that the word 'sex' in the Sex Discrimination Act 1975 (SDA) should be interpreted to include 'sexual orientation'. The reasoning was that there was ambiguity on the question of whether the word sex included the concept of sexual orientation. That ambiguity in the SDA should be resolved by bringing the law into line with the ECHR. As it had just been decided under the Convention that the practice of dismissing homosexual service personnel breaches Article 8 of the Convention,[40] the word 'sex' in the Sex Discrimination Act was therefore interpreted to include 'sexual orientation'. The Act on its face is not ambiguous, but by making reference to the jurisprudence of the ECHR, ambiguity, in the view of the EAT, was revealed. Once revealed, the tribunal could act as they have always believed they can, to resolve the ambiguity to comply with the Convention. By allowing courts to consider the ECHR case law in order to reveal ambiguity in the first place, the HRA greatly enhances the potential role of the ECHR in domestic law.

The second way in which the Act has wider scope than at first appears is that although only binding on public authorities directly,[41] that term is fairly widely defined. 'Public authority' includes any body whose functions are 'of a public nature'. The exact meaning of the term is not yet clear, and caused much debate during the passage of the Act through both Houses of Parliament. It clearly covers the acts of government departments, local authorities and the police.[42] It is further defined to include any person 'certain of whose functions are functions of a public nature'.[43] This wider definition of public authority may help overcome some of the difficulties courts have experienced in making a realistic and practical distinction between public and private bodies in the realm of judicial review.[44] The debate in the context of judicial review case law, about whether the status of an organisation as public or private is dependent on the nature of the organisation[45] or the public nature of its activities,[46] is circumvented in relation to the HRA by the statement that bodies certain of whose *functions* are public are public authorities.

---

[39] Decision of Court of Session on 1 June 2001.

[40] *Smith v UK* (2000) 29 EHRR 493.   [41] HRA s 6.

[42] 17 June HC Debs Col 409.   [43] HRA s 6(3).

[44] See for example: H. Woolf, 'Public Law—Private Law: Why the Divide?' (1986) PL 220, G. Morris and S. Fredman, 'The Costs of Exclusivity' (1994) PL 69 and G. Morris and S. Fredman, 'Public or Private? State Employees and Judicial Review' (1991) 107 LQR 298, D. Oliver, 'Common Values in Public and Private Law and the Public/Private Divide' (1997) PL 630. For a general discussion of the impact of public law on employment law see P. Davies and M. Freedland, 'The Impact of Public Law on Labour Law 1972–1997' (1997) ILJ 311.

[45] *R v Disciplinary Committee of the Jockey Club, ex p Aga Khan* [1993] 2 All ER 853.

[46] *R v Panel on Takeovers and Mergers, ex p Datafin* [1987] 1 All ER 564. See generally P. Craig, 'Public Law and Control over Private Power' in M. Taggart (ed), *The Province of Administrative Law* (1997) Hart Publishing, Oxford.

The extension of the ambit of the HRA to bodies with a public function is welcome to the extent that it allows many private organisations to be subject to the Convention. Part of the difficulty for judicial review jurisprudence has been that the distinction between private and public bodies has become increasingly ambiguous in recent years. The privatisation of many public utilities, and the contracting out of many of the traditional functions of the public sector (such as the running of prisons) to private contractors, some of which also continue their traditionally private functions, has led to increasing difficulty in maintaining a meaningful distinction between the two sectors, with many organisations retaining a 'mixed' or 'hybrid' status.[47] Of course, only time will tell whether the extended definition of public authorities will work in practice.[48] It may well be that the difficulties with the concept in the context of judicial review will be replicated in relation to the HRA, despite the attempts of the drafters of the Act to avoid this problem.

Moreover, having circumvented some of the difficulties in defining public authorities by giving a wide definition, the HRA then introduces an alternative distinction between acts of a public nature and those of a private nature. This distinction does not apply to overtly public authorities, such as local government. But an otherwise private body, which is a public authority because it carries out some public functions, is only bound to comply with the Convention in relation to those public functions. Acts of a private nature, carried out by bodies of mixed status, are therefore not directly covered. Deciding whether an *act* is public or private in nature may in time create parallel difficulties to those that arise in deciding whether a *body* is public in nature so as to be susceptible to judicial review. Furthermore, the assumption that overtly public authorities are always susceptible to review under the HRA may give rise to anomalies, given that they too can engage in acts of a private nature. For example, NHS trusts are clearly public bodies but they carry out a limited amount of what in any other context would be viewed as private work. Because of their overtly public status, however, even these private acts could be subject to review.[49] In contrast, the private acts of mixed bodies are not subject to review.

Despite the anticipated difficulties in determining whether a function is public or private, it is anticipated from the position in the law of judicial review that employment matters will be viewed as being of a private nature.[50] Thus, for 'mixed' or 'hybrid' bodies, as for purely private bodies, the employment relationship will not be covered by the Convention because of its

---

[47]   See G. Morris, 'The Human Rights Act and the Public/Private Divide in Employment Law' (1998) ILJ 293.

[48]   For some of the anticipated difficulties that might arise see Morris, ibid. See also D. Oliver, 'The Human Rights Act and Public Law/Private Law Divides' (2000) EHRLR Issue 4, 343.

[49]   See further Morris, ibid.

[50]   *McClaren v Home Office* [1990] ICR 824 establishes that employment disputes are viewed as private matters in relation to judicial review.

private nature. To an extent this reflects the current position in employment law where the employment relationship is governed in much the same way whether the employer is public or private,[51] that is, via the common law contract of employment, with additional protection provided by statutes such as the Employment Rights Act 1996. Although the employment position of civil servants is slightly different,[52] many public sector employees, such as teachers and health workers, are not classified as civil servants in this country, and are clearly governed by a contract of employment. Given that many traditional public sector functions are now carried out by private companies, the classification of the employment relationship as private does make some practical sense. Many of the new private sector 'public service providers' continue to operate simultaneously within the private sector. A private company that runs a prison and runs private security for private premises could have the same staff working for both parts of the business. According to the HRA, all members of staff of such a company would enjoy the same protection for the exercise of the right to free speech. Whether staff worked in the private security part of the business (a private function) or the prison (a public function), the acts of the employer would be acts of a private nature.

However, those who work for 'obviously' public authorities such as government departments and local authorities will be directly covered in relation to their employment.[53] This may give rise to fairly serious anomalies, given the increasing part played by the private sector in many areas which were traditionally part of the public sector. For example, some of those working in the prison service will be directly covered by the Convention, and some will not, depending on which prison they work for. In avoiding the anomaly for private 'mixed function' companies of having some employees covered by the Convention and some not (depending on which part of the business they work for), the Act creates an alternative anomaly as between employees doing the same job, such as prison officers, some of whom are covered and some of whom are not, depending on the identity of the employer. These difficulties can only be overcome if the Act is amended to make all bodies directly subject to the Convention, public or private. Although such a change is unlikely in the foreseeable future, support for such an amendment can be found in the case law of the ECtHR which makes clear, in the context of privatised public service providers, that the protection of Convention rights should not be avoided by contracting out of services by the state.[54]

The fact that the law is unlikely to be amended to cover private bodies or the private activities of mixed status bodies is not as grave a restriction in the

[51] S. Fredman and G. Morris, *The State as Employer: Labour Law in the Public Services* (1989) Mansell, London.
[52] See ibid and S. Deakin and G. Morris, *Labour Law* (1995) Butterworths, London, at 169.
[53] The Home Secretary Jack Straw, 17 June HC Debs Col 409.
[54] See *Costello-Roberts v UK* (1993) 19 EHRR 116, and Morris, n 47 above at 304.

HRA's protection as it at first seems. This is because the term 'public author-ity' includes courts and tribunals,[55] which are therefore bound, in any hear-ing between private parties, to uphold Convention rights. This is the final way in which the HRA reduces the impact of the failure to directly incorporate the Convention, and it is the mechanism with perhaps the greatest significance for employment law. It means that the Convention must be taken into account in interpreting the common law and any statutes, even where they govern totally private matters. This provides enormous potential for the Convention rights to infiltrate the workplace, and indeed many other private relationships, *indirectly*.

An example of the potential indirect effect of the HRA can be found in the statutory remedy of unfair dismissal, and the fairness of a dismissal under Employment Rights Act 1996 s 98(4). In assessing the fairness of a dismissal, employment tribunals will need to consider the question of whether the dismissal infringes one of the Convention rights, in order to comply with their obligation as public bodies to comply with the Convention. Where a dismissal touches on a Convention right, the question of whether it was 'reasonable' to dismiss in the circumstances will need to be answered with reference to the Convention standard. This will necessitate a consideration of whether the dismissal was proportionate and necessary in a democratic soci-ety. Cases raising such issues include dismissals for breaches of dress codes, where rights to freedom of expression (Article 10) and to respect for private and family life (Article 8) apply;[56] and dismissals relating to speaking out about concerns at work, where Article 10 rights arise.[57] The impact of the requirements of proportionality and necessity on the standard of reasonable-ness could be significant in these cases, which are otherwise judged accord-ing to the usual standards operating in business,[58] and may well result in a more stringent standard of 'reasonableness' being applied in other cases in order for consistency to be achieved in all cases under the Employment Rights Act.[59]

---

[55] HRA s 6.

[56] The Sex Discrimination Act 1975 could also apply here if different dress codes operate for men and women; the SDA would also be interpreted subject to the Convention, and the decision in *Smith v Safeway PLC* [1996] IRLR 456 could need revisiting in the light of *Stevens v UK* (1986) 46 D&R 245. See G. Clayton and G. Pitt, 'Dress Codes and Freedom of Expression' [1997] EHRLR 54. For discussion of dress codes as forms of expression see Chapter 2.

[57] The Public Interest Disclosure Act 1998 would also apply here, and would also need to be interpreted in accordance with the Convention.

[58] *Rolls Royce Ltd v Walpole* [1980] IRLR 343, *Richmond Precision Engineering Ltd v Pearce* [1985] IRLR 179.

[59] This will be discussed in more detail in Chapter 5 on unfair dismissal and the Public Interest Disclosure Act. For discussion on whether the 'proportionality' test will amend the '*Wednesbury* unreasonableness' test in judicial review, see R. Singh, *The Future of Human Rights in the United Kingdom* (1997) Hart Publishing, Oxford, Chapter 3 and M. Hunt, *Using Human Rights Law in English Courts* (1997) Hart Publishing, Oxford.

Furthermore, the impact of the Convention on the employment relationship could be dramatically increased if Convention rights are incorporated into the employment contract, obliging both parties to abide by the Convention. This may be possible following the wide scope given to the duty of trust and confidence by the House of Lords in *Malik v BCCI*.[60] Here the duty of trust and confidence was described as a 'portmanteau, general obligation not to engage in conduct likely to undermine the trust and confidence required if the employment relationship is to continue in the manner the employment contract implicitly envisages'.[61] It is unlikely that either party would envisage a relationship at odds with the fundamental rights protected in international law, and thus Hepple has suggested that in the future one might see cases where the Convention rights are implied into the contract of employment.[62] In *Johnson v Unisys Ltd*[63] the House of Lords seems to have put a halt on extending the implied duty of trust and confidence, in a decision that might be taken to suggest that further developments of the type suggested by Hepple have become unlikely. However, in *Johnson v Unisys* the focus was on awarding damages for the manner of dismissal and it was accepted that the duty of trust and confidence can continue to develop in relation to the ongoing relationship between employer and employee. Indeed, Lord Hoffman referred to the fact that the employment relationship must involve the observance of fundamental human rights as well as recognising general economic interests.[64] Only time will tell whether courts will take up Hepple's suggestion that an implied duty to comply with the rights contained in the ECHR might be developed based on the duty of trust and confidence. Even if they do, breach of Convention rights would still not give rise to a direct cause of action under the Convention unless the employer is clearly a public authority. Breaches of Convention rights would instead be breaches of contract, and could give rise to damages claims. In particular, breach of a Convention right could give a right to treat the contract as terminated and claim constructive dismissal.[65]

The HRA thus creates significant potential for the Convention to be used within the private sphere.[66] This position is to be welcomed, not least because it can be difficult to maintain clear and meaningful distinctions between the public and private sector. Perhaps more importantly, governments are not the only parties who can interfere with human rights. The restriction of the Convention to protection against state action reflects the view that the main

---

[60] [1997] 3 All ER 1.   [61] Lord Nicholls [1997] 3 All ER 1 at 5.
[62] B. Hepple, 'Human Rights and Employment Law', Amicus Curiae (8 June 1998) 19–23. See also S. Palmer, 'Human Rights: Implications for Labour Law' [2000] CLJ 168.
[63] [2001] UKHL 13, [2001] IRLR 279.
[64] Lord Hoffman [2001] UKHL 13 at para 37.
[65] *Western Excavating (ECC) Ltd v Sharp* [1978] QB 761.
[66] See M. Hunt, 'The "Horizontal Effect" of the Human Rights Act' (1998) PL 423.

threat to human rights comes from the state. However, that view is increasingly difficult to sustain in the modern world, as private corporations expand their power into areas once seen as the preserve of the state,[67] such as health care, transport, pensions, water, gas and electricity supplies. It is right that the jurisprudence of the Convention should apply in these areas. The fact that the application is only indirect in relation to mixed or hybrid bodies may, over time, become of less significance, although this will depend on courts being prepared to be bold in the use of their powers of interpretation under the HRA.

USING THE HUMAN RIGHTS ACT TO PROTECT FREEDOM OF SPEECH AT WORK

In order to comply with the HRA, courts and tribunals will need to consider the ECHR whenever they are interpreting the rights and obligations of employees at common law and under statute. Since coming into force in 1953, the European Court of Human Rights and the European Commission on Human Rights[68] have developed a huge and ever-increasing body of case law that can provide guidance on the meaning of the rights contained in the Convention. Under s 2 of the HRA, judgments and decisions of the European Court and the Commission on Human Rights must be taken into account when considering Convention rights in domestic law. Interestingly, however, domestic courts are not bound to follow the European decisions, only to take them into account. They remain free to develop their own applications of the Convention. If domestic interpretation is more restrictive than that available at the ECtHR in Strasbourg, the individual's right to appeal to the ECtHR remains, notwithstanding the existence of the HRA. The fact that domestic courts are not bound by the European jurisprudence, then, should be of most significance in allowing them to provide more generous protection than that available in the European Court.

Because of its Treaty status, the only party bound by the ECHR is the state, and as noted above, this position is maintained in the HRA in that Convention rights only apply to public bodies, and cannot be used directly in the private sphere.[69] Moreover, even in relation to public sector employers the ECtHR has been fairly slow to recognise that the Convention protects human rights within the sphere of work. In two major decisions in the 1980s the ECtHR held that the Convention does not cover access to a job. In *Kosiek*

---

[67] See discussion in Chapter 2 on the audience interests in speech relating to the private sector.

[68] The European Commission on Human Rights no longer exists after the coming into force of Protocol 11 on 1 November 1998. All cases are now heard by the European Court of Human Rights.

[69] See generally, A. Clapham, *Human Rights in the Private Sphere* (1993) Oxford University Press, Oxford and A. Clapham, 'The Privatisation of Human Rights' (1995) EHRLR 20.

v Germany,[70] where a probationary lecturer was dismissed from his post because of his active membership of the National Democratic Party, it was
stated that the Convention did not cover access to public office. Similarly, in
Glasenapp v Germany,[71] a probationary secondary school teacher was dismissed, amongst other things, for refusing to certify in writing that she did
not support the German Communist Party, the KPD. The ECtHR held again
that the issue was one of access to the civil service, and thus not covered by
the Convention.[72] Although these cases involved refusal of permanent
employment because of membership of political parties, the reasoning is of
wider significance. It suggests that dismissal involves no prima facie breach of
the Convention. The Convention right is not infringed *per se*, just the right to
a job, a right that is not recognised in the Convention. This reasoning could
mean that employees dismissed for exercising the right to freedom of speech,
including speech on matters relating to their work, would be unprotected
against work based sanctions.

This position has been applied in a number of Commission cases under
Article 9 guaranteeing freedom of conscience and religion. In 1981 in
Ahmad[73] a teacher claimed that his Article 9 rights were breached when he
had to resign after being refused permission to arrange his working hours so
as to be able to attend the local Mosque for prayer. His claim was ruled inadmissible. More recently, in 1997, in the case of *Stedman*[74] an employee was
dismissed for refusing to work on a Sunday. Again a claim that this breached
Article 9 was ruled inadmissible. In both cases, the employees in question
were said to be able to exercise their religious freedom, as they were free to
resign their employment. The freedom to resign was viewed as adequate
protection for their freedom to practise their religion.

In contrast to the restrictive approach by both the Court and Commission
in these particular cases, there is support elsewhere within the Strasbourg
case law for the view that work based penalties such as dismissal for exercising the right to freedom of expression may well breach the Convention. As
J. S. Mill said, 'men might as well be imprisoned, as excluded from the means
of earning their bread'[75] and in *Van Der Heijden v the Netherlands*[76] this was
recognised by the Commission in its finding that to dismiss for exercising the

---

[70] (1986) 9 EHRR 328.   [71] (1987) 9 EHRR 25.

[72] See also *Leander v Sweden* (1987) 9 EHRR 433 where the applicant claimed that the
refusal to offer him a job as a museum technician, because certain secret information allegedly
made him a security risk, was in breach of Article 10. The application was dismissed
on the basis that the right to recruitment to the public service was not recognised by the
Convention.

[73] *Ahmad v UK* (1981) 4 EHRR 126.   [74] *Stedman v UK* (1997) 23 EHRR CD 168.

[75] 'Men are not more zealous for truth than they are for error, and a sufficient application of
legal or even of social penalties will generally succeed in stopping the propagation of either . . .
men might as well be imprisoned, as excluded from the means of earning their bread.'
J. S. Mill, 'On Liberty', in S. Collini (ed), *On Liberty and Other Writings* (1989) Cambridge
University Press, Cambridge, at 31 and 34.

[76] (1985) D&R 101.

right to free speech is to restrict and penalise that freedom, and that this can be just as strong a deterrent to speech as total prohibition. The threat of dismissal operates as a very real restraint on speech on sensitive issues. Moreover, in the admissibility proceedings in *Glasenapp*[77] it was said that 'the scope of Article 10(1) may be wider than merely to forbid the complete interruption or prevention of freedom of expression, and may extend further to protect the individual against certain other restrictions or penalties which result directly from the expression or holding of an opinion'.

The inhibiting effect of threats of dismissal on speech was finally accepted by the ECtHR in 1995. In *Vogt v Germany*[78] the majority of the Court took the view that dismissal was sufficient interference with the right to free speech to warrant the protection of the Convention. Like *Glasenapp* the case involved the dismissal of a teacher for being a member of the German Communist Party. The Court distinguished *Kosiek* and *Glasenapp* on the basis that they concerned probationary employees and therefore *access* to the civil service. Vogt, in contrast, was already a permanent civil servant at the time of her dismissal. This meant that the Court could no longer avoid the issue of whether dismissal amounted to an interference with the rights guaranteed under the Convention, and decided that it did.

Although the margin in favour of finding that the dismissal amounted to an interference warranting protection was very narrow (ten votes to nine), even the dissenting judges accepted that the dismissal was an interference with free speech. The dissenters differed from the majority only in finding that the interference met the requirements of Article 10(2) as being proportionate and necessary in pursuit of a legitimate aim. The majority in *Vogt* distinguished the earlier cases of *Kosiek* and *Glasenapp* in which dismissal was not an interference with speech on the basis that they involved probationary staff, in contrast to Vogt's permanent position. However, as Judge Jambrek pointed out in his partly dissenting judgment, such a distinction is impossible to maintain on any principled basis, and perhaps really reflects a change in policy by the Court. One would hope that this is the case, and that in the future the ECtHR will make this explicit, although the later Commission case of *Stedman*[79] on Article 9 makes this less than certain. Indeed the 1999 case of *Wille v Liechtenstein*[80] suggests that the ECtHR is continuing with the distinction between access to the civil service and dismissal from it. The case involved a dispute between the Prince of Liechtenstein and Dr Wille, President of the Liechtenstein Administrative Court, who had given a public lecture in which he claimed that the Administrative Court was competent to decide on the interpretation of the constitution in cases of disagreement with the Prince. The Prince took exception to the comments as violating the spirit and letter of the constitution, and reprimanded Wille, stating that he would not be

---

[77] *X v Germany* (1983) 5 EHRR 471.   [78] (1996) 21 EHRR 205.
[79] *Stedman v UK* (1997) 23 EHRR CD 168.   [80] (2000) 30 EHRR 558.

appointed to his office again. The Court concentrated on the reprimand rather than the threat not to reappoint and, following *Vogt*, decided that this was in breach of Article 10. However, it should be noted that the Court maintained the position taken over temporary staff in *Kosiek* and *Glasenapp*.

The decision in *Vogt*, that dismissal involves a prima facie breach of the Convention, must be preferable to those that contradict it, and it should apply whether or not employment is permanent. After all, such a finding does not automatically mean that a dismissal in fact breaches the Convention. That question would await the application of the test in Article 10(2) and allows the necessity and proportionality of any restriction to be assessed. The decisions in *Kosiek*, *Glasenapp*, *Stedman*, and *Ahmad* that dismissal does not interfere with Convention rights (because one is still free to exercise the right in question by leaving employment) means that those issues are never addressed. It is to be hoped that the decision in *Vogt* will be followed by UK courts when applying the Convention in HRA cases; after all, under HRA s 2, they are not bound to follow the equivocal case law of the ECtHR and Commission on this issue.

Despite the apparent change of policy in *Vogt* towards an acceptance that dismissal can infringe the right to free speech, two uncertainties remain in relation to the impact of the Convention rights on employment protection. First, *Vogt* involved public sector employment, and so it may be argued that the jurisprudence of the ECHR cannot apply in the private sector, whatever the mechanics of the HRA allowing this to take place. Second, the case did not deal explicitly with the position of employees who contract out of their free speech rights. Where these issues have been raised explicitly, they suggest that a certain degree of contracting out of free speech rights is allowed in the context of employment.[81] This could cause difficulty for those seeking to rely on the HRA to protect the right to free speech at work, as most employees are subject to contractual duties of loyalty, fidelity and confidence, any or all of which can be breached by the exercise of free speech.

Taking the first point first, on the application of the Convention to private sector employment, the fact that the Convention only directly binds states does not cause insuperable hurdles to be overcome by private sector staff. It has long been accepted by the Commission and Court that a failure to enact legislation to protect employees from breaches of the Convention can be imputed to the state. This was confirmed in *Young, James and Webster v UK*[82] where failure to provide domestic legislation to prohibit dismissal for non-membership of a union, raising rights under Article 11, was the responsibility of the state[83] and could therefore be imputed to the state for the purposes

---

[81] See G. Morris, 'Fundamental Rights: Exclusion by Agreement?' [2001] ILJ 49.

[82] [1981] IRLR 408.

[83] Under Article 1. Article 1 is not covered by the HRA; however, the government is of the view that this is unnecessary because the HRA itself imposes a duty on the state to safeguard Convention rights.

of bringing the case. Arguably, then, any failure by the domestic courts adequately to protect the free speech of employees even in claims against private sector employers could similarly give rise to a claim against the state. The fact that *Vogt* indirectly creates a private sector right to free speech as well as a public sector right means that all employees should be able to claim the protection of the Convention at work either directly or indirectly via the mechanisms set up under the HRA, discussed above.

The second difficulty, posed by the fact that both the Court and Commission have allowed individuals to contract out of their rights to freedom of expression, suggests that an employer might successfully argue that the employee agrees to restrict the right to free speech by entering the employment contract, for example by signing a confidentiality or loyalty clause. However, cases arising under Article 10[84] have made clear that although employees can contract out of the right to freedom of speech, any such contractual restriction will need to be capable of flexible interpretation, allowing courts to assess the proportionality and necessity of the restriction in the particular case, before it will be viewed as compatible with Article 10. If national courts were to enforce or uphold absolute rights for employers to impose contractual restrictions on the free speech of staff, this would breach the state's responsibility to safeguard the rights of employees, in the same way as the absence of legislative protection for employees against the closed shop practices breached the state's obligations under the Convention in *Young, James and Webster*. Instead, states (via their courts) must allow for a degree of flexibility in the enforcement of contractual restrictions on speech, to ensure that the requirements for proportionality and necessity for the restriction can be met.[85]

This was the outcome in *Rommelfanger v FDR*[86] where a doctor in a Roman Catholic hospital was dismissed for writing a letter to the press disapproving of the Church's attitude to abortion. His complaint that his dismissal infringed his right to freedom of speech was ruled inadmissible by the Commission, as involving no direct state interference with the applicant's freedom of expression. His contractual duty of loyalty to the hospital had been breached by the letter, and the Commission was of the view that the enforcement of contractual duties, freely entered into, did not constitute an interference by a public authority with his Convention rights. This seems to suggest that where the employee has contracted out of the right to free speech, the scrutiny required under Article 10(2) is not necessary. There is then no need to address the question of whether the restrictions on speech are necessary and proportionate to achieve a specified legitimate aim. However, the case is not in fact good authority for the proposition that employees

---

[84]   See *Vereniging Rechtswinkels Utrecht v The Netherlands* (1986) 46 D&R 200 on the ability to contract out of the right to free speech.
[85]   See G. Morris, 'Fundamental Rights: Exclusion by Agreement?' [2001] ILJ 49.
[86]   (1989) 62 D&R 151.

can contract out of their Convention rights. The Commission pointed out that although Rommelfanger had contracted out of his right to free speech by signing a loyalty clause, the national law included provisions to ensure that the demands of the duty of loyalty were reasonable. The local law under which the legality of his dismissal was assessed included a degree of flexibility and discretion, allowing the domestic court to weigh up the competing interests of employer and employee, in particular the applicant's interests in free speech against the employer's corresponding right to free speech. This meant that the employee was adequately protected by the domestic law, even though in this instance the discretion was exercised against him. The Commission therefore concluded that there was no duty on the state to provide additional protection beyond that already provided in the domestic law, and so there was no breach of the state's obligation to protect freedom of speech. For this reason, the contracting out of the right to free speech was allowed on this occasion. If the domestic law had been applied in an absolute manner, with no consideration of the employee's right to free speech, the Commission might well have found there to be a prima facie interference with speech that needed to be subject to review under Article 10(2).

Further support for this interpretation of the decision in *Rommelfanger* can be gained from the decision in *Vogt* where the court found that the restriction on speech did breach Article 10. Although the case can be distinguished on the basis that the state was the direct employer, and the issue of contracting out of rights was not addressed, the court did point out that the restriction on speech involved in the case applied automatically to all civil service staff, with no provision for individual circumstances to be considered, and this seems to have been influential in the decision.[87] The flexibility and discretion in the application of contractual restrictions on speech required in *Rommelfanger* therefore did not arise.

After *Rommelfanger* and *Vogt*, the argument that employees are not entitled to employment protection if they contract out of the right to free speech when entering employment should not succeed, and the HRA should be interpreted to protect free speech in the workplace. The two cases provide authority for the proposition that freedom of expression survives entry to the workplace, and that employees should thus be able to require that any contractual duties restricting speech be interpreted to afford adequate protection for the right to free speech. Any work based penalties imposed for the exercise of free speech should comply with Article 10(2) and be necessary and proportionate responses to the speech.

Under the HRA, then, public sector staff will have a directly enforceable right to have their freedom of speech protected at work, to the extent that this is compatible with the limitations contained in Article 10(2). Those in the

---

[87] 'The absolute nature of that duty . . . is striking . . . The duty is always owed, in every context.' *Vogt v Germany* (1996) 21 EHRR 205 at para 59.

private sector will be able to require that their employment rights be interpreted to accord, as far as possible, with this Convention right. An employee
who is dismissed for exercising the right to free speech, or a member of staff
who faces a breach of confidence case, could face the claim that they have
contracted out of their free speech rights and that the jurisprudence of the
ECHR does not apply. However, such staff should be able to ask the court
hearing their case to consider the ECHR case law on Article 10 in assessing
whether the dismissal is fair, or whether there is a breach of confidence in the
circumstances. The application of the law in both cases is subject to a degree
of discretion and flexibility; and that discretion should be exercised in a way
that is compatible with the Convention.

The extent to which our domestic law, both statutory and common law,
will protect the right to freedom of speech at work will, with the HRA in force,
depend on the scope of the protection under the ECHR as those hearing
cases which involve free speech issues take the case law of the ECtHR and
the European Commission on Human Rights into account in interpreting
domestic law. The remainder of this chapter will consider in more detail the
case law of the ECtHR and Commission of Human Rights on the scope of
the right to freedom of expression in order to see what the courts will find
when they look to the Convention for guidance.

THE HUMAN RIGHTS ACT AND
THE JURISPRUDENCE OF ARTICLE 10
OF THE ECHR

Article 10 of the European Convention on Human Rights states:

1. Everyone has the right to freedom of expression. This right shall include freedom
to hold opinions and to receive and impart information and ideas without interference by public authority and regardless of frontiers. This article shall not prevent
States from requiring the licensing of broadcasting, television or cinema enterprises.
2. The exercise of these freedoms, since it carries with it duties and responsibilities,
may be subject to such formalities, conditions, restrictions or penalties as are prescribed by law and are necessary in a democratic society, in the interests of national
security, territorial integrity or public safety, for the protection of health or morals, for
the protection of the reputation or rights of others, for preventing the disclosure of
information received in confidence, or for maintaining the authority and impartiality
of the judiciary.[88]

In Chapter 2, the right to free speech was considered as of dual significance:
a fundamental personal freedom, and an important political right. This is
recognised by the ECHR. Its preamble provides that the 'fundamental free-

---

[88] See generally, P. van Dijk and G. van Hoof, *Theory and Practice of the European Convention
on Human Rights* (2nd edn, 1990) Kluwer, the Netherlands.

doms which are the foundation of justice and peace in the world are best maintained . . . by an effective political democracy . . .'; and the ECtHR has recognised that freedom of speech is central to the achievement of those aims. In one of its first cases on freedom of expression the ECtHR stated that 'freedom of expression constitutes one of the essential foundations of [a "democratic society"], one of the basic conditions for its progress and for the development of every man'.[89]

Article 10(1) protects holding and expressing opinions, and imparting and receiving information. The protection covers all types of information and opinion, whether 'favourably received' or of a type to 'offend, shock or disturb the State or any sector of the population'.[90] However, the level of protection varies according to a number of factors including the type of information imparted; and the protection is not absolute, but limited by the operation of Article 10(2), which recognises that freedom of expression carries with it duties and responsibilities, and that in some cases freedom of expression must be limited.

ARTICLE 10(2): LIMITATIONS ON THE RIGHT TO FREEDOM OF EXPRESSION

Even though the right to freedom of expression does seem to apply to speech by employees, the right itself is far from absolute. The consideration of the case law that has been developed by the ECtHR will indicate the extent to which the HRA will protect a right to free speech at work. As will be seen, plenty of scope exists within the case law on Article 10(2) for the protection of the rights of employers to confidence and loyalty from staff, and indeed for their own free speech. Article 10(2) sets out a number of grounds on which free speech can be legitimately restricted. The circumstances in which the restrictions on speech are allowed are themselves limited under Article 10(2). They must be prescribed by law; they must be for one of the reasons listed in the section; and they must be necessary in a democratic society. All three of these conditions must be met before a restriction or interference with freedom of expression will be acceptable under the Convention.

Prescribed by Law

Sunday Times v UK[91] contains the classic definition of what is needed for a restriction to be 'prescribed by law':

First the law must be adequately accessible: the citizen must be able to have an indication that is adequate in the circumstances of the legal rules applicable to a given case. Secondly, a norm cannot be regarded as a 'law' unless it is formulated with sufficient precision to enable the citizen to regulate his conduct: he must be able to

---

[89] *Handyside v UK* (1981) 1 EHRR 737. See also *Sunday Times v UK* (1979) 2 EHRR 245, *Lingens v Austria* (1986) 8 EHRR 407, *Barthold v Germany* (1985) 7 EHRR 383.
[90] *Handyside v UK* (1981) 1 EHRR 737.   [91] (1979) 2 EHRR 245.

foresee, to a degree that is reasonable in the circumstances, the consequences which a given action may entail. Those consequences need not be foreseeable with absolute certainty: experience shows this to be unattainable.[92]

Most of the types of interference with speech experienced by employees will meet this description. Employees could face disciplinary action or dismissal for breach of loyalty,[93] or be subject to defamation claims, or to claims for breach of confidence. Although none of these areas of law operate without uncertainty, and outcomes can at times be difficult to predict, they are probably within the bounds of acceptable uncertainty envisaged by the ECtHR in the *Sunday Times* case.

The issue was discussed in *Goodwin v UK*[94] which involved the 'interests of justice' exception to the protection of sources under the Contempt of Court Act 1981. Whether or not the exception applies depends upon a balancing exercise undertaken by the judges between competing public interests. The ECtHR was of the view that the law did not involve the use of an unlimited discretion by the judiciary as case law and precedent provided some parameters within which the discretion was exercised. The law was thus sufficiently foreseeable to meet Convention requirements of certainty. The same approach would undoubtedly apply in breach of confidence cases. The interpretation of the concept of the public interest does involve the use of judicial discretion, but sufficient guidance can be drawn from case law on the use of that discretion for the outcome to be predicted with an acceptable degree of certainty.

Legitimate Aims in Article 10(2)

If an employee speaks about matters of concern at work, and restrictions on that speech are provided by law, the restriction must be for a purpose listed in Article 10(2) if it is to comply with the Convention. The purposes most likely to be applicable in the context of free speech and the workplace are the protection of the reputation or rights of others and the prevention of the disclosure of information received in confidence. In some cases the interests of national security may also warrant a restriction.

The protection of the reputation of others is clearly covered in the UK by the law on defamation. Thus the employee's right to free speech may be legitimately curtailed in circumstances where the speech is defamatory. Restrictions placed on the employee's speech could be by way of damages claims by the subject of the defamation. Alternatively, an employer could

---

[92] *Sunday Times v UK* (1979) 2 EHRR 245 at para 49. See also *Hodgson and others v UK* (1987) 51 D&R 136 where the Commission said that 'The mere fact that a legislative provision may give rise to problems of interpretation does not mean that it is so vague and imprecise as to lack the quality of "law" in this sense.'

[93] In *Barthold v Germany* (1985) 7 EHRR 383 the 'law' was not limited to national laws but extended to professional rules and codes of conduct. Discipline or dismissal of an employee may therefore be 'prescribed by law' where this is provided for by a professional code of conduct.

[94] [1996] 22 EHRR 123, para 31 ff.

choose to discipline or even dismiss an employee on the basis that the speech injures the reputation of another. In such a case, the employer could show that the interference served a legitimate aim under Article 10(2). However, any restriction would still need to meet the third requirement, that it be necessary in a democratic society.

Similarly, restrictions on speech under the Official Secrets Acts will serve the interests of national security, an aim listed in Article 10(2), and will be allowed, subject to the needs of proportionality and necessity. The need to protect confidential information is another common reason for employers to restrict the free speech of their staff, and again this is recognised by Article 10(2). Dismissal and disciplinary action taken against staff who disclose confidential information will therefore also comply with Convention standards on free speech protection, subject to the need for the action to be proportionate and necessary in a democratic society.

Probably the most extensive ground for legitimately restricting speech is the protection of the rights of others. Exactly which 'rights of others' need such protection is not specified, but this category clearly extends beyond protecting rights to reputation and to the maintenance of confidence. In the employment context it could cover the rights of the employer to free speech, and to enjoy the loyalty and fidelity of staff. In fact, this ground is potentially extremely wide, as there seems to be no requirement that the rights of others have to be legally enforceable rights. Although the restrictions on speech themselves have to be prescribed by sufficiently clear laws, the aims of those rules do not have to be clear to anywhere like the same degree. In *Ahmed v UK*[95] the rights of others to effective political democracy was a ground for restricting the political speech of local government workers. Members of the public were also said to have a right to expect that the members that they vote into office will be advised in a politically neutral manner.[96] While one might want to protect such rights, it is perhaps unwise to allow the restriction of important human rights on grounds that are too unclear and indeterminate. Not only does an over-extensive interpretation of 'the rights of others' make the other aims specified in Article 10(2) redundant,[97] but as the dissenting judges in *Ahmed* pointed out, such an interpretation risks the notion of the rights of others 'being stretched so far as to lose almost all distinct meaning'.[98] If courts are too ready to find new 'rights of others' where rights are exercised at work, any right to free speech at work will become extremely vulnerable.

Even given the breadth of the 'rights of others' category, in a few cases it might be possible to argue that restrictions on speech serve no legitimate aim. For example, if the information disclosed relates to a matter of public

---

[95] (2000) 29 EHRR 1.   [96] At para 53.
[97] See G. Morris, 'The political activities of local government workers and the European Convention on Human Rights' (1999) PL 211 at 216.
[98] Joint dissenting opinion of Judges Spielmann, Pekkanen and Van Dijk at para 1.

interest no duty of confidence arises.[99] Nor is there any breach of confidence if employee speech relates to matters that are in the public domain.[100] Where information is not confidential, any restrictions on the communication of the information would be without a legitimate aim and so would breach the Convention. Similar outcomes would occur where speech by an employee was not defamatory because covered by a defence of justification, fair comment or qualified privilege.[101] If this were accepted by a court or tribunal in a particular case, there would be no need to undertake the additional assessment of whether the restriction would be necessary in a democratic society. However, reliance on the defences to claims of defamation and breach of confidence will not necessarily create a large area of free speech to be enjoyed by employees, and in any event, other aims, such as the catch-all 'protection of the rights of others', could still give rise to a legitimate restriction in relation to the same speech.

Necessity in a Democratic Society

Since in most cases restrictions on speech are prescribed by law and serve a legitimate aim, it is in relation to the necessity of the interference that the supervision of the ECtHR really comes into play, and where domestic courts will have most to learn from its jurisprudence. The standard of review by the ECtHR under this heading is fairly high. There needs to be a 'pressing social need' before a restriction is necessary, and the ECtHR has made clear that 'necessary' means more than just 'useful', 'reasonable', or 'desirable'. Moreover, for any restriction to be necessary, it must be proportionate to the legitimate aim pursued.[102] In order for a measure to be proportionate it must be important enough to warrant limiting an important right, the measure must be linked to the objective to be achieved, and the means used must be no more than is necessary to achieve the objective. The more serious the infringement of human rights, the more important the legitimate objective must be.

Despite the high level of review suggested by the ECtHR by phrases such as 'pressing social need', the Court has also recognised that states need a certain flexibility in their observance of the Convention. Thus a 'margin of appreciation' is allowed to states in setting the parameters of free speech under domestic law. The theory is that this flexibility is limited, being at all times subject to European supervision. The concept of the 'margin of appreciation' as a way to allow flexibility to states was first used in Article 15 cases involving derogation from the Convention in times of national emergency. Its infiltration into the interpretation of the 'personal freedoms' in the rest of the

---

[99] *Gartside v Outram* (1856) 26 LJ Ch 113.
[100] *Woodward v Hutchins* [1977] 1 WLR 760.
[101] See generally, P. Carter-Ruck, *Peter Carter-Ruck on Libel and Slander* (4th edn, 1992) Butterworths, London.
[102] *Handyside v UK* (1981) 1 EHRR 737, at para 48.

Convention (Articles 8–11) has been gradual but extensive,[103] so that now the ECtHR tends to consider the margin of appreciation in most cases as part of the consideration of the necessity and proportionality of a restriction. The extent to which this concept can dilute the protection of the Convention, and the extent to which it may be used by domestic courts, will be considered later.

Although its reasoning is not usually extensive, and many of the cases do not involve employment based sanctions, consideration of case law can provide useful guidance on the factors considered within the Convention jurisprudence in determining whether a restriction on speech is necessary in a democratic society. In turn, these cases are likely to be used by domestic courts and tribunals in assessing whether measures taken by employers against employees for exercising the right to free speech are compatible with the HRA.

FACTORS DETERMINING THE NECESSITY OF AN INTERFERENCE

Although the ECtHR and Commission recognise that the interests in freedom of speech can outweigh the duty of confidentiality owed by employee to employer,[104] as a starting point it is accepted that employment brings with it responsibilities towards one's employer which can involve restrictions on speech.[105] The factors that the ECtHR has taken into account in assessing when such restrictions are disproportionate and therefore unnecessary include: the nature of the restriction on speech; the nature of the applicant's job; the applicant's conduct in the post; the channel of communication; the truth of the information; and the nature of the speech itself.

The Nature of the Restriction on Speech

Interference with free speech can vary in gravity, from injunctions against speaking backed up by criminal sanctions, to disciplinary measures imposed at work. Where the speech of an individual is effectively barred altogether, on pain of criminal sanctions, the ECtHR is understandably more likely to find that the sanction is unnecessary. In *Lingens v Austria*[106] and *Thorgierson v Iceland*[107] criminal defamation proceedings were brought in respect of the publication and writing of articles criticising a senior politician and the police respectively. The speech was effectively barred altogether on pain of criminal

---

[103] See H. Yourow, *The Margin of Appreciation Doctrine in the Dynamics of European Human Rights Jurisprudence* (1996) Kluwer Law International, The Hague; London; T. O'Donnell, 'The Margin of Appreciation Doctrine: Standard in the Jurisprudence of the European Court of Human Rights' (1982) Human Rights Quarterly 474; T. Jones, 'The Devaluation of Human Rights Under the European Convention' (1995) PL 430; and P. Mahoney, 'Universality versus Subsidiarity in the Strasbourg Case Law on Free Speech: Explaining Some Recent Judgments' [1997] EHRLR 364.

[104] *Goodwin v UK* (1996) 22 EHRR 123.

[105] See *E v Switzerland* (1984) 38 D&R 124.   [106] (1986) 8 EHRR 407.

[107] (1991) 14 EHRR 843.

sanction. The threat represented by criminal proceedings would inhibit contribution to public debate, and so in both cases the penalties for the expression of opinion were found to be in violation of the Convention. The same point was made again in *Incal v Turkey*,[108] a case which involved the prohibition of the distribution of a leaflet which was critical of the way in which the local authorities had dealt with the local Kurdish population. The publisher, the leader of an opposition political party, was also prosecuted. These actions were found to be in contravention of Article 10, a decision influenced by the nature of the restriction imposed. The ECtHR was concerned at the 'radical nature of the interference' and noted that 'its preventative aspect by itself raises problems under Article 10'.[109]

In contrast, where speech is not totally banned, the protection of the Convention has been more limited. In *Jacubowski v Germany*[110] an injunction was granted to prevent a journalist circulating among a number of journalists a set of newspaper cuttings that were critical of his former employer. One of the reasons given by the ECtHR for deciding that the injunction did not constitute a violation of Article 10 was that it did not prevent every expression of the opinion, but only prevented publication of the particular circular. The same approach was taken in *Vereniging Rechtswinkels Utrecht v Netherlands*[111] where the applicant's permission to run an advice centre in a prison was withdrawn because he breached the terms of the agreement upon which that permission was granted by reporting a particular incident to the press. The Commission, in deciding that the case was inadmissible, pointed out that the applicant was not prevented from expressing his views, but was merely prevented from doing so whilst continuing with the agreement to run the advice centre. Similar approaches can be found in a number of other cases. In *Ahmad*[112] and *Stedman*[113] the Commission was of the view that the freedom of the applicants to resign effectively guaranteed their Convention rights, as they remained free to exercise the right after their employment ended.

An employee who suffers a detriment at work for expressing an opinion on a work related matter is not prevented from expressing the view altogether, just prevented from expressing the view and remaining in employment. It is likely, in the light of this case law, that a restriction such as dismissal or disciplinary action at work will be said to be proportionate. This approach is understandable, when one considers the range of restrictions on speech considered under the ECHR. Clearly an outright ban on speech is a more serious infringement on the right to free speech than a restriction which only impinges at work. However, as has been recognised from Mill

---

[108] (2000) 29 EHRR 449.
[109] *Incal v Turkey* (2000) 29 EHRR 449 at para 56.   [110] (1995) 19 EHRR 64.
[111] (1986) 46 D&R 200. Note, however, that it was not an employment case.
[112] *Ahmad v UK* (1981) 4 EHRR 126.   [113] *Stedman v UK* (1997) 23 EHRR CD 168.

onwards,[114] restricting people's access to a livelihood can in practice involve a greater deterrent to free speech than other legal sanctions; and so the effect of a threat of dismissal is not dissimilar, in practice, to a ban on speech. This was recognised in *Van Der Heijden v the Netherlands*[115] where the Commission accepted that dismissal from employment acts as a strong deterrent to speech by employees. The case involved the dismissal of the director of an immigration centre on account of his political activities. The Commission stated that although the case concerned only the effects of exercising the right of free speech, not the removal of the freedom itself, nonetheless the termination of employment did restrict and penalise freedom of speech. In the event, the case was declared inadmissible as the measure was necessary in a democratic society; his political activity was on behalf of a party that was hostile to the presence of foreign workers and was clearly incompatible with his job.

Thus, the view that dismissal interferes with the right to free speech does have some support in the Convention case law. Nonetheless, there is also no doubt that an absolute ban on speech would be viewed as a more serious infringement on free speech by the ECtHR. The HRA is unlikely to be of much help to employees who are dismissed or disciplined for exercising the right to free speech unless other factors can be found in favour of protecting staff against work based penalties for exercising the right to free speech at work.

The Nature of the Applicant's Job

The fact that certain roles involve a greater degree of restraint on freedom of speech is recognised in the Strasbourg case law. In *E v Switzerland*[116] a judge, who was reprimanded for distributing a leaflet that commented on pending legal proceedings, argued that the interference with his free expression was not necessary for the maintenance of the authority and impartiality of the judiciary. The Commission disagreed and in finding the complaint inadmissible said that the judge should, as a public official serving in the judiciary, show restraint in the exercise of his freedom of expression. In *Morrisens v Belgium*[117] an application to the Commission was declared inadmissible where a teacher was dismissed following a television interview in which she had made various allegations against the provincial authorities and made 'unacceptable insinuations' concerning the heads of the school. The Commission considered that by entering the civil service, the applicant had accepted certain restrictions on the exercise of her freedom of speech.

Again, in *B v UK*[118] the Commission commented that restrictions on the speech of employees in government service were prima facie reasonable. This

---

[114] J. S. Mill, 'On Liberty', in S. Collini (ed), *On Liberty and Other Writings* (1989) Cambridge University Press, Cambridge, at 31 and 34, referred to above.
[115] (1985) D&R 101.   [116] (1984) 38 D&R.
[117] (1988) D&R 56.   [118] (1986) 45 D&R 41.

is effectively confirmed by the decision of the ECtHR in *Ahmed v UK*[119] where the restrictions on political speech imposed on local government staff by regulations made under the Local Government and Housing Act 1989 were found to be acceptable under Article 10(2). The restrictions applied only to staff who might be involved in giving policy advice to elected local government officials. The ECtHR noted that the number of staff covered by the restriction was, according to the evidence of the government, kept as small as necessary for the purpose of ensuring political neutrality of advice, and staff who felt that their jobs had been inappropriately subject to the restrictions could apply for exemption. The implication is clear that the nature of the jobs of the more senior local government staff covered by the regulations meant that restrictions on speech were appropriate.

Restrictions on the speech of certain employees can clearly be necessary in a democratic society. As noted in Chapter 2, the status of the employee can impact upon the extent to which free speech should be protected at work. More senior staff may owe greater levels of loyalty to the employer and may represent the views of the employer to the public. Moreover, in certain types of employment, such as the judiciary and the civil service, more discretion may be required of staff because of the sensitive nature of the information handled as part of the job. However, it is worth pointing out that at times these same people may have a special duty to contribute to public debate on matters of public, and at times political, importance, by virtue of their expertise and status. Elsewhere in the case law on Article 10(2) the importance of debate on such issues is clearly stressed,[120] and it may be that the nature of the applicant's job will be viewed as of lesser importance where the subject matter of speech warrants the full public debate.

There is a second, more practical way in which the nature of the applicant's job may impact on the protection of speech, particularly where he or she has specialist skills. In *Vogt*[121] the majority referred to the fact that dismissal was a particularly severe sanction as it had the effect of preventing Mrs Vogt from getting a job as a teacher anywhere else. In Germany, where teachers are civil servants, dismissal from the civil service effectively precluded her from work in this capacity. In the UK, apart from civil servants, there are usually a number of employers even for staff working in the public sector. For example, health service staff can work for different hospital trusts and teachers for different local authorities. To an extent then, dismissal is likely to be a less severe penalty than it was for Mrs Vogt, who could not work as a teacher again. In *Smith v UK*[122] the ECtHR gave a *Vogt* wide application. The case involved the investigation and subsequent dismissal of the two applicants from the Royal Air Force on the basis of their homosexuality. Both applicants had long service records in skilled work with the RAF. Pointing out that the applicants'

---

[119] (2000) 29 EHRR 1.   [120] *Lingens v Austria* (1986) 8 EHRR 407.
[121] *Vogt v Germany* (1996) 21 EHRR 205.   [122] (2000) 29 EHRR 493.

skills would be of use in civilian life, the ECtHR also noted that they would encounter difficulties in obtaining civilian posts in their specialisms, reflecting the seniority and status they had enjoyed in the RAF. Despite the fact that the applicants could find alternative work, the fact that suitable and comparable work would be hard to come by was a factor the court took into account in finding that the investigations and dismissals were a disproportionate interference with the applicant's right to privacy.

This reading of *Vogt* may be very helpful to staff seeking to rely on the ECHR jurisprudence to aid claims under the HRA, because in many cases the practical difficulties of finding another job for which one is trained and experienced are likely to be severe following a dismissal for exercising the right to free speech. This is particularly the case where speech has taken place as part of a public debate. Public criticism of the employer is highly likely to lead to publicity. In some cases, the employee may even gain a level of local or national notoriety. In such cases, the fact that an alternative employer exists will not necessarily help the dismissed employee find new employment. New employers may well be wary of employing someone who is known to have exercised their freedom of speech in such a way as to have been dismissed in the past. According to *Vogt*, it is possible that where this is a factor, it may weigh against a dismissal being found to be a proportionate response to the exercise of free speech.

The Applicant's Conduct at Work and Work-Related Speech

A further argument accepted by the Commission and the ECtHR in *Vogt* was that Mrs Vogt's conduct at work had always been beyond reproach. She had not sought to indoctrinate her pupils towards her political views, neither had she personally made anti-constitutional statements, although she was a member of a political party that advocated such views. Thus dismissal from her job was a disproportionate interference with her speech. The personal conduct of the employee at work was taken into account in assessing the proportionality of the work based interference with speech. A sanction such as dismissal was not a proportionate response because Mrs Vogt's personal behaviour at work had been exemplary.

An additional issue in *Vogt* was that an employment based sanction was imposed for speech that was not essentially employment based. Mrs Vogt was an active member of a political party, but did not carry out any political activity at work. The sanction imposed did not bear much relation to the speech being sanctioned. Her exemplary work record could thus be used to show that a disciplinary sanction was disproportionate. Had the speech related to work, however, then the outcome might have been different. The speech itself might then have undermined the 'exemplary record' of the employee at work, and dismissal may have been said to be a proportionate response.

The fact that there is a good work record may thus help employees dismissed for exercising the right to free speech at work, and this may particularly be the case when speaking about matters not related to the work-place. A teacher taking part in public debate on health matters or a doctor taking part in debate on education might both be able to challenge the pro-portionality of any resulting dismissal or disciplinary sanction on this ground.

However, where the employee's speech does relate to the workplace, the contrary will apply, and it might be said to be proportionate to impose a work based sanction on the speech, because the speech itself may be classed as conduct affecting work. Even in such a case, however, the alternative may be arguable, as the speech of employees taking part in public debate about matters relating to their workplace may bear no relation to the conduct of the employee in the practice of her job. For example, if a surgeon participates in public debate on funding for the NHS, this will not interfere with her ability to carry out surgery. Even if it is argued that the functions of a surgeon extend beyond carrying out surgery, to include maintaining confidence in the NHS, that does not necessarily preclude taking part in discussion on how that is best achieved. The speech is thus not connected to the employee's *conduct* in the job, and dismissal should not necessarily be proportionate.

The Manner of the Expression

In two unreported decisions,[123] the Commission ruled applications inadmis-sible on the basis that the employees involved had been intemperate in the way in which they had spoken. In such cases, the fact that the ECtHR takes account of the employee's conduct at work will make it harder to show that dismissal is disproportionate. In *Tucht v FRG*[124] a public health professional, who had been unsuccessful in seeking promotion, was dismissed after send-ing numerous complaints about his superiors and the organisation for which he worked to those superiors, to the regional parliament, trade unions, professional bodies, colleagues and political parties. His dismissal was for disciplinary offences such as publishing abusive criticism and disclosing con-fidential information. The Commission took the view that the dismissal was not for making the criticism *per se* but for the abusive and offensive way in which it had been made. Similarly, in *De Jong v the Netherlands*[125] the Commission found that the dismissal of a police officer for publicly and pri-vately criticising the policies and conduct of his employer and the judiciary did not infringe the Convention because of the abusive way in which the crit-icism was voiced. It seems that the right to free speech encompasses a right to criticise one's employer, but not in an overly critical or abusive manner. The approach in the employment context can be contrasted with that which applies in other contexts, where the Court has made clear that the protection

---

[123] Quoted in J. Bowers, J. Mitchell and J. Lewis, *Whistleblowing: The New Law* (1999) Sweet and Maxwell, London, at 130.
[124] (1982) Case No 9336/81 (unreported).
[125] (1984) Case No 10280/83 (unreported).

of the Convention applies to speech that offends, shocks or disturbs, and not just to inoffensive matters.[126]

These two cases, although perhaps understandable on their facts, create a danger for employees as it may become too easy for employers to argue that they are not dismissing or disciplining an employee because he exercised the right to free speech, but because of the manner in which he did so. It is obviously necessary to allow employers to dismiss on the basis of misconduct: one danger of providing employment protection for whistleblowers has been said to be that staff may try to use it to protect themselves against dismissal on other grounds.[127] An employee might decide to disclose wrongdoing as a way of preventing being chosen for redundancy or disciplined for misconduct. Clearly safeguards are needed against this, the most obvious being that the employer can show that dismissal was not caused by the exercise of free speech, but by some other cause, such as redundancy or misconduct. But where the misconduct causing dismissal is conduct relating to the manner or mode of the speech, the issues are different. The danger is then that it may too readily be used by employers to justify dismissal on the basis of the manner of expression. It would be preferable for other features of the particular case, such as the importance of the subject matter of the speech, to take precedence in the assessment of proportionality in such cases. If the employee says something that the public should hear, then the intemperate manner of speech should not prevent a finding that dismissal is disproportionate. Otherwise, the chilling effect of such a sanction may prevent the public from hearing speech that it is in their interests to hear.

The Channel of Communication

Both the Commission and the Court have considered the mode of communication of ideas when assessing the proportionality of a restriction on speech. In *Morrisens v Belgium*[128] the applicant made statements on television that were critical of her employer. The public nature of the allegations and the fact that they were made on television were not viewed favourably by the Commission and were factors taken into account in its finding that her dismissal did not breach her Convention rights. By way of contrast, in *Grigoriades v Greece*[129] an army conscript was required to spend more time in the army by way of a disciplinary penalty for writing a letter highly critical of the army and sending it to an officer and one of his colleagues. The language used in the letter was intemperate and abusive, factors that could have weighed against the applicant. However, the Court and Commission were influenced

---

[126] *Handyside v UK* (1981) 1 EHRR 737. It has also taken into account that journalistic devices can include a degree of provocation and exaggeration, stating that this should not preclude protection. See *De Haes and Gijesls v Belgium* (1998) 25 EHRR 1.

[127] See J. Gobert and M. Punch, 'Whistleblowers, the Public Interest and the Public Interest Disclosure Act' (2000) 63 MLR 25.

[128] (1988) D&R 56.   [129] (1999) 27 EHRR 464.

in their finding that the sanction was disproportionate and therefore unnecessary in a democratic society by the fact that the letter was only circulated internally within the army, and not published or disseminated to a wider audience.

Where concerns are raised internally, severe penalties are less likely to be proportionate. This is clearly right, given that the interests of others, including the employer, suffer less harm if speech is restricted to a small number of recipients. However, the converse, whereby public speech is more likely to warrant restrictions, may cause difficulty for those who wish to participate in public debate. If the aim of speech is to contribute to general debate on an issue, it can only be effective if made with publicity. In such cases, it is to be hoped that the medium through which the speech is communicated will not be given too much weight, so that other factors, such as the subject matter of the speech, can result in a finding that an interference is unnecessary. In support of such an approach, there are strong indications in the case law on Article 10 that the press and other media are to be afforded special protection as 'public watchdogs'.[130] If the press are to fulfil this vital role, then the same special protection should extend to those who provide information which, in the public interest, the media publishes.

The Truth of the Information

In concluding that the disciplinary sanction imposed in *Morrisens*[131] was proportionate, the Commission pointed out that the applicant's accusations against her superiors had not been supported by any evidence. This suggests that whether any information disclosed is true or not may be a further factor influencing the question of whether an interference is necessary in a democratic society. This was certainly the case in *Bergens Tidende v Norway*.[132] The case involved newspaper reports of allegations by cosmetic surgery patients that their surgeon, Dr R, had provided inadequate care. The penalties imposed on the newspaper by Norway's domestic courts in respect of Dr R's successful defamation claim were ruled by the ECtHR to breach the newspaper's Article 10 rights to freedom of expression. In coming to this conclusion, the Court attached considerable weight to the fact that the allegations at the heart of the case were correct and accurately recorded.

In *Bergens* the Court also considered another issue related to the truth of the information. The newspaper article which was the subject of the dispute had in fact been written in response to an earlier article reporting that Dr R was opening a new clinic offering cosmetic surgery. This original article presented a favourable picture of Dr R's practice and did not mention any complaints. It was in reaction to this article that a number of readers had

---

[130] *Thorgierson v Iceland* (1992) 14 EHRR 843, para 63; *Barthold v Germany* (1985) 7 EHRR 383, para 58; *Jersild v Denmark* (1995) 19 EHRR 1, para 31.
[131] (1988) D&R 56.   [132] (2001) 31 EHRR 16.

written in to the paper reporting their bad experiences at the hands of Dr R. Only then had the newspaper undertaken further research and put together the second article to which Dr R objected. In its judgment the Court points out that the second article was a response to the earlier favourable article, and seems to take account of the fact that a particular image had been presented to the public, giving rise to a corresponding public interest in indicating the falsity of that image where there was clear evidence to that effect. In essence, the Court seemed to suggest that there is a public interest in setting the record straight.[133]

Other cases suggest a broader approach by the Court on the issue of the truth of the information discussed. In *Thorgierson*[134] the Court recognised that establishing the truth of some types of allegation is a near impossible task. The writer in that case had made allegations of police brutality based on reports made to him by others. There was thus some basis for the concerns, but they could not be proven. Given that the matter was one of public concern, this was not a reason to deny protection. Similarly in *Lingens*,[135] the Commission accepted that Article 10 protection extends to the expression of opinions and value judgments that are not susceptible to proof. Again, the extent to which this factor will be relevant is thus dependent on the type of speech in issue.

The Type of the Speech

The type of the speech is probably the single most important factor in determining the proportionality of any restriction on speech. The Court and Commission have made clear that the protection of the Convention extends to all types of speech including speech that offends, shocks or disturbs, not just to inoffensive matters.[136]

Where the speaker raises an issue of public concern or interest, then restrictions are more likely to be disproportionate to any legitimate aim pursued. The main way in which the Court and Commission reflect the different treatment of different types of speech is via the mechanism of the margin of appreciation, whereby individual states are given a degree of flexibility in their application of the Convention. The extent of the margin allowed depends in large measure on the type and subject matter of the speech.[137] In *Handyside* where the concept was used in relation to Article 10(2), the Court was concerned with the prosecution of a publisher under the Obscene Publications Acts. The book that had been published, *The Little Red*

---

[133] The approach echoes that of the Court of Appeal in *Woodward v Hutchins* [1977] 1 WLR 760 where Lord Denning held that where a party builds up a particular image to gain advantageous publicity, the public interest will be served where it is demonstrated that the image fostered is untrue.

[134] *Thorgierson v Iceland* (1992) 14 EHRR 843.

[135] *Lingens v Austria* (1986) 8 EHRR 407.   [136] *Handyside v UK* (1981) 1 EHRR 737.

[137] 'The scope of the domestic power of appreciation is not identical as regards each of the aims listed in Article 10(2).' *Sunday Times v UK* (1979) 2 EHRR 245, at para 59.

Schoolbook, was aimed at school aged children and contained a number of pages with information relating to sex and drugs, with no mention of the illegality of the drugs, nor of the illegality of sexual intercourse between underage boys and girls. In deciding that the prosecution involved no breach of the Convention, the Court recognised that there is no uniform European concept of morals and that individual states are in a better position to decide necessary limits on freedom of speech in such matters. The margin of appreciation referred to by the Court allowed such discretion to be introduced into the concept of necessity in the Convention.

In contrast, in *The Sunday Times v UK* (involving an injunction to prevent publication of details about litigation that was in progress) the need to maintain the authority of the judiciary could be judged more objectively than the moral questions in *Handyside*,[138] and a narrower margin of appreciation was applied, with the Court finding that the UK was in breach of the Convention. Thus, where speech raises a matter of public concern, or otherwise serves the public interest, the Court allows domestic courts a narrower margin of appreciation in their compliance with the Convention, thereby imposing a stricter standard in its review of the legality of any interference with freedom of speech.

In *Hertzel v Switzerland*[139] the applicant was banned from stating in a journal article that food prepared in microwave ovens was a health hazard, and from using images of death in the accompanying illustrations. The Commission noted that he was expressing views on public health, and that free expression on matters of public importance for the community was of special importance. As a result, the ban was not proportionate to the aim of protecting the reputation and business interests of the manufacturers of the microwave ovens. The Court recognised that a margin of appreciation was necessary in allowing states to regulate commercial matters, especially in complex and fluctuating areas such as unfair competition, but went on to say that 'it is necessary to reduce the extent of the margin of appreciation when what is at stake is not a given individual's purely "commercial" statements, but his participation in a debate affecting the general interest, for example, over public health'.[140] Even though the applicant was not barred from expressing the views altogether (a factor that makes the Court more ready to allow a restriction on speech),[141] the restriction was found to be dispro-

---

[138] 'Precisely the same cannot be said of the far more objective notion of the "authority" of the judiciary. . . . Accordingly, here a more extensive European supervision corresponds to a less discretionary power of appreciation.' (*Sunday Times*, see n 137 above at para 59.) Also see T. O'Donnell, 'The Margin of Appreciation Doctrine: Standard in the Jurisprudence of the European Court of Human Rights' [1982] Human Rights Quarterly 474 and T. Jones, 'The Devaluation of Human Rights Under the European Convention' [1995] PL 430.

[139] (1998) 28 EHRR 534.

[140] *Hertzel v Switzerland* (1998) 28 EHRR 534 at para 47.

[141] He remained free to publish in non-economic spheres such as scientific or academic journals. *Hertzel v Switzerland* (1998) 28 EHRR 534 at para 44.

portionate, mainly because the subject matter of the speech was a matter of general public concern.[142]

The concerns that have been viewed as worthy of special protection are not limited to issues of public health. In a case involving a newspaper's challenge to defamation proceedings, arising out of its reports of violations of the seal hunting regulations in Norway, the Court accepted that issues of local or national importance should be given special protection against restrictions. It noted that careful scrutiny was needed where sanctions discourage the participation of the press in debates over matters of legitimate public concern.[143] Although the case was raised in the context of defamation proceedings against a newspaper, rather than an employment sanction against an employee for raising a work related issue, the broad classification of issues of public interest would apply, whatever the context in which the speech arose.

The Court has also recognised that the dealings of businessmen involved with large public companies are worthy of public scrutiny and discussion. In *Fayed v UK*[144] the Court stated that 'the limits of acceptable criticism are wider with regard to businessmen actively involved in the affairs of large public companies than with regard to private individuals. . . . Persons . . . who fall into the former category of businessmen inevitably and knowingly lay themselves open to close scrutiny of their acts . . . above all by bodies representing the public interest.'[145] Moreover, it was noted that where information had been used in public by the Fayeds to build a good reputation, they could not complain of moves to demonstrate that the information was false.[146] The case shows that the Court recognises a wide range of information as being in the public interest. This category of information may be of particular importance for employees in large companies exercising the right to free speech. It demonstrates that the Court recognises the powerful position of large companies in today's world, and will not assume that the only threat to freedom of speech comes from the state.

A second example of the Court recognising that the right to free speech extends to the discussion of prominent businessmen, on the basis that it serves the public interest, can be found in *Fressoz and Roire v France*.[147] The case involved publication of details of a pay rise awarded to the chairman of a major public company, Peugeot. The publication was made in the context of an industrial dispute over pay at Peugeot, in which the management were refusing a pay rise to the general workforce. In the government's view the restriction on speech was justified as the speech related to a personal matter.

---

[142] See also *Bergens Tidende v Norway* (2001) 31 EHRR 16, where the ECtHR also protected speech relating to public health despite the fact that the speech damaged the subject's reputation.

[143] *Bladet Tromsø and Stensaas v Norway* (2000) 29 EHRR 125.

[144] (1994) 18 EHRR 393.   [145] Ibid at para 75.

[146] Cf *Bergens Tidende v Norway* (2001) 31 EHRR 16, discussed above.

[147] (2001) 31 EHRR 1.

The Court disagreed, stating that in the context of a dispute over the refusal of a pay rise, the disclosure of the chairman's large pay rise contributed to a general debate on a matter of public importance. The Court went as far as to state that 'issues concerning employment and pay generally attract considerable attention. Consequently, an interference with . . . press freedom cannot be compatible with Article 10(2) unless it is justified by an overriding requirement in the public interest.'[148] Again the recognition by the Court that the internal affairs of a business may be the subject of legitimate public debate could aid employees using the HRA, and seeking to show that discipline or dismissal for speaking in public about matters relating to the workplace breaches their Article 10 rights.

Although the Court recognises a wide range of information as being in the public interest, extra special protection is given to speech which upholds one of the stated aims of the Convention, such as the maintenance of a democratic society. The Court recognises that 'freedom of political debate is at the very core of the concept of a democratic society which prevails throughout the Convention'.[149] As a result, the Court has made clear on a number of occasions that it is particularly reluctant to sanction interference with speech which has political implications.

In *Lingens* the applicant was convicted of criminal defamation after publishing two articles that criticised the Austrian Chancellor. In holding that this violated Article 10, the Court recognised that the limits of acceptable criticism are wider as regards a politician than as regards a private individual. Despite the fact that it was for the legitimate aim of protecting the reputation of others, the political nature of the speech meant that the restriction was disproportionate to that aim. The Court also pointed out that public opinion provides a means of accountability for those who hold public power. A free press is the best way for that opinion to be informed, and for people to learn the views and opinions of political leaders. In *Castells v Spain*,[150] the Court held that the conviction of the applicant for insulting the government was in violation of Article 10, even though it served the legitimate aim of preventing public disorder and protecting the reputation of others. Again the Court pointed out that '[i]n the democratic system the actions or omissions of the government must be subject to the close scrutiny not only of the legislative and judicial authorities but also of the press and public opinion'.[151] In these cases, the Court recognises the vital role of the press in informing public opinion on political and other matters of public interest.[152] Taken together they indicate that the Court will be reluctant to sanction infringements on the

---

[148] *Fressoz and Roire v France* (2001) 31 EHRR 1 at para 51.
[149] *Lingens v Austria* (1986) 8 EHRR 407.   [150] (1992) 13 EHRR 445.
[151] Ibid at para 46. See also *Schwabe v Austria* (1993) 14 HRLJ 26 and *Oberschlick v Austria* (1991) 19 EHRR 389.
[152] See also *Thorgierson v Iceland* (1992) 14 EHRR 843, para 63; *Barthold v Germany* (1985) 7 EHRR 383, para 58; *Jersild v Denmark* (1995) 19 EHRR 1, para 31.

freedom of expression of those who speak about matters that can be said to be of political importance.

The cases demonstrate the way in which greater public accountability of public bodies can be achieved by allowing freedom of expression, where the speech relates to the conduct of those bodies. They also show that the Court recognises that the democratic process is dependent upon freedom of political cal speech. The reasoning here echoes that of Meiklejohn[153] who took the view that a truly democratic system requires a well informed electorate, and that members of the public therefore need all relevant information before them when playing their part in the democratic process.

The extent to which this reasoning is applicable to all areas of the public sector is unclear. In *Janowski v Poland*[154] the applicant intervened when some municipal guards requested some street vendors to move to a nearby market-place. Janowski pointed out, in the presence of some bystanders, that the guards were acting without legal authority. He also used some offensive language to them, calling them 'oafs' and 'dumb'. He was charged with the criminal offence of having insulted the municipal guards while they were carrying out their duties and with having acted with flagrant contempt for legal order. In assessing whether these sanctions were proportionate to the aim of preventing disorder, the Commission took the view that civil servants, like politicians, could legitimately be subject to wider criticism than others, and should accept that the criticism may sometimes be harsh or expressed in a strong form. However, the Court disagreed. First it pointed out that Janowski's comments did not form part of an open discussion of matters of public concern. Second, while accepting that civil servants may be open to greater criticism than ordinary members of the public, it was not the case that civil servants knowingly lay themselves open to close scrutiny of their every word and deed to the extent that politicians do. Thus the sanctions were proportionate.

The decision of the Court was not unanimous, however. One of the five dissenting judges pointed out that the abuse or excess of authority by the public officials was indeed a matter of public concern, and speech pointing this out should therefore have been protected.[155] This is probably the preferable view. It may be the case that not all civil servants, by virtue only of being public sector employees, should be open to constant close scrutiny. However, speech that uncovers abuses of power and authority, particularly within the public sector, should be protected as relating to matters of public concern.

---

[153] A. Meiklejohn, *Free Speech and its Relation to Self Government* (1972) Kennikat Press, New York, discussed in Chapter 2.

[154] (2000) 19 EHRR 705.

[155] Dissenting opinion of Judge Sir Nicolas Bratza. Another, Judge Bonello, took the view that the case failed to find a 'proper equilibrium . . . between sheltering those who were abusing public order, and those who, exceeding the limits of permissible speech, abused the abusers of the law'.

The *Janowski* case can be contrasted with that of *Thorgierson v Iceland*,[156] where the Court refused to accept that a lesser level of protection was needed for speech that did not relate to political issues. The applicant had been convicted of defamation for writing newspaper articles criticising the police. The government of Iceland sought to argue that the restrictions allowed by Article 10(2) varied according to the type of speech or expression, with political speech accorded the greatest level of protection. Since the opinions expressed by the applicant did not relate directly to the participation of citizens in a democracy, they did not amount to political speech, and therefore interference would be more readily justified. The Court did not accept the argument. It stated that the restrictions on freedom of expression should be narrowly interpreted and that there is no warrant in case law for distinguishing between one type of speech and another. The state's argument that 'nonpolitical' speech deserved less protection was not accepted. It seems then, *pace* the decision in *Janowski*, that the 'type of speech' can be used to argue only for more protection under the Convention, and not for less.

As these cases demonstrate, the subject matter of speech is probably the most important of the factors determining the level of protection afforded to free speech by the ECHR. Although the Convention protects freedom of speech regardless of content, the importance of the subject matter of the speech is introduced by the Article 10(2) restrictions. Where the public interest is served by speech, it will be harder to show that restrictions are proportionate, even though they may serve one of the legitimate aims listed in Article 10(2). Employees who seek to use the HRA to argue that their freedom of speech should be protected at work will be in a strong position when that speech relates to a matter of public concern. Domestic courts, taking account of the jurisprudence of the ECHR, will need to note the special protection afforded by the Convention to political or other public interest speech. This means that other aspects of employees' speech that might otherwise militate against its protection (for example the fact that the speech is made in public, and relates to the workplace) should be outweighed. The extent to which this is so will, however, depend on the way in which the ECHR's concept of the margin of appreciation is used by domestic courts in applying the Convention rights in UK courts.

THE MARGIN OF APPRECIATION

As mentioned above, the margin of appreciation is the mechanism whereby individual states are given a degree of flexibility in their application of the Convention. It depends for its scope on the type and subject matter of the speech. Before considering whether the margin of appreciation will apply under the HRA, it is worth considering its role in ECHR jurisprudence more

---

[156] (1992) 14 EHRR 843.

generally, as it is questionable whether it is a justifiable concept even at the European level.

According different types of speech differing margins of appreciation possibly reflects the dual purposes of free speech protection: self fulfilment and enabling participation in democracy.[157] The narrower margin in relation to political speech suggests that in reality the basis of much of the protection of Article 10 is that free speech helps maintain the democratic process. The fact that it also helps maintain the individual right to personal autonomy and human dignity seems to be of lesser importance. As a result, in any clash between interests, the right to free speech tends to yield in cases where the protection would be based on personal autonomy. By way of illustration, in *Otto-Premiger Institute v Austria*[158] the Court granted a wide margin of appreciation to the state in finding that the seizure of a blasphemous film did not breach Article 10. In contrast, in *Goodwin v UK*,[159] the Court upheld a journalist's freedom to withhold the name of the source of confidential information that he had published, on the basis that it served the public interest. The Court appears to grant a wider margin of appreciation where free speech enables self fulfilment, thereby reducing its supervisory role. If speech enables wider public participation in decision making, and can be classed as 'political', then a narrow margin is also used.

Whether this approach is justified is open to question. For example, the distinction between artistic speech and 'political' speech can be difficult to maintain on a principled basis: is there sufficient difference between a blasphemous film[160] and a film exposing racism[161] to justify different standards of protection?[162] The danger can be that a wide margin of appreciation, and consequently reduced European supervision, results in the erosion of protection afforded to 'personal' speech. However, a certain margin of appreciation is probably necessary for the Convention to be workable, given that there is always room for judicial discretion in interpretation, and especially given the rather vague language of the Convention.

The effect of the margin of appreciation is that the Convention effectively offers weaker protection to speech which serves personal autonomy, rather than the public interest. This may impact on the use of the Convention by those exercising the right to freedom of speech at work. Where the employee engages in whistleblowing speech, which refers to immediate and urgent concerns about serious wrongdoing, there is little problem. Reference by

[157] *Handyside v UK* (1981) 1 EHRR 737. Also, see P. Mahoney, 'Universality versus Subsidiarity in the Strasbourg Case Law on Free Speech: Explaining Some Recent Judgments' [1997] EHRLR 364.
[158] (1995) 19 EHRR 34.   [159] (1996) 22 EHRR 123.
[160] *Otto-Premiger Institute v Austria* (1995) 19 EHRR 34.
[161] *Jersild v Denmark* (1995) 19 EHRR 1.
[162] See A. Lester, 'Universality versus Subsidiarity: A Reply' [1998] EHRLR 73.

domestic courts to the jurisprudence of the ECHR, under the mechanisms set out in the HRA, should lead the speech to be protected. According to the Convention case law, interference with speech in whistleblowing cases may not even serve a legitimate aim, let alone be classed as necessary in a democratic society. In addition, the strong protection granted under Article 10 where the speech can be shown to be of a political nature could aid employees disciplined or dismissed for engaging in political speech.[163] The difficulty comes when considering the individual who raises more general concerns about matters of public importance, drawing on experience at work. If the domestic courts take into account the case law of the ECHR here, they will need to reflect the fact that such speech is often classified as 'personal', or as an aspect of self fulfilment, and the level of protection is consequently limited. Only if the public interest in allowing such speech is recognised will sufficient protection be granted. The difference in approach in *Janowski* and *Thorgierson* on the importance of speech critical of public authorities does not give cause for great optimism that the public interest in general comment on matters at work would be readily recognised by the Strasbourg Court, and this could also be reflected in domestic court decisions.

A further difficulty with the current use of the margin of appreciation is that, although it is a necessary concept, it can be used too readily by the ECtHR to avoid setting consistent and high standards of protection for freedom of expression. These concerns have been recognised by some members of the Court, such as the dissenting judges in *Jacubowski v Germany*.[164] The majority of the ECtHR held that there was no breach of Article 10 where an injunction was allowed preventing the applicant from circulating to journalists newspaper cuttings which were critical of his former employer. They said that although this amounted to an infringement of the applicant's freedom of expression, it was not disproportionate (and was therefore necessary) bearing in mind the wide margin of appreciation needed in complex and fluctuating matters such as unfair competition. The three dissenting judges argued that the majority had given excessive significance to the doctrine of the margin of appreciation and, as a result, the Court had not undertaken the effective supervision required by the Convention.

The dissenting judges have a legitimate concern: too wide a margin of appreciation results in 'weak and unpredictable' case law, and a lack of principled interpretation and application of the right to free speech.[165] Where a wide margin of appreciation is given, the Court can avoid setting universal standards by relying too heavily on the findings of domestic courts. It then

---

[163] Subject to any special restrictions imposed on the employee. See the decision in *Ahmed v UK* (2000) 29 EHRR 1, discussed above.

[164] (1994) 19 EHRR 64.

[165] A. Lester, 'Universality versus Subsidiarity: A Reply' [1998] EHRLR 73 at 78, and P. van Dijk and G. van Hoof, *Theory and Practice of the European Convention on Human Rights* (2nd edn, 1990) Kluwer, the Netherlands.

becomes difficult to see how this squares with the Court's statement (above) that 'necessity' means more than just 'reasonable'. The Court's commitment to the concept of proportionality as governing the question of the necessity of restrictions on speech is also undermined.[166]

THE MARGIN OF APPRECIATION AND THE HUMAN RIGHTS ACT 1998

Although not without its critics, the margin of appreciation is well established in the Convention case law. What is not yet certain is how the concept will translate into domestic law under the HRA. If introduced directly into domestic law it is probable that the concept of the margin of appreciation would be used to dilute the protection available. Although introduced to the ECHR to allow flexibility in times of emergency, the need for a margin of appreciation to apply at international level is clear in non-emergency cases too. This is especially in cases involving moral issues, where standards can vary across the different states who are party to the Convention. This is even more the case given the expansion of the Council of Europe[167] into eastern Europe. However, the need for a margin of appreciation internationally does not mean that the concept is necessary at a domestic level.

In the discussion of the HRA in Parliament the applicability of the margin of appreciation in domestic courts was discussed. The Home Secretary, in a rather opaque statement, confirmed that the margin of appreciation would be available to judges, in that they are to take account of the case law of the Court and Commission in interpreting the Convention in domestic courts, including case law on the margin of appreciation, although domestic courts are not bound by those decisions.[168] Those opposed to incorporation seemed to suggest that the margin of appreciation could be used by judges in the UK to allow flexibility in the interpretation of the Convention.[169] On this view, a court could consider the European case law and then apply a margin of appreciation itself. The danger of such an approach is that it would weaken the protection of the Convention even further, allowing a form of judicial review of decisions, which will then only be overturned if outside the standards of *Wednesbury* reasonableness. Although *Wednesbury* unreasonableness and the margin of appreciation are not the same concepts, in both cases the court does not view its task as standard setting, but overturns decisions only if they are outside a certain range, or margin, of reasonableness. Such a standard of review would be very weak compared to that potentially available under the HRA.[170] It could also open up avenues of appeal to Strasbourg on the basis that the Convention has not been correctly applied.

[166] N. Lavender, 'The Problem of the Margin of Appreciation' [1997] EHRLR 380.
[167] Comprised of the member states to the Convention.
[168] HRA s 2.   [169] See HC Debs 3 June 1998 col 423–4.
[170] See both Singh and Hunt, above, for a discussion of the difference between the concept of 'proportionality' under the Convention, and *Wednesbury* reasonableness.

The lack of clarity on this issue on the face of the Act and in the parliamentary debates was addressed by the House of Lords in *R v DPP*, *ex p Kebilene*,[171] decided prior to the Act's coming into force. The case does not concern the application of Article 10, and so may not be followed in HRA cases involving freedom of expression, but the decision does give an indication of the House of Lords approach to the issue. In *Kebilene*, their Lordships made clear that the margin of appreciation does not apply in domestic courts. However, they substituted an alternative. They pointed out that many cases will not be clear cut and that courts will have a discretionary area of judgment in deciding whether Convention rights have been infringed. Lord Hope pointed out that the Convention rights are expressions of principle, not strict rules, and that application of these principles require questions of balance and proportionality to be decided. In such cases, some flexibility is required. Thus, in many cases courts will want to recognise that decision making bodies have a sphere of discretion which is theirs to exercise, which should not be interfered with unnecessarily, especially where the decision making body is democratically elected. Although the weakness inherent in accepting the margin of appreciation at domestic level is avoided by the decision in *Kebilene*, the alternative 'discretionary area of judgment' may not be very different. The suggestion from the House of Lords seems to be that courts should be wary of substituting their views for those of the decision making body, reflecting the well established but restricted role for the courts to be found in both judicial review and employment law.[172] Whilst there is clearly a need for some area of discretion or flexibility in the application of the broadly stated rights of the Convention, it is to be hoped that its use will not undermine the potential for the HRA to improve the protection of fundamental rights in domestic courts.

CONCLUSION

Of all the UK's international obligations relating to workplace rights, those that arise under the ECHR have the greatest potential to change domestic law. Under the HRA domestic law will need to be interpreted to comply with the ECHR. Where staff are subject to work based sanctions for exercising the right to free speech the legality of those sanctions will fall to be considered in the light of the jurisprudence of the Convention. As has been seen, the European case law has potential to improve the protection of those who exercise the right to free speech at work. A number of areas, both statutory and common law, which are of relevance to employees who raise concerns at work could be affected by being interpreted to comply with Article 10. Some of

---

[171] [2000] 2 AC 326.
[172] See *UCATT v Brain* [1981] IRLR 224: it is not the job of the tribunal to substitute its own judgment for that of the employer.

these have been mentioned above and include the development of the concept of 'reasonableness' in relation to unfair dismissal, the scope of the duty of confidence and the meaning of the public interest. The extent to which the law in these areas may be interpreted to provide greater protection for the free speech of employees is dependent, to an extent, on the type of speech involved.

WHISTLEBLOWING SPEECH

Where an employee raises a serious concern about wrongdoing or safety at work, the protection already available in domestic law could be enhanced by reference to the jurisprudence of the ECHR. The case law on Article 10 makes clear that where a person discloses matters that, in the public interest, should be made known, the speech should be protected. This is the case even where disclosure is on a wide scale, a factor that can otherwise weigh in favour of the maintenance of confidentiality. The rights of the audience to hear what is said, and the role of the press in acting as a watchdog for the public to alert them to potential wrongdoing, are given great weight in Convention jurisprudence. These issues could be used by whistleblowers to argue for an interpretation of domestic law which would accept as lawful disclosures of important information to the press.[173]

POLITICAL SPEECH

Where speech has political implications, then Article 10 could be relied on to argue for improved protection for workers. The recognition in the Strasbourg case law that political speech requires the greatest protection on the basis of its democratic importance, and the recognition that dismissal can act as a significant chill on free speech, could both be used to aid an employee who challenges work related restrictions on speech with political overtones. This is particularly the case where work based restrictions are imposed for speech that is unconnected with work. However, where political speech relates to work, the case law on Article 10 provides much less encouragement. The decision in *Ahmed v UK*[174] makes clear that an employer's need for political neutrality can easily be found to outweigh the free speech rights of the employee.

PERSONAL VIEWS AND GENERAL COMMENT

Where speech relates to matters of personal interest, or the expression of personal views, the protection of the Convention is more limited. Article 10 does recognise such personal speech as worthy of protection under the Convention, but provides a wider margin of appreciation to states in the protection

---

[173] See Chapter 5 below on the interpretation of the Public Interest Disclosure Act, which provides protection for workers who blow the whistle on wrongdoing.
[174] (2000) 29 EHRR 1.

they provide. This reflects the emphasis within the jurisprudence on protecting audience and democratic interests in speech rather than on protecting speech as a matter of personal autonomy and human dignity. The limits on free speech, set out in Article 10(2), such as the protection of the rights of others, are more likely to prevail where speech expresses a personal view, and where the claim for protection can only be based on the speaker's right to autonomy. However, where general comment or personal views relate to public interest matters, reliance on Article 10 may improve the protection available. The Convention case law recognises a wide range of issues as of public interest, albeit not of direct political importance. Information relating to national and local issues and views on public (but not political) figures, such as prominent businessmen, have all been accepted as serving the public interest. If a matter is classed as in the public interest, then the audience interest in hearing what is said comes into the equation. In such cases, the balance to be achieved between the right to free speech and the rights of others who may be offended by the speech is much finer, and will not necessarily result in the lawful restriction of speech. The wide range of public interests recognised by the ECtHR means that reference to the jurisprudence of the Convention could be of help to employees in domestic courts, even where the speech appears at first to be merely a personal viewpoint or a matter of general comment.

Thus far, the prospects for the use of the Convention in domestic law via the HRA have been fairly promising. The chances of employees who have spoken out about matters at work successfully challenging the legality of any resulting work based sanctions in domestic courts and tribunals should be greater if they can rely on the protection of the right to free speech in Article 10 of the ECHR. The mechanisms set out in the HRA should allow them to do so, directly or indirectly, depending on whether they work for public or private sector employers.

However, this optimistic outlook has to be subject to some serious reservations. First, although it is clear that the Convention is to be used to develop the common law,[175] the exact weight to be attached to the Convention rights is not yet clear. In relation to statutes, s 3 of the HRA 1998 states that legislation must 'as far as possible' be interpreted to comply with the Convention. This means that as far as statutory interpretation is concerned, Convention rights are supreme. Where a declaration of incompatibility is made, Parliament should legislate to remedy the deficiency in domestic law. Whether it does so or not, and with what speed, will be a matter of political choice for the government.[176] The same supremacy of Convention rights is not explicit in relation to the common law. The influence of the Convention on the develop-

---

[175] Lord Chancellor, HL Debs 24 November 1997 col 783.
[176] Even if it chooses not to legislate, after a declaration has been made, the victim would still be able to take a case to Strasbourg.

ment of the common law is more indirect, via the obligation on the courts as 'public authorities' themselves to comply with the Convention. It is not clear whether the Convention rights are, to use Dworkin's phrase, to 'trump' the common law, or just to have the status of guiding principles.[177] Given the supremacy of Convention rights in relation to statutory interpretation, it is to be hoped that the courts will take a parallel approach to the interpretation of the common law, and give primacy to the Convention rights. Otherwise anomalies may well appear. Within employment law, common law and statutory rights are closely interrelated: common law determines the content of the contract, breach of which can give rise to (common law) wrongful and (statutory) unfair dismissal claims. It is clearly preferable that Convention rights be given the same weight whatever the basis of protection.

The second restriction on the use of the ECHR to protect those who exercise the right to freedom of expression is inherent in the structure of the HRA. The additional protection of the Convention is only available to the worker where the employer is the state. In the case of private sector staff, protection is dependent on finding a common law or statutory right which can be interpreted to include the rights protected by the Convention. Moreover, even this level of private sector protection is dependent on the courts accepting that the HRA does have a degree of horizontal effect, so that it can be used to regulate private relationships.[178] Whether or not they will take the opportunity to do so provided by the Act is yet to be seen.

This leads on to the final and perhaps most serious caveat to any assumption that the HRA heralds a new dawn in human rights protection in the UK. This is the fact that domestic courts have been using the Convention jurisprudence for some time to interpret domestic law, and yet the result has not always been extra protection for freedom of speech. Although prior to the HRA, the courts could not rely directly on Article 10 in reaching their conclusions, they had a chance to refer to the jurisprudence in interpreting the law. In many cases their conclusions have been that the law already complies with the standards set out in Article 10. This suggests that allowing Convention rights to be relied on directly may not have much impact on the law.[179]

In a number of cases, the courts have expressly considered the case law of the ECHR in reaching their conclusions. However, they have usually been quick to confirm that their deliberations have only confirmed that UK law on freedom of speech already complies with the requirements of the Convention. In *Attorney General v Guardian Newspapers Ltd (Spycatcher) (No 2)*,[180]

---

[177] The concept of rights as trumps and rights as guiding principles is discussed by Dworkin in *Taking Rights Seriously* (1977) Duckworth Press, London.
[178] See M. Hunt, 'The "Horizontal Effect" of the Human Rights Act' (1998) PL 423.
[179] See A. McColgan, 'Article 10 and the right to freedom of expression: workers ungagged?', in K. Ewing (ed), *Human Rights at Work* (2000) Institute of Employment Rights, London.
[180] [1990] 1 AC 109.

considering the injunctions against publication of details of the book *Spycatcher*, Lord Goff claimed that he could see 'no inconsistency between the English law on this subject and article 10 of the European Convention on Human Rights'. Indeed he went on to say: 'we may pride ourselves on the fact that freedom of speech has existed in this country perhaps as long as, if not longer than, it has existed in any other country in the world'.[181] In fact, the ECtHR disagreed with the House of Lords and found that the continuation of the injunctions after publication of the information in the United States did interfere with Article 10 rights.[182] In the light of this decision, the confidence with which Lord Goff asserted that domestic law complies with the law on Article 10 seems rather overstated. Nonetheless, it has subsequently been referred to as correctly stating the position.[183] In *Reynolds v Times Newspapers*[184] this was confirmed by Lord Nicholls who stated that 'the common law approach accords with the present state of the human rights jurisprudence'.[185] Again, in *Camelot Group PLC v Centaur Communications Ltd*[186] Schiemann LJ looked at the common law on confidentiality and the public interest in the light of the case law of the ECHR and found that the principles involved were substantially the same.

Throughout this chapter it has been argued that the HRA can offer extra protection to those facing work based sanctions for exercising the right to freedom of speech at work, as it enables the courts to take account of the jurisprudence of the ECHR. However, judging by past performance, as illustrated in the cases above, one might think that courts will not jump at the chances offered by the HRA to change current interpretations of the common law to provide that extra protection. Yet some of the early cases decided with reference to the HRA either just before, or soon after, its entry into force suggest that the courts may indeed be willing to exploit the opportunities offered by the Act. Whereas the cases prior to the HRA indicate that courts have been unwilling to find domestic law to be in conflict with Convention case law, some of the cases decided with reference to the Act have been more bold.

In *R v Offen*,[187] where the Court of Appeal gave the word 'exceptional' the opposite of its usual meaning, the court considered that it could have come to the same conclusion using pre-HRA methods of statutory interpretation, the intention of Parliament having been to protect the public only from those who posed a significant risk to the public. To an extent it can be suggested that the existence of the HRA was unnecessary to the court's decision. However,

---

[181] [1990] 1 AC 109 at 283.
[182] *The Observer and the Guardian v UK* (1991) 14 EHRR 153 and *The Sunday Times v UK* (1991) 14 EHRR 229.
[183] See *Derbyshire CC v Times Newspapers* [1993] AC 534 at 551G.
[184] [1999] 3 WLR 1010.   [185] Ibid at 1026.   [186] [1998] 1 All ER 251.
[187] [2001] 1 WLR 253.

it is not insignificant that despite several opportunities to do so,[188] that inter-pretation was not given until after the HRA was in force. Another example of the courts' more bold use of the HRA can be found in *Arthur JS Hall & Co (a firm) v Simons*[189] where the House of Lords, making reference to the need to comply with the ECHR, overturned the traditional immunity from suit for negligence in the handling of civil and criminal proceedings enjoyed by advocates.[190] Further examples include *R v DPP, ex p Kebilene*,[191] and *MacDonald v Ministry of Defence* in the EAT[192] discussed above, where the courts used the HRA to interpret domestic law very broadly so as to provide increased human rights protection.

The HRA, with its potential application to both public and private rela-tionships, thus clearly has the power to increase the protection afforded to employees' right to freedom of speech. Yet the potential for the Act to effect radical change remains crucially dependent on the extent to which those who interpret the law are minded to make such changes.[193] The flexibility in-herent in the Strasbourg jurisprudence gives scope for both conservative and radical interpretations. Whether or not the HRA fulfils its potential to provide increased protection for freedom of expression rights in domestic law depends on the extent to which our judges are willing to exploit these opportunities.

---

[188] *R v Kelly* [1999] 2 Cr App R (S) 178, *R v Buckland* [2000] 2 Cr App R (S) 217.
[189] [2000] 3 WLR 543.   [190] Per Lord Millet, at 624.
[191] [2000] 2 AC 326.   [192] [2000] IRLR 748.
[193] See M. Hunt, 'The Human Rights Act and Legal Culture: The Judiciary and the Legal Profession' (1999) JLS 86, on the extent to which the HRA requires a change in culture among lawyers and judges, including a change in the way in which cases are presented and decided.

4

Freedom of Speech and The Contract of Employment: The Concept of the Public Interest

One of the legitimate restrictions on the exercise of freedom of speech by employees arises where it interferes with the rights of others. The fact that the right to free speech is not an absolute right is accepted in all the main charters on human rights, including Article 10(2) of the European Convention on Human Rights (ECHR), which allows freedom of speech to be restricted in order to protect others' rights, and to prevent the disclosure of information received in confidence. This chapter will consider the contract of employment and the various duties owed by employees that may restrict the right to freedom of speech to be enjoyed by those who work. The main contractual duties which will have an impact on freedom of speech for employees are the duty of mutual trust and confidence; of co-operation and fidelity; and duties in relation to confidential information. These duties may be contained in express terms of the employment contract, or may be implied into the contract by the common law. Whether express or implied, they will be subject to an exception where the speech serves the public interest. This means that the question of whether the public interest is served by speech is of pivotal importance in assessing the contractual duties of the employee. The case law on the scope of the public interest in the disclosure of information has mainly arisen in relation to the duty of confidentiality, and this case law will be explored in detail in the chapter, but the understanding the cases give of how courts have interpreted the public interest is equally applicable to the other duties owed by the employee.

EMPLOYEE DUTIES IMPACTING ON FREEDOM OF SPEECH

THE DUTY OF MUTUAL TRUST AND CONFIDENCE

A disclosure of information relating to the workplace may well involve the breach of the implied term of mutual trust and confidence, which includes a duty of co-operation and fidelity. Although known as the duty of mutual trust and confidence, the word confidence in this context refers to employer and employee having confidence in each other, rather than to the concept of confidentiality. In order to distinguish it from the specific duty of confidence owed in relation to confidential information, discussed further below, the duty of mutual trust and confidence will be referred to as the duty of mutual trust in this chapter.

In most cases, the duty of mutual trust will not form an express term of the contract. Instead it is implied into the employment contract by the common law. Terms are implied into contracts to give effect to the presumed intention of the parties, and to facilitate the business efficacy of the contract. In the case of the duty of trust, it can safely be assumed that both parties to the contract would intend there to be a degree of trust and confidence between them in entering the new relationship. A duty of mutual trust is also necessary for the employment contract to operate effectively; any attempt to carry on an employment relationship without some basis of trust between the parties would be likely to run into difficulty rather fast. The implied duty of mutual trust is a very broad based duty owed between employer and employee, and is essential to the smooth functioning of the employment relationship.

In *Malik v BCCI*,[1] the key case on the duty of mutual trust, the duty is referred to as 'the portmanteau, general obligation not to engage in conduct likely to undermine the trust and confidence required if the employment relationship is to continue in the manner the employment contract implicitly envisages'.[2] The exact parameters of the duty are still being defined, but employers have been found to be in breach where they have falsely accused the employee of theft;[3] have failed to investigate a complaint about health and safety;[4] or have provided a reference for an employee that referred to complaints made against her without having previously informed her of those complaints.[5] In fact, the duty of confidence implied into the contract of employment can also be understood to form part of the more general duty of mutual trust as currently understood. Although these examples of the duty of mutual trust have involved the duties of employers, it is stressed in each case that the duty is mutual, and is equally owed by employee to employer. For example, in the case of *Malik* itself the breach of the duty of mutual trust arose out of the employer's actions that cast a stigma on the employees. In a second case arising out of the collapse of the BCCI bank, *BCCI v Ali*,[6] the High Court recognised that employees' actions could equally cast a stigma on the employer.

Examples of the duty as it is owed by employees can be found in *Ticehurst v British Telecommunications plc*[7] where a duty to exercise discretion

---

[1] [1997] IRLR 462.   [2] Per Lord Nicholls, at para 13.
[3] *Robinson v Crompton Parkinson* [1978] ICR 401.
[4] *British Aircraft Corporation v Austin* [1978] IRLR 332.
[5] *TSB Bank PLC v Harris* [2000] IRLR 157.   [6] [1999] IRLR 226.
[7] [1992] IRLR 219.

faithfully in the interests of the employer was implied into the contract of employment. A withdrawal of good will as part of industrial action was found to be a breach of this contractual duty. Although implied in the context of industrial action, it indicates an approach by the courts to employees' implied duties that extends beyond the strict confines of job descriptions and express terms, to a more general duty of faithful service. In *Thornley v ARA Ltd*[8] the 'fundamental, common sense, contractual obligation upon a servant not to let his master down'[9] was said to be breached where the employee disclosed confidential information to the press. Thornley had raised matters of concern about the design of aircraft in which he was involved. He had raised his concerns internally at first but, following what he believed was an unsatisfactory response by the employer, he then disclosed the confidential information to the press. It was this external disclosure that the EAT viewed as the breach of the implied term of the contract not to let the employer down.[10] After the *Malik* case, both these duties can be understood to form part of the general duty of mutual trust.

The actions of an employee who speaks in public about matters relating to work, or makes statements of opinion unfavourable to the employer, could have the effect of breaching the duty of mutual trust owed between employer and employee, resulting in a breach of contract. The duty of mutual trust could therefore cause difficulties for employees who wish to exercise the right to free speech at work, particularly if they participate in debate on sensitive issues, as any such participation could constitute a breach of its terms. In Chapter 2 a number of employer interests were identified that could be threatened by an employee's exercise of free speech. These included the employer's financial interests, its interests in autonomy and the public interest in good management and the efficient running of the business. Any action that interferes with these interests puts a good working relationship between employer and employee under threat. This may potentially undermine the employment relationship, and so breach the general duty of mutual trust between employer and employee.

Employees who blow the whistle on wrongdoing at work may well cause the enterprise financial loss, as well as damaging its good reputation. In this way, the duty of mutual trust may be breached, subject to the determination of the public interest issue discussed below. Likewise, an employee who exercises the right to free speech to make political comments with which the employer disagrees could be said to breach the duty of trust, especially

---

[8] *Thornley v Aircraft Research Association Ltd*, 14 September 1976, 539/11 and 11 May 1977 EAT 669/76.
[9] 1977 EAT 669/76, at 8 para g–h.
[10] '. . . the real gravamen of the employer's complaint . . . was that *by sending the letter to The Guardian on the 7th June 1976 he was in breach of trust to his employers*'. *Thornley*, at 8 f (italics supplied).

if they are unpopular views. Continuing to employ an individual who has expressed unpopular opinions could cause disruption among others in the workforce or bring the enterprise itself into disrepute. In any such case, the speech could be said to interfere with the duty of mutual trust, again subject to the determination of the public interest issue. Engaging in principled dissent or other adverse comment on an employer's actions or policies is also liable to a potential finding that the employer's interests have been damaged. This will be the case especially if the views are expressed publicly and they damage the reputation of the employer.

THE DUTY OF CONFIDENCE

The duty of confidence owed by an employee to his employer has a number of legal bases. It is contained in the employment contract as part of a general duty of good faith,[11] so to that extent it is a contractual obligation. However, it also exists as an equitable obligation, arising out of the relationship between giver and recipient of confidential information.[12] In both its forms,[13] the duty of confidence arises from the recognition in law that it is 'in the public interest that when information is received in confidence—for a limited purpose, as it always is—it should not be used for other purposes'.[14] Courts tend to take a flexible, pragmatic approach to the issue of the legal basis of the duty of confidence, using whichever jurisdiction gives the best protection for the information, equitable or contractual. Concepts and case law from one jurisdiction are used in proceedings in the other when considering the meaning of terms such as the public interest. For the purposes of the discussion of the employment context in this chapter, the basis of the duty of confidence will be assumed to be contractual, although many of the cases considered involve the equitable duty.

All employment contracts contain a duty of confidence. In many cases this duty is expressly stated in a clause requiring that employees maintain the confidentiality of information to which they are privy as a result of their employment. Confidentiality clauses may also be incorporated into a contract from an outside source, such as from a collective agreement, works rules, company handbooks, or professional codes of conduct. In addition, confidentiality clauses are sometimes imposed after the employment contract has terminated as part of a negotiated settlement. Where there is no express term covering confidentiality, one will be implied by the courts. As with the duty of

---

[11] *Robb v Green* [1895] 2 QB 315.

[12] *Coco v AN Clark (Engineers) Ltd* [1969] RPC 41.

[13] Additional obligations of confidence have in the past been based on the law of property and tort. See Chapter 2 of Y. Cripps, *Legal Implications of Disclosure in the Public Interest* (2nd edn, 1994) Sweet & Maxwell, London.

[14] *Norwich Pharmacal Co v Commissioners of Customs and Excise* [1972] RPC 743 per Lord Denning.

mutual trust, the duty of confidence meets the general requirements for implied terms, reflecting the intentions of the parties and being necessary for business efficacy: both employer and employee can be taken to intend there to be a degree of confidence between them in entering the contract, and a duty of confidence is necessary for the employment contract to operate effectively.

A specific form of the duty of confidence has been developed in relation to confidential information from the need for businesses to preserve commercial secrets. Since information can be exploited for economic gain it is clearly necessary to allow those who invest in invention and discovery of new processes and products to reap the benefits of such industry. An implied term of confidence therefore prevents employees from disclosing confidential information during the course of their employment, and from disclosing trade secrets even after employment has ceased.[15] Apart from this specific duty in relation to commercial secrets, a more general duty of confidence also exists in relation to information gained by the employee in the course of employment. This duty can be breached where an employee discloses information of a confidential nature in the course of exercising the right to free speech. Employees who raise matters of concern about wrongdoing at work may well disclose confidential information in the process. For example, disclosures relating to fraud or other financial irregularity could well involve disclosures of confidential financial information. In many cases, the raising of broader concerns will not involve confidential information, as the subject of the speech will already be known to the public. However, where the employee's speech involves commercially sensitive information which the employer may have expressly categorised as confidential, the duty will be breached. Examples could include disclosures relating to staffing levels in a hospital as part of a general discussion of health policy, or discussions of education policy backed up with real examples in a particular school. Although the information is only used in such cases to add weight to a personal or political opinion it could be classed as confidential, and so its use could involve a breach of the contractual duty of confidence.

Although it may seem obvious that the disclosure of information already known to the public cannot involve a breach of duty of confidence, in fact the case law on the duty of confidence suggests that this may not be the case where the contract of employment is concerned. Whilst it is clear that where information is in the public domain there is no confidence to be breached,[16] deciding whether something is in the public domain or not has given rise to some difficulty. It is not something that can be determined in absolute

---

[15] *Faccenda Chicken v Fowler* [1986] ICR 297.
[16] See Lord Denning in *Woodward v Hutchins* [1977] 1 WLR 760 at 764.

terms, but may be a question of degree.[17] Information may be known to a small number of people but not to the wider public and still retain the inaccessibility characteristic of confidential information. It is then unclear at what point the number of people knowing the information becomes large enough to be classed as the public for the purpose of showing that the information is in the public domain, and so not confidential. Similar uncertainties remain where information is used by a person who came across the information in circumstances of confidence, even though the information is accessible to the public should they wish to find it.

On the question of the number of people who can know information before it loses its quality of confidence, it seems that as long as it is made clear to those who receive the information that it is confidential, it can retain this status even though it has been widely disseminated and is known to a large number of people.[18] Where information is disseminated among a large group of people, such as the workforce of a large employer, care needs to be taken by the employer to ensure that those who receive it are aware of its confidentiality. Otherwise, an employee may be able to argue that any disclosure or discussion of the information does not amount to a breach of the duty of confidence as it is too widely known for confidentiality to exist.

A second uncertainty about when a duty of confidence will be owed by employees arises where the information, although known to others, is obtained in circumstances of trust. It might be assumed that no duty of confidence is owed where information is published or widely disseminated, for example outside the workplace. However, such an assumption needs to be guarded following the decision in *Schering Chemicals v Falkman Ltd*[19] which suggests that a duty of confidence will be imposed on a person to whom information is provided in confidence, even where that information is available from public sources to any other person who cares to investigate. The case involved a drug, 'Primodos', which had been used as a pregnancy test until it was found to be linked to abnormalities in new born children. Although the drug was withdrawn from use, the manufacturer, Schering Chemicals, received a lot of adverse publicity and decided to provide public relations training for its executives, so that they would be better able to present the company's point of view. Falkman Ltd was engaged to provide the training. One of its sub-contractors was David Elstein, who was provided with information about 'Primodos', which he

---

[17] Per Lord Donaldson MR in the Court of Appeal in *Attorney-General v Guardian Newspapers (Spycatcher) (No 2)* [1990] 1 AC 109 at 107, quoting Cross J in *Franchi v Franchi* [1967] RPC 149.

[18] *Sun Printers v Westminster Press Limited* [1982] IRLR 292. 'There is nothing . . . to prevent the fullest communication between management and workforce under a seal of confidentiality', per Donaldson LJ at 295.

[19] [1982] QB 1.

accepted was confidential. He subsequently made a television programme about the drug with Thames TV, using information obtained by a researcher from research papers, periodicals, newspapers and magazines. Schering Chemicals applied for an injunction to restrain what they saw as a breach of confidence. Elstein claimed that the information was already in the public domain. Yet despite the fact that all the information used in the programme came from material already in the public domain, the injunction was granted.

According to the view of the majority of the Court of Appeal, the fact that the information was in the public domain did not relieve Elstein of the duty of confidence. Although others were free to make programmes about the drug, Elstein had voluntarily undertaken the duty not to disclose and so could not use the information himself. Elstein was not an employee of Schering Chemicals, but the reasoning could easily be applied in the context of the contract of employment. It would mean that employees who have an insider's informed view on an issue would be in breach of the duty of confidence if they were to contribute to public debate, even where the facts used in the contribution were already known to the public.

In the '*Spycatcher*' litigation[20] the extent to which the duty of confidence no longer applies once information reaches the public domain was also discussed at length. Although the final outcome supports the view that no duty exists once the information is in the public domain, that conclusion was never as straightforward as one might have expected given the general proposition that information cannot be confidential if it is generally known. The cases form part of the long running, international legal saga arising out of the publication in Australia of the memoirs of Peter Wright, an ex-member of the secret intelligence service MI5. His book contained a number of details which the government viewed as damaging to the security services, and it argued that the book also amounted to a breach of the lifelong duty of confidence owed by security services staff to the government. The government brought proceedings in Australia for breach of confidence and an account of the profits from the book. When those proceedings were commented on by the press in the UK, the Attorney General sought injunctions against the newspapers involved.

By the time of the appeal hearings for the interlocutory (temporary) injunctions, the book was widely published abroad, and as a result, reasonably easily accessible to anyone in the UK who wished to obtain it, either by buying it from abroad using a phone and credit card, or by bringing it home from travel abroad. Nonetheless, the temporary injunctions were maintained by the House of Lords. Lord Brandon argued that for information to be in the public domain, it had to be known by the public as a

---

[20] *Attorney-General v Guardian Newspapers Ltd (Spycatcher)* [1987] 1 WLR 1248, and *Attorney-General v Guardian Newspapers (Spycatcher) (No 2)* [1990] 1 AC 109.

whole, not just to the small proportion of the public who cared enough to find it. Lords Oliver and Bridge dissented strongly from the majority. They argued that, as the information was in the public domain, further publication should not be restrained. As Lord Bridge put it: 'The present attempt to insulate the public in this country from information which is freely available elsewhere is a significant step down [a] very dangerous road. The maintenance of the ban, as more and more copies of the book *Spycatcher* enter this country and circulate here, will seem more and more ridiculous.'[21] He predicted that the government would face condemnation and humiliation before the ECtHR if it persisted with the ban, and 'long before that they will have been condemned at the bar of public opinion in the free world'. [22] In fact the temporary injunctions were found not to be in breach of the ECHR when the matter reached the ECtHR, probably reflecting the caution with which that court treats matters involving national security. They did, however, find that once the information was readily available from abroad, there was no need for the injunctions.[23] The government was therefore not totally humiliated at the ECtHR, although Lord Bridge may have been right about public opinion in the free world.

The views of Lords Oliver and Bridge were vindicated when the cases again reached the House of Lords for a second time in the applications for the temporary injunctions to be made permanent. In this second round of hearings, the wide availability of the book did finally lead to the lifting of the injunctions.[24] Lord Goff pointed out that no obligation to preserve confidence can exist where there is no confidence left to preserve. The wide availability of the book *Spycatcher* meant that no obligation of confidence was owed in respect of its contents.

The cause of the lack of confidentiality in the *Spycatcher* case was the easy availability of the book abroad, and the ease with which it could be brought into the country. The easy availability of information is likely to cause increasing difficulties for those seeking to prevent disclosure in future because of easy access to information across national borders afforded by the internet. This was the factual background to a second security services case, in which *Spycatcher* was applied. In *Attorney-General v Times Newspapers*[25] the Court of Appeal allowed publication of extracts from a book published by a former member of the Secret Intelligence Services, Richard Tomlinson. The book was to be published in Russia, America and in many parts of Europe. It would be available in the UK via the internet. The Court

[21] *Attorney-General v Guardian Newspapers Ltd (Spycatcher)* [1987] 1 WLR 1248 at 1286 G.
[22] Ibid.
[23] *The Observer and the Guardian v UK* (1991) 14 EHRR 153 and *The Times v UK* (1991) 14 EHRR 229.
[24] *Attorney-General v Guardian Newspapers (Spycatcher) (No 2)* [1990] 1 AC 109.
[25] [2001] 1 WLR 885.

allowed publication on the basis that the information was in the public domain.

Although the decisions in *Spycatcher No. 2* and the *Attorney-General v Times Newspapers* cases may suggest that the courts have retracted from the earlier position in *Schering*, such a conclusion may be premature. Lord Oliver, in the interlocutory hearing before the House of Lords in *Spycatcher*, showed that *Schering* can be distinguished from the *Spycatcher* case in a way that may have important implications for employees seeking to exercise freedom of speech. In *Spycatcher*, the parties against whom the breach of confidence was claimed were not the original recipients of the confidential information. That had been Peter Wright, the ex-employee, who had written the book, and Heinemann, his publisher. The papers were merely reporting on the proceedings that arose out of the book. In contrast, in the *Schering* case, Elstein and Falkman, against whom the breach of confidence was claimed, had been the original recipients of the information. This could mean that they owed a duty of confidence in respect of the information, despite the fact that it was available to others and in the public domain. This distinction leaves employees who are the original recipients of confidential information in danger of being found to be in breach of their contractual duty of confidence, even though the information is in the public domain and others are free to publicise the information. The freedom of speech of employees would be much better protected if the dissenting views of Lord Denning in *Schering* and the views of the House of Lords in *Spycatcher No 2* were to be followed in relation to all recipients of information. Although confidentiality can remain in information that is known to a finite number of people, once the wider public has access to the information there is no reason to uphold a duty of confidence in relation to one particular person.

Modern technology means that it is increasingly easy to make information available to the public, which in turn makes it increasingly difficult to maintain confidentiality. However, even where there is no breach of confidence, because information is in the public domain, employees may still risk being in breach of contract for exercising the right to free speech, because of the additional duty of mutual trust owed by employees to the employer. In *Schering*, the argument was that Elstein could not use the information because he had learnt it as a result of his fiduciary relationship with the company. As has been argued above, that view does not stand up to close scrutiny when one is looking at whether the information was confidential or not because of the public domain issue. Yet the fact that the information could not be used because of the nature of the relationship between the giver and recipient of the information is of relevance to the employment relationship. It is arguable that the faithful and loyal employee should not disclose to the outside world information relating to his employment, especially where it is unfavourable to the employer, even though that information is obtainable through other sources. The information may not be confidential if it is in the public domain, but that does not prevent it being a breach of trust to discuss it or publicise it further.

THE EMPLOYMENT CONTRACT AND THE CONCEPT OF THE PUBLIC INTEREST

The exercise of free speech by employees thus has the potential to breach the terms of the contract of employment in a variety of ways. The two relevant contractual terms, the duty of mutual trust and the duty of confidence, can both be breached by employees who exercise the right to free speech, whether that speech takes place in work or outside, and whether or not the speech relates to the workplace. Most obviously, speech which involves revealing information about the workplace to the public is likely to breach the duty of confidence, but even speech that is unrelated to work may involve a potential breach of the duty of mutual trust if it damages the legitimate interests of the employer. In each case, however, the contractual duties owed by the employee are subject to an exception where the speech of the employee serves the wider public interest. The concept of the public interest as a limit on the contractual duties of employees is used explicitly in relation to the duty of confidence, and it applies whether the duty of confidence is express or implied. The public interest exception also operates implicitly in relation to the duty of mutual trust.

The Public Interest and the Duty of Confidence

The fact that the implied duty of confidence is not absolute and does not apply where it is in the public interest that information be disclosed was recognised in the employment context in *Initial Services v Putterill*.[26] The case involved a sales manager for the plaintiff's laundry, who handed in his notice and at the same time handed documents belonging to the employer to a national newspaper. The documents showed that the laundry had given false information to customers. It had raised its prices, and had published a circular for customers telling them that the price rise was mainly due to a new employment tax, when in reality the increased price created extra profits for the business. The documents also showed that the laundry had agreed with other laundries to keep up their prices, a practice which was in breach of the Restrictive Trade Practices Act 1956. The plaintiff employer applied to the court for an injunction to prevent disclosure of the information on the basis that it would amount to a breach of confidence, but it was unsuccessful. Lord Denning held that the obligation of confidence is subject to exceptions, including where information is disclosed relating to 'any misconduct of such a nature that it ought in the public interest to be disclosed to others'. The information in the case had this public interest nature, and so the newspaper

---

[26] [1968] QB 396.

article was allowed to be published. The existence of the public interest exception is crucial to the operation of the duty of confidence. Where it is in the public interest that information be disclosed, no duty of confidence arises. The disclosure of public interest information in the course of the exercise of free speech by an employee will not involve a breach of the contractual duty of confidence.

In many cases, contracts of employment will contain an express duty of confidence with no public interest exception, or only a limited one. Yet whether or not it is referred to in an express term, the public interest exception will still apply, because express or incorporated terms will, where possible, be interpreted so as not to conflict with the duties implied into the contract by common law. In order to resolve any apparent conflict between express and implied terms, the first step is to look at the intention of the parties involved. If all parties intended a public interest exception to apply, the confidentiality clause can be interpreted to include it. Where the intentions of the parties cannot be ascertained, the court itself will have to determine the scope of the employee's duty. The general rule is that express terms take precedence, as courts cannot imply into a contract something that is expressly excluded. However, any ambiguities or omissions in an express term will be interpreted so as not to conflict with the terms usually implied into contracts.[27] Thus, where an express confidentiality clause mentions no exceptions, the public interest exception can be implied into that clause because it has not been expressly excluded. Where potentially ambiguous terminology is used, for example requiring that matters be reported to an appropriate person, it will be interpreted so as to comply with the law on the implied duty of confidence. This could, where the public interest so demands, result in even the media being viewed as appropriate recipients of information.

Moreover, any attempt expressly to exclude the public interest exception to the duty of confidence is unlikely to be successful. As a matter of public policy, express terms will only be upheld to the extent that they do not conflict with a recognised public interest. This was made plain in *Initial Services v Putterill*[28] where it was said that an express term prohibiting the employee from disclosing matters that it is in the public interest to disclose would be void for reasons of public policy.[29] Equally void would be a term limiting disclosure to particular recipients such as a chosen regulator, when the information is such that it ought to be made available on a wider basis.[30] Thus whether or not there is an express confidentiality clause in the contract of employment, the exercise of freedom of speech where that speech

---

[27] *Johnstone v Bloomsbury Health Authority* [1991] IRLR 118 CA.

[28] [1968] 1 QB 396.

[29] Evidence of courts refusing to uphold express terms on the basis that they are void for public policy reasons can be found in the case law in other contexts, for example, on the enforcement of post-employment restrictive covenants.

[30] See *Initial Services v Putterill* [1968] 1 QB 396 at 409 and 412.

serves the public interest should involve no breach of the employment contract.

The Public Interest and the Duty of Mutual Trust

Just as the duty of confidence is subject to a public interest exception, the duty of mutual trust must be too. The duty of mutual trust is an implied contractual duty, the exact parameters of which are not yet set,[31] and a public interest exception almost certainly forms part of its terms. As was stated in *Initial Services v Putterill*,[32] if a contract contained a term expressly limiting the disclosure or discussion of information even where it is in the public interest that it be disclosed or discussed, such a term would not be enforced for reasons of public policy. If an express term of that kind is unsustainable, courts will clearly not imply such a term into a contract. The same must apply to the implied duty of mutual trust. Its exact parameters may be unclear, but it will not extend so far as to operate against the general public interest. Thus it should make no difference whether an incident of free speech breaches the duty of confidence, or the duty of mutual trust: where it is in the public interest that the speech be allowed, there is unlikely to be a breach of any term of the employment contract.

How Have Courts Defined the Public Interest?

The question of whether the public interest is served by speech is of prime importance in assessing the contractual duties of the employee. In determining when the public interest requires that information be disclosed, a distinction needs to be drawn between information that is *in the public interest* and information *of public interest*, that is, merely interesting to the public. The contractual duty to maintain mutual trust and confidentiality within the employment relationship will not be outweighed by the fact that the public find particular information interesting or even fascinating. Alternatively, where it is in the public interest that information be disclosed, disclosure will not be in breach of contract, however great the personal interest of the 'owner' of the information in keeping it private and out of the public view.

The court will consider a variety of factors when looking at whether the public interest requires disclosure and thus whether the disclosure involves a breach of the contract of employment. These include: the type of information disclosed; the identity of the recipient of the information; the timing of the disclosure; the motive for disclosure and other behaviour surrounding disclosure; and the status of the facts disclosed. Most of the cases in which these factors have been considered have arisen in the context of the duty of confidence, and it is in these cases that guidance can be found on

---

[31]   J. Lindsay, 'The Implied Term of Trust and Confidence' (2001) ILJ 1.
[32]   [1968] 1 QB 396.

how courts have interpreted the concept of the public interest. However, the scope of the public interest revealed in these cases would apply equally in cases where the contractual duty under consideration was the duty of mutual trust.

The Type of Information

The early cases in which the concept of public interest disclosure was developed concerned confidentiality in respect of crimes or civil wrongs. The public interest definitions accepted in the cases seemed to be limited to the disclosure of such information. Hence statements in the early cases such as '[t]here is no confidence as to the disclosure of iniquity'[33] and 'the duty to the public to disclose the criminal or illegal intention may properly be held to override the private duty to respect and protect the client's confidence'.[34] In later cases, however, the categories of information that may be disclosed in the public interest have increased, representing a welcome expansion to the concept of the public interest, albeit at the cost of certainty. In order to gain an understanding of how this issue is approached, it is necessary to consider in some detail some of the cases that have come before the courts.

In *Initial Services v Putterill*[35] the public interest exception was not restricted to cases of crime or civil wrong, but extended to 'any misconduct of such a nature that it ought in the public interest to be disclosed. . . . The exception should extend to crimes, frauds and misdeeds, both those actually committed as well as those in contemplation.'[36] Thus, misleading circulars suggesting that price rises were attributable only to increased employment tax, when in fact they included increased profits for the business, were matters that could be disclosed in the public interest, as well as the illegal conduct entailed in the breach of the Restrictive Trade Practices Act 1956. Again in *Fraser v Evans*[37] the view was that '[iniquity] is merely an instance of just cause or excuse for breaking confidence. There are some things which may be required to be disclosed in the public interest, in which event no confidence can be prayed in aid to keep them secret.'[38]

In subsequent cases many types of information apart from that relating to illegal conduct have been said to be eligible for disclosure in the public interest. In *Hubbard v Vosper*[39] it was held that a book describing courses run by the Church of Scientology could be published despite the fact that the information contained in the book was obtained in breach of confidence. '[T]he courses . . . indicate medical quackeries of a sort which may be dangerous if practised behind closed doors . . . There is good ground for thinking that those courses contain such dangerous material that it is in the public interest

---

[33] *Gartside v Outram* (1856) 26 LJ Ch 113.
[34] *Weld-Blundell v Stephens* [1919] 1 KB 520 at 527.   [35] [1968] 1 QB 396.
[36] Per Lord Denning, at 405.   [37] [1969] 1 QB 349.
[38] Per Lord Denning, at 362.   [39] [1972] 2 QB 84.

that it should be made known.'[40] There was no suggestion that the information revealed illegal conduct, just that it was 'medically dangerous'. The need to extend protection beyond disclosures of misconduct and misdeeds to protect other disclosures was also recognised in *Malone v Commissioner of Police*,[41] a case which involved telephone tapping. Malone had been accused of participation in a crime, and as part of their investigation the police had arranged for his telephone to be tapped by the Post Office. Malone challenged the legality of the telephone tapping, and as part of the case argued that it involved a breach of confidence. On this issue, Megarry V-C said: 'there may be cases where . . . there is a just cause or excuse for breaking confidence. The confidential information may relate to some apprehension of an impending chemical or other disaster, arising without misconduct, of which the authorities are not aware, but which ought in the public interest to be disclosed to them.'[42]

Again in *Lion Laboratories v Evans*[43] the type of information that could serve the public interest was not restricted to illegal behaviour. The case involved the disclosure of internal company documents which cast doubt on the reliability of breathalyser machines manufactured by the plaintiff company and used by police to provide evidence of intoxication in drink-driving cases. The documents were being offered to newspapers by two ex-employees who had worked as technicians at Lion Laboratories. At an ex parte hearing, an injunction against publication of the documents was granted, but this was not upheld at appeal. The Court of Appeal refused to limit the public interest defence to the disclosure of misconduct or illegal behaviour. It allowed disclosure to the press by the former employees because the information affected 'the life, and even the liberty, of an unascertainable number of Her Majesty's subjects'. Lion Laboratories were the only manufacturer of the breathalyser devices licensed by the Home Office and this imposed on them a very strong obligation to ensure that the manufacture and accuracy of the machines was to the highest standard. There was very clear public interest in avoiding wrongful convictions based on unreliable evidence and this outweighed any duty of confidence owed by the employees to their former employer.

Perhaps the widest classification of information that can be in the public interest was given in *Woodward v Hutchins*[44] where a public relations agent to some well known singers (professionally known as Tom Jones, Engelbert Humperdinck, Gilbert O'Sullivan and Gordon Mills) had written a series of articles for a national newspaper disclosing information relating to the singers' private lives, conduct and personal affairs. Lord Denning pointed out that the singers had sought publicity in order to present themselves

---

[40] Per Lord Denning, at 96.   [41] [1979] Ch 344.
[42] Ibid at 635 c. Malone took his case to the ECtHR, and was successful. *Malone v UK* (1984) 7 EHRR led to the introduction of the Interception of Communications Act 1985.
[43] [1985] QB 526.   [44] [1977] 1 WLR 760.

in a favourable light and so that audiences would come to hear them and support them. He went on to say that there was a public interest in knowing the truth and that where a party builds up a particular image to gain advantageous publicity, the public interest will be served where it is demonstrated that the image fostered is untrue. It was in the public interest that the information be published because '[t]he public should not be misled'.[45] This statement admits a very broad concept of the public interest, but is unlikely to be used to introduce a 'defence of truth' into claims for breach of the employment contract. However, where a particular message has been given to the public, the case is authority for the fact that information indicating the falsity of the message might be viewed as serving the public interest.

The trend to widen the categories of information that may be disclosed is not uniform, however. In *Beloff v Pressdram Ltd*,[46] a case involving breach of copyright, the public interest was given a more restrictive interpretation: 'The defence of public interest clearly covers, and in the authorities does not extend beyond, disclosure . . . in the public interest, of matters carried out or contemplated, in breach of the country's security or in breach of law, including statutory duty, fraud, or otherwise destructive of the country or its people, including matters medically dangerous to the public; and doubtless other misdeeds of similar gravity. . . . Such public interest, as now recognised by the law, does not extend beyond misdeeds of a serious nature and importance to the country and thus, in my view clearly recognisable as such.'[47] This is a very different approach. Information relating to the reliability of breathalysers may not be regarded as in the public interest according to this formulation, let alone information about the private lives of pop stars, whatever the message presented to the public.

British Steel Corporation v Granada Television[48] gives a further example of the courts taking a restrictive approach to the definition of the public interest. The case was not a breach of confidence case, nor did it involve a breach of any other term of the employment contract, but it did turn on the meaning of the public interest and so is of relevance here: the different legal context in which the term was discussed does not significantly alter its meaning. At the centre of the case was a documentary about the 1980 steel strike, which made use of internal company documents which had been leaked by an employee at British Steel (BSC). The action before the House of Lords was for an order to make Granada disclose the source of its information. Granada argued that there was a public interest in newspapers and broadcasters not having to reveal details of their sources, and that this public interest would be harmed if it was forced to give the name of the 'mole'. The documents disclosed evidence of mismanagement at BSC, then a state owned company, as well as

[45] Ibid at 764 B.   [46] [1973] 1 All ER 241.
[47] Per Ungoed-Thomas J at 260 g.   [48] [1981] AC 1097.

showing that the government had intervened in the steel strike, intervention that it had previously denied. The House of Lords in the final appeal had to decide where, on balance, the public interest lay: in protecting journalists' sources or in maintaining the rights of BSC to know the identity of the 'mole'? The majority of their Lordships upheld the order for Granada to reveal its source. They conceded that the public interest could be served by the public knowing about the steel strike, and knowing of the attitude of BSC and the government towards the settling of the strike, but would not allow that these revelations could amount to revelations of the type of misconduct required to overcome the duty of confidence owed by the 'mole' to his employer; they amounted only to revelations of 'mismanagement and government intervention'.

The conclusion on where the public interest lay in *British Steel* was, arguably, unduly restrictive, and lacked proper recognition of the public nature of the corporation and the consequent public interest in knowing something of the causes of its financial difficulties. The decision was not unanimous, and in a powerful dissenting judgment, Lord Salmon argued that the public interest was served by the disclosure of the information leaked to Granada, as it related to a publicly owned industry. He referred to the amount of public money used to bail BSC out of its financial difficulties: the state had loaned BSC (in early 1980s prices) £700 million in one year and £450 million in the next, to cover losses, together with a £3 billion loan for new equipment and machinery. Even with this level of public subsidy, BSC was not operating with the same degree of efficiency as its European competitors. In Lord Salmon's view this was a public interest matter: 'it is a nationalised industry . . . If it operates at a serious loss, it causes serious harm to the nation . . . It is not surprising that the public should wish, and indeed are morally entitled to know how it is that BSC is in such a parlous condition.'[49] A similar approach had been taken by Lord Denning at the hearing before the Court of Appeal where he said that the documents raised a number of points 'of considerable public interest . . . Especially as the British Steel Corporation was a public corporation accountable to Parliament.' Lord Denning also pointed out that the documents revealed that there had been government intervention in the steel strike, which had previously been denied. If his approach in *Woodward* had been adopted, this could have provided alternative grounds for allowing disclosure as the public had been misled as to the government involvement in the strike.[50] The views of Lords Denning and Salmon in the *British Steel* case are preferable to those of the prevailing majority, as they give appropriate recognition of the competing rights involved in cases of disclosure, and in

---

[49] [1981] AC 1097 at 1187–1189.
[50] However, Lord Denning was of the view that Granada's irresponsible handling of the documents was such that it forfeited the right to the protection of its source.

particular, recognition of the strength of audience interests in cases involving the enterprises which receive public funding.

Despite the disappointingly narrow interpretation of the public interest in the *British Steel* case, it is worth noting that the categories of information that may be in the public interest are not closed; courts have accepted that they may 'alter from time to time . . . as social conditions and social legislation develop'.[51] Furthermore, now that the interpretation of the public interest is to be developed in the light of the jurisprudence on the ECHR with the entry into force of the HRA,[52] disclosures should more readily be found to be in the public interest. Indeed if the issue is viewed as a matter of freedom of speech for the person making the disclosure, the assumption should be made that disclosure is allowed, with restriction only being allowed on one of the grounds specified in Article 10(2), for the protection of the rights of others or preventing the disclosure of information received in confidence, where it is proportionate and necessary in a democratic society. The requirement that restrictions be proportionate ought to result in stronger protection for disclosures of information, as the European Court of Human Rights has made clear that protection of the right to free speech extends to speech that is offensive, shocking or disturbing, and not just to inoffensive matters.[53] Where it aids the maintenance of a democratic society (one of the stated aims of the Convention), the Court will be particularly reluctant to sanction any restriction on speech. In particular, the Court's commitment to protecting free political debate is clear, and it is usually reluctant to prevent any disclosure of information with political overtones.[54] Although it accepted the temporary injunctions in the *Spycatcher* case, the case did involve a risk of breaching national security, a matter over which the Court usually allows states a very wide margin of appreciation. In cases without national security implications, the disclosure of information that relates to public sector industries or services should be more readily protected once the law on the public interest is interpreted to comply with Article 10 ECHR.

To an extent, disclosures of government information already appear to be treated differently by domestic courts, with the onus on the government to show why disclosure should be restrained, rather than on the speaker to justify disclosure. The reason for distinguishing between government secrecy and private sector confidence is explained by Lord Goff in *Spycatcher No. 2*:[55] 'in the case of Government secrets the mere fact of confidentiality does not alone support . . . a conclusion [that confidential information should be

[51]   *D v NSPCC* [1977] 1 All ER 589 at 605 b, per Lord Hailsham.
[52]   See discussion of the impact of the HRA in Chapter 3 above.
[53]   *Handyside v UK* (1981) 1 EHRR 737.   [54]   *Lingens v Austria* (1986) 8 EHRR 407.
[55]   *Attorney-General v Guardian Newspapers Ltd (Spycatcher) (No 2)* [1990] 1 AC 109.

protected], because in a free society there is a continuing public interest that the workings of government should be open to scrutiny and criticism'.[56] The Court's approach on this issue does seem to accord with that of the ECtHR in providing greater protection to political speech.

Of course, information relating to the public sector is not limited to government information, and political significance can be claimed for a wide range of information, not just government secrets. It is arguable that the public have an interest in knowing some of what occurs within all industries and services funded by them, whether or not they are publicly owned, and that they should be open to scrutiny and criticism as the government is. Such a line does have some judicial support, such as in the judgments of Lord Denning and Lord Salmon in the *British Steel* case.[57] Although this line of reasoning has yet to be adopted by the majority, it is arguable not only that it should be, but that it should be extended to cover the recently privatised sector and those parts of the private sector providing services previously provided by the public sector. As was suggested in Chapter 2, the operation of the public sector including local government, education and the NHS are issues of public and political importance and the public interest is served by having information relating to them available. As with government secrets, there will be times where freedom of speech by employees needs to be restrained; in respect of government information, restraint may be needed for national security reasons, and in respect of other employers it may be needed in respect of some commercial information. But the basic rule should be to promote openness, and there should be very clear reasons for restraining the disclosure of information relating to such public service bodies. This argument is less clear in relation to the purely private sector. Information indicating mismanagement, or disclosing how particular spending decisions are made, is far less likely to be viewed as a public interest issue, whereas such information relating to the public sector may well be. However, as suggested in Chapter 2,[58] it is not so much the status of the enterprise that is relevant to the question of whether free speech should be protected, but the subject matter of the speech. Where an enterprise enjoys a near monopoly position in the market, or where it provides essential services, it is arguable that there may be a public interest in knowing more of its affairs whether it is public or private in nature. Moreover, where information reveals illegal, wrongful or dangerous conduct, the type of information involved means that the public interest will be served by its disclosure regardless of the sector in which the industry or service operates.

Of the four categories of speech identified in Chapter 2, whistleblowing, political speech, principled dissent and personal views, it appears that, on

---

[56] *Attorney-General v Guardian Newspapers Ltd (Spycatcher) (No 2)* [1990] 1 AC 109 at 280.
[57] [1981] AC 1097 at 1123 and 1187–1189A.
[58] See Chapter 2, The status of the employer and the public/private divide.

the basis of its subject matter, whistleblowing involving disclosure of wrong-doing, illegality and public danger has the greatest likelihood of being found to serve the public interest. Whether a particular incident is found, overall, to serve the public interest will of course depend on the other factors considered by courts, such as the channel of communication, discussed below. Most cases of political speech by employees will not raise issues of confidentiality, but may involve breaches of other duties owed to the employer such as the duty of mutual trust. It is not clear from the case law that a court would find that political speech serves the public interest on the basis of the subject matter, unless it indicates that the public has been misled on a matter of political importance. The case law suggests that there must be an element of wrongdoing or danger before the public interest is served. Political significance is probably not sufficient. It is to be hoped that once the common law is interpreted to comply with the requirements of the ECHR, this will change, to reflect the greater protection afforded to political speech by the ECtHR.[59] As for principled dissent, again this may not always raise issues of confidentiality, but may breach the duty of mutual trust. Where this is the case, it seems unlikely that the subject matter would be said to serve the public interest unless it involves danger or wrongdoing. Even though other factors may still favour disclosure, the subject matter of speech remains one of the key factors affecting the definition of the public interest and it will be unusual for disclosures to be found to meet the definition where the subject matter is not inherently one that serves the public interest as interpreted by the courts. This will make it unlikely that the current law will be able to provide adequate protection for employees who engage in principled dissent, even though it may serve the wider audience interests identified earlier.

Information of an Advantageous Nature

It is notable that all the cases suggest that the public interest is served by disclosure either of danger, or at least of information that relates to misdeeds or wrongdoing. Cases have not involved disclosures of information about more positive matters. It is not clear what approach courts would take to interpreting the public interest if information were of such a beneficial nature. For example, if an employee working for a drugs company believed that a cure for AIDS had been found, but that the company had commercial reasons for suppressing that information (preferring, for example, to wait until a more profitable vaccine can be produced), it is not clear whether courts would say that the public interest would be served by allowing that disclosure. The more restrictive interpretations of the public interest in the case law suggest that the disclosures that are in the public interest must relate to illegal behaviour, or misdeeds. The more generous approach still suggests

---

[59] See Chapter 3, The type of information.

information must relate to a detriment to the public before it is in the public interest to disclose it.[60] It is arguable that withholding a known treatment for a fatal disease does amount to a detriment to the public and a moral wrong of such proportions that it can be classed as a misdeed, which would make it much easier to show that the public interest is served by its disclosure. However, less extreme examples, where there may be genuine reasons for maintaining secrecy, are easy to imagine. A company may wish to maintain the confidentiality of the make-up of a drug; an employee knowing that the drug could be produced much more cheaply discloses this information. The case law on trade secrets provides strong protection for employers against employees who disclose information that is commercially sensitive and may deprive the employer of the profit that he could otherwise expect from the goods he manufactures.[61] There is no indication that the rule allowing employers to protect trade secrets[62] is subject to the public interest exception except where that information discloses wrongdoing or misconduct, or at the very least, discloses a potential harm, as opposed to a benefit, to the public.

The Identity of the Recipient of the Information

A second factor considered by courts when determining whether a particular disclosure is in the public interest or not is the identity of the person or organisation to whom the information is given. Whilst it may be in the public interest that the information is revealed to someone, it is not necessarily the case that the public interest is served by disclosure to all. In *Initial Services v Putterill*,[63] which involved a disclosure to the press, the point was made that in some cases disclosure to the general public via the media may not be justified, although disclosure to a relevant official might be (in that case the registrar responsible for enforcing the Restrictive Trade Practices Act 1956). Later cases have also taken the line that the public interest may be served by disclosure to some, but not to all.

In *Spycatcher No 2*,[64] the House of Lords held that even where disclosure was in the public interest, it did not follow that publication should be via the media. In some cases it would be better to disclose to some other body who could investigate. Where security personnel wished to claim that a disclosure was in the public interest they would need to show that they had tried inter-

---

[60] For example the concern over the reliability of the breathalyser in *Lion Laboratories*, or the public interest in disclosing impending disasters suggested in *Malone v Commissioner of Police (No 2)*, n 43 and n 41 above.

[61] See 'Employee Competition and Confidentiality', IDS Employment Supplement 72, Incomes Data Services Ltd, December 1994.

[62] *Faccenda Chicken v Fowler* [1986] ICR 297.   [63] [1968] 1 QB 396.

[64] [1990] 1 AC 109.

nal channels before resorting to disclosure to the press. In *Re a Company's Application*,[65] the compliance officer for a financial services company threatened to reveal financial irregularities to FIMBRA (the financial services regulatory body) and the Inland Revenue. He had been dismissed by the company and threatened the disclosures as part of the negotiation of his compensation package. The plaintiff's chief executive, to whom the threat had been made, regarded it as blackmail, and obtained an interlocutory injunction against the defendant prohibiting him from disclosing confidential information outside the company. At the hearing of the application for the injunction to be made permanent, the plaintiff company was unsuccessful in relation to disclosures to FIMBRA and the Inland Revenue. Disclosure to such recipients would involve no breach of confidence. The fact that disclosure was to be to a relevant regulatory body overrode the malicious motive for the disclosure.[66]

Similarly, in *W v Egdell*,[67] limited disclosure of a medical opinion among those involved in the patient's care was not a breach of patient confidence, although wider publication probably would have been. W was a schizophrenic who had been detained for killing five people in a shooting incident. His case was to be reviewed by a mental health review tribunal, and his solicitors sought a medical report from Dr Egdell for use in those proceedings. His report stated that the patient was still dangerous and raised a number of new concerns that had not been raised by the medical team advising the Home Office about W's future care. As a result, W withdrew his application from the tribunal, and the report was not used. Dr Egdell, concerned that the content of the report should be known by W's medical team and by the Home Office, sent a copy to both parties without W's consent. In holding that the public interest in the parties knowing the contents of the report overrode any breach of confidence involved, the Court of Appeal pointed out that the information was only disclosed to other professionals involved in W's care. The point was made that disclosure for other purposes, for example, in an academic journal, would not have been in the public interest.

On the other hand, in *Initial Services v Putterill*[68] the court recognised that in certain circumstances disclosure on a wider scale can be justified, and indeed disclosure via the press has been allowed in many cases on the basis that it serves the public interest. *Initial Services* itself concerned an unsuccessful attempt to prevent disclosure of price fixing in a newspaper article, with the Court of Appeal finding that, at times, the person with a proper interest in receiving information may be the press. Similarly, in

---

[65] [1989] Ch 477.
[66] See discussion under 'Motive and behaviour surrounding disclosure' below.
[67] [1990] Ch 359.   [68] [1968] 1 QB 396.

Fraser v Evans[69] and *Woodward v Hutchins*[70] disclosures by journalists, and in *Hubbard v Vosper*[71] disclosure in a book, were not prevented. In *Lion Laboratories v Evans*,[72] where the injunction was sought against the disclosure of information about the breathalyser to the press, no issue was raised about the identity of the person to whom the disclosures were made. The information was important for the proper administration of justice as the machine could be used to provide evidence in criminal prosecutions. Clearly the general public should have access to information that could be important in defending criminal charges;[73] thus disclosure on the widest possible scale was justified. This was approved in *Spycatcher No 2* where it was agreed that in circumstances such as those in *Lion Laboratories*, media publication was acceptable.

Despite the cases indicating a willingness by courts to allow publication via the press, it is not the case that employees are left free to use the media to raise concerns whenever they wish, particularly if other channels have not been exhausted. Staff with concerns about illegal or irregular or unsafe conduct would be expected to raise matters internally at first. Once any internal procedure is exhausted, or if an adequate response is not received, or if internal disclosure is unsuitable (for example the concern relates to internal management), then disclosure to other bodies, such as a regulatory body, trade union, or an MP, may be acceptable as necessary in the public interest. Equally, where such steps have been taken, but without a satisfactory response, it may be that disclosure on an even wider scale will be in the public interest. Clearly, where concerns are very urgent and relate to a serious matter such as public health and safety, internal disclosure will not be appropriate, even as a starting point: instead, the quickest way to reach the widest number of people will be by disclosure via the media. Express terms attempting to restrict the categories of persons to whom information may be disclosed will be void to the extent that they conflict with the public interest. It would therefore not be open to an employer to rely on a contractual clause that prevents external disclosure where the public interest is served by such a disclosure.[74]

The need to use the least public channel of communication possible when making a disclosure does not cause great difficulty to the whistleblower. Some concerns will be able to be reported internally or to a regulatory body, other more serious or urgent concerns may be suitable for

---

[69] [1969] 1 QB 349. 'There are some things which are of such public concern that the newspapers, the Press, and, indeed, everyone is entitled to make known the truth and to make fair comment on it.' per Lord Denning, at 12 D.

[70] [1977] 1 WLR 760.   [71] [1972] 2 QB 84.   [72] [1985] QB 526.

[73] 'We are here dealing with a machine on the accuracy of which may depend a person's livelihood, or even his liberty' [1984] 2 All ER 417 per Griffiths LJ at 433.

[74] See the judgment of Winn LJ in *Initial Services v Putterill* [1968] 1 QB 397.

external disclosure. Greater difficulty on this issue is faced by staff wishing to use work based experience to participate in public debate on a matter of public interest, or to voice principled dissent or personal views about a work related policy. By definition, such employees want to catch the public eye, most obviously via the media. It has already been noted that the subject matter in these cases is unlikely to be found to need disclosure on a wide scale, and it may therefore be that a court would not find the public interest served by the speech. The only way to counter such a conclusion is to raise the argument made above that, particularly where it relates to public sector institutions, public debate serves the public interest. To be effective, the discussion needs publicity; thus the public interest is served by wide public disclosure. If the right to free speech is to be adequately protected at work, such an approach needs to be accepted by the courts. Given the approach to the issue in the cases such as *Fraser v Evans*,[75] *Woodward v Hutchins*[76] and *Hubbard v Vosper*[77] where wide disclosures were allowed, and the significance of the role of the media in maintaining freedom of speech under the ECHR, it is not impossible that it may be accepted in the future.[78]

Timing of Disclosure

In determining where the public interest lies, the courts also consider whether the public will be protected by disclosure of the information. Where the disclosure of information is likely to prevent harm to the public, courts are unlikely to require the maintenance of confidentiality. In *Lion Laboratories v Evans*,[79] the information about reliability of breathalysers could bring immediate benefit to any person facing criminal charges based on evidence from such machines, and so the court allowed its wide publication. Where a concern relates to a future danger, then again the courts appear to favour disclosure. In *Initial Services v Putterill*[80] Lord Denning held that the public interest exception to the duty of confidence should extend to 'crimes, frauds and misdeeds, both those actually committed as well as those in contemplation',[81] and in *Malone v Commissioner of Police*[82] Megarry V-C held that information relating to 'some apprehension of an impending chemical or other disaster' should, in the public interest, be disclosed.[83]

However, if information is going to come into the public domain soon in any event, then there may be no public interest in early disclosure. In *Camelot Group plc v Centaur Communications Ltd*[84] an employee leaked the annual

---

[75] See note 69 above.   [76] [1977] 1 WLR 760.   [77] [1972] 2 QB 84.
[78] See discussion in Chapter 3 on the channel of communication in the ECHR case law.
[79] [1985] QB 526.   [80] [1968] 1 QB 396.   [81] Ibid at 405 F.
[82] [1979] Ch 344.   [83] Ibid at 635 c.   [84] [1998] 1 All ER 251 CA.

accounts of Camelot to the press a week before they were due to be published. Although the publication of the accounts was in the public interest, given the amount of public money spent on the lottery and the public nature of the 'good causes' funded by it, their publication a week earlier than scheduled did not significantly further the public interest. Indeed, generally, the early release of financial information harms the public interest as it can facilitate insider trading by giving some traders an unfair advantage in the market; and the continued presence at work of the person who leaked the documents was likely to harm working relationships. The court was therefore willing to order the disclosure of the source of the leaked information, so that the company could discipline or dismiss its disloyal employee. The court considered the ECHR jurisprudence in coming to its opinion, in which it was said that the identity of journalists' sources should usually be kept secret in order for the press to fulfil its role as watchdog.[85] It said that the need to discover the identity of a disloyal employee would not always mean that disclosure of the source of information was in the public interest. However, on the facts of this case, in particular, the fact that the case did not involve iniquity by the employer and so was not a whistleblowing case, the public interest was not served by protecting the source of the disclosure.

The case law is more contradictory in relation to the disclosure of past misconduct. In *Schering Chemicals Ltd v Falkman Ltd*[86] Shaw LJ argued that because the drug 'Primodos' had been withdrawn from the market and the immediate threat to health had therefore passed, the public interest was not served by disclosure of the information. However, the fact that the threat to the public had passed was raised by Lord Denning in his dissenting judgment in *Schering*, to the opposite effect. The publication of material revealing information about the drug Primodos could not affect its sales as it had been withdrawn from the market long since, and this was one reason he used to argue that the information should be revealed.

Given the contradictory case law on this issue, it is difficult to anticipate how courts would view the matter if an employee's disclosure relates to past wrongdoing. In most cases, the outcome will probably be decided with reference to the other features of the case, so that the issue of timing remains neutral. Alternatively, the court's approach could be influenced by whether the employee owes an express duty of confidence to the employer. Where confidentiality is imposed as an express term of a contract, courts may make a presumption in favour of confidence; the fact that a threat is not current means that there is no good reason to upset that presumption and disclosure is unlikely to be acceptable. Where there is only an implied duty of confidentiality, courts may make a presumption in favour of disclosure; the fact that the threat is past will mean that there is no good

---

[85] *Goodwin v UK* (1996) 22 EHRR 123.   [86] [1982] QB 1.

reason for a restriction and publication should therefore involve no breach of duty.

Motive and Behaviour Surrounding Disclosure

There are some indications that courts will consider the motives of the person who reveals information and may more readily find there to be a breach of confidence where information is disclosed out of malice, spite or for material gain. In *Initial Services v Putterill*[87] it was made clear that disclosure would not have been approved in the case had it been made out of spite or for financial reward. This view is also reflected in comments made by the court when upholding the injunction against disclosure of information in *Schering*:[88] Templeman LJ pointed out that Elstein had obtained the information because he 'agreed for reward' to take part in the training session. He had then used that information 'for his own gain'.[89] He went on to say that if the injunction were not granted the court would enable 'a trusted adviser to make money out of his dealing in confidential information'.[90] Shaw LJ spoke of the lack of protection for 'mercenary betrayal'.[91] Concern was also expressed in the *Spycatcher* cases about publication of information disclosed by disloyal employees for financial gain.[92]

This view has not been taken in all cases. In *British Steel Corporation v Granada*[93] the informer's motive was said to be irrelevant,[94] and in *Lion Laboratories*[95] it was said that the public have a right to know some confidential information 'even if [it] has been unlawfully obtained in flagrant breach of confidence and irrespective of the motive of the informer'.[96] Moreover, the fact that financial gain was made from the disclosures did not prevent the court from allowing the disclosures in *Woodward v Hutchins*[97] and *Hubbard v Vosper.*[98]

In *Re a Company's Application*[99] the possible malicious motive of the defendant was explicitly referred to and still did not prevent a finding that the disclosure could be allowed. Scott J reasoned that if the alleged breaches of FIMBRA rules had taken place, then they ought to be reported. If they were untrue, FIMBRA would discover this, and no harm would be done to the company. In neither case was the public interest in the investigation taking place affected by the motive of the discloser. This reasoning suggests courts will treat the motive of the person making the disclosure as secondary to other factors when weighing up whether or not to allow disclosure.

---

[87] [1968] 1 QB 396.   [88] [1982] QB 1.   [89] Ibid at 37.
[90] Ibid at 40.   [91] Ibid at 27.
[92] See Lord Griffiths in *Attorney-General v Guardian Newspapers Ltd (Spycatcher) (No 2)* [1990] 1 AC 109 at 279.
[93] [1981] AC 1097.   [94] See comments of Lord Fraser, at 1202 D.
[95] [1985] QB 526.   [96] Per Stephenson LJ at 422 j.   [97] [1977] 1 WLR 760.
[98] [1972] 2 QB 84.   [99] [1989] Ch 477.

One further factor that may possibly be considered by courts in assessing where the public interest lies is the behaviour of those who disclose information and the behaviour of those to whom it is disclosed. This has been considered in the context of contempt of court proceedings and so may not directly apply to cases involving breach of the employment contract. However, in the cases prior to the Contempt of Court Act 1981 the question in issue was where the public interest lay and so the case law may have relevance in cases involving the public interest concept. In the *British Steel* action to make Granada disclose the source of its confidential information,[100] Granada argued that the public interest would be harmed if it was forced to give the name of its 'mole'. Apart from the fact that the type of information did not sufficiently justify protection of the source, a number of adverse comments were made about the behaviour of Granada in relation to the document in question, and about the wrongful behaviour of the 'mole'. In the Court of Appeal and the House of Lords, unfavourable comments were made about the behaviour of journalists at Granada who had tampered with, and 'mutilated', the document to conceal the identity of its source.

Following the introduction of the Contempt of Court Act 1981, the question of whether journalists should reveal their sources is not decided according to a public interest test. Different criteria are used, 'the interests of justice' being the closest to the old public interest.[101] Although therefore only of tangential relevance to the definition of the public interest, it is worth noting that the behaviour of the discloser of information remains of relevance to the court. *X Ltd v Morgan Grampian (Publishers) Ltd*[102] involved an application for disclosure of the identity of the source of a journalist's confidential information. The House of Lords upheld the applicant company's claim that disclosure of the source was in the interests of justice. In reaching this conclusion, the relationship between the importance of the information and the behaviour of the discloser was discussed: 'if it appears that the information was obtained illegally, this will diminish the importance of protecting the source, unless, of course, this factor is counterbalanced by a clear public interest in publication of the information as in the classic case where the source has acted for the purpose of exposing iniquity.'[103] The fact that the information was obtained 'tortiously'[104] was an additional factor in concluding that the interests of justice required revelation of the source.

Clearly these cases arise in a different legal context to contractual claims in relation to free speech at work, and so will not directly apply. However, given the indeterminate nature of the public interest concept, and the way in which it is affected by a number of different issues, they may be of some relevance.

---

[100] [1981] AC 1097.   [101] Contempt of Court Act 1981 s 10.
[102] [1990] 2 All ER 1.   [103] Ibid at 10.   [104] Ibid at 6.

The Contempt of Court Act cases suggest that the courts will not look favourably on what they see as wrongful conduct by those who exercise the right to free speech. If an employee were to speak about work related matters using information that was obtained unlawfully this may be a factor that would weigh against a finding that the speech serves the public interest. However, as the House of Lords made clear in *X Ltd v Morgan Grampian*, this could easily be outweighed by other factors in favour of allowing speech, such as the subject matter of speech. This was confirmed by the ECtHR when the journalist in the *Morgan Grampian* case took the case to Strasbourg. In *Goodwin v UK*[105] the ECtHR held that the company had a legitimate interest in terminating the employment of the disloyal employee, but that it was outweighed in this case by the interest in a free press.

Where the subject matter justifies the disclosure, neither motive nor the behaviour surrounding the disclosure is likely to affect a decision on whether to allow actual publication of information. The decision to publish is dependent instead on issues such as the type of information. However, these issues may be relevant to the question of whether employment protection is available for the employee who makes the disclosure. Although where the public interest is served by disclosure there may be no breach of confidence, nor any breach of mutual trust, a bad motive or what is viewed as wrongful behaviour by the employee may affect the remedy available to the dismissed employee. First, any financial reward already obtained in payment for the disclosure could affect the remedy available. The remedy could similarly be affected in an unfair dismissal case where compensation must be just and equitable.[106] Secondly, a bad motive or bad behaviour on the part of the employee could be relevant in deciding whether dismissal on the basis of conduct is fair.[107]

The Truth of Facts Disclosed

The public interest is unlikely to be served by disclosure of unfounded suspicions of wrongdoing. It has been suggested that the public interest is only served by disclosure where the employee can show that she has reasonable grounds for the belief that the information sought to be disclosed is true. Thus, the exception will not be allowed 'upon a mere roving suggestion . . . or even, perhaps, on a general suggestion [that there might be wrongdoing]';[108] and 'the generic defence to breach of confidence, that it is in the

---

[105]   (1996) 22 EHRR 123.
[106]   ERA 1996 s 123. Where information is disclosed for financial reward there may be a danger of committing an offence under the Prevention of Corruption Acts 1906 and 1916 and the Public Bodies Corrupt Practices Act 1889. See Y. Cripps, *Legal Implications of Disclosure in the Public Interest* (2nd edn, 1994) Sweet & Maxwell, London, at 173 ff.
[107]   See Chapter 5 below.
[108]   *Gartside v Outram* (1856) 26 LJ Ch 113 at 114.

public interest to publish, must be supported by evidence to show why the plaintiff should not be given interlocutory relief'.[109] This point was repeated in *Spycatcher No 2*[110] when it was said that 'it is not sufficient to set up the defence merely to show that allegations of wrongdoing have been made. There must be at least a prima facie case that the allegations have substance.'[111] This approach also corresponds with that of the European Commission on Human Rights in *Morrisens v Belgium*,[112] where a teacher was dismissed after she had made various allegations against the provincial authorities and made unacceptable insinuations concerning the heads of the school in a television interview. The Commission, in finding that a disciplinary sanction was proportionate, pointed out that the accusations were not supported by any evidence.

However, this requirement is not absolute. The ECtHR has pointed out that it can be difficult to establish the truth of some allegations. In such cases, if the matter is one of public concern, this is not a reason to deny protection.[113] Furthermore, the European Commission on Human Rights has suggested[114] that the amount of evidence needed to support an allegation may vary depending on where disclosure is made. Domestic law on this issue complies with these suggestions from the European case law. In *Re a Company's Application*,[115] Scott J refused to consider whether the allegations of breaches of FIMBRA regulations and tax irregularities were true; these were issues that would be considered by FIMBRA and the Inland Revenue after the disclosures had been made to them. If the allegations were substantiated action would follow, and if unsubstantiated they would be ignored. There was no need for the judge hearing the case to be concerned with the veracity of the claims. However, *Spycatcher No 2*[116] was distinguished on the basis that the case dealt with disclosure on a wide scale via the media. In such cases the court would need to consider whether there was reasonable basis to the allegations. In contrast, where there is no more than 'disclosure to a recipient which has a duty to investigate matters within its remit, it is not . . . for the court to investigate the substance of the proposed disclosure'.[117]

Balancing the Public Interest Factors

Where a court must decide whether speech serves the public interest, all the above factors can influence the decision. In effect, the court undertakes a balancing exercise in which each factor can work in favour or against a finding

---

[109]   *Lion Laboratories v Evans* [1985] QB 526 per O'Connor LJ at 431f.
[110]   *Attorney-General v Guardian Newspapers (Spycatcher) (No 2)* [1990] 1 AC 109.
[111]   Ibid at 266.   [112]   (1988) D&R 56.
[113]   See *Thorgierson v Iceland* (1992) 14 EHRR 843.
[114]   *Lingens v Austria* (1986) 8 EHRR 407.   [115]   [1989] Ch 477.
[116]   *Attorney-General v Guardian Newspapers (Spycatcher) (No 2)* [1990] 1 AC 109.
[117]   *Re a Company's Application* [1989] 2 Ch 477 at 252d.

that disclosure is necessary. If overall the factors in favour of allowing disclosure outweigh those in favour of restriction, then the court will allow the disclosure. *Re a Company's Application* illustrates the balancing exercise that courts undertake. The threatened disclosure was to a regulatory body, not to the general public, a factor that weighs in favour of the disclosure being made. The disclosure was motivated by malice, a factor that can weigh against disclosure. Other factors weighed in favour of disclosure; the disclosure was to a limited audience with a proper interest in the information, and the information was of a type that it was clearly in the public interest to disclose, tax irregularities and breaches of FIMBRA rules both being 'misdeeds'. A permanent injunction against disclosure of the information to the regulatory bodies was therefore not granted: on balance, the general public interest was served by allowing the disclosure.

FREEDOM OF SPEECH AND THE EMPLOYMENT CONTRACT

The exercise of the right to freedom of expression by an employee involves a potential breach of contract, either of the implied duty of mutual trust or of an express or implied duty of confidence. However, where the court decides that it is in the public interest for information to be known, any disclosure or discussion of the information by an employee will not involve a breach of these contractual duties. Where an employer takes action against an employee for speech which serves the public interest, the employee is likely to have a legal remedy. In contrast, where speech involves a breach of contract by the employee, because it does not serve the public interest, it will be easier for the employer to justify imposing work based sanctions on the employee.

As far as disciplinary actions short of dismissal are concerned, any such actions will be lawful where the employee is in breach of contract. The employee would not be entitled to resign, nor claim breach of contract by the employer. Conversely, if the employee's speech does not breach the employment contract, because it serves the public interest, then any action short of dismissal would instead involve a breach of contract by the employer. This can give grounds to the employee to resign and claim constructive dismissal. Contractual remedies would be available for such a dismissal as it is unlikely in the case of resignation that the employer will have provided adequate notice. Such action is also likely to give rise to a remedy for unfair dismissal (discussed in Chapter 5) as it is unlikely that the employer will have complied with the procedural requirements for a fair dismissal in a case where the employee has resigned due to the employer's breach of contract. Where the employer dismisses the employee for the exercise of free speech, the question of whether the employee was in breach of contract is of less direct relevance, and it is not determinative of the question of whether the resulting dismissal is fair.

A breach of the employment contract can therefore form a legal basis for disciplinary action to be taken against the employee, the most serious being dismissal. Of course the reverse is also true: where a disclosure is not found to be in the public interest, an employee will have no defence in any contractual case taken against him based on breach of confidence or breach of mutual trust. In order for employee freedom of speech to be adequately protected, therefore, it is vital that courts strike the correct balance between the public interest in disclosure and that of protecting the employment relationship of trust and of confidence.

Understanding the extent to which any incident of speech may serve the public interest is therefore an important step in considering the extent to which employees enjoy a proper measure of freedom of speech on matters relating to work. An assessment of the adequacy of the law to protect different types of employee speech (identified in Chapter 2 as whistleblowing, political speech, principled dissent and personal views) requires a consideration of the correlation between the common law public interest defence and the requirements for protection suggested in Chapter 2.

Whistleblowing

Employees who blow the whistle on serious wrongdoing at work should, according to the case law considered above, find it relatively easy to argue that their speech involves no breach of contract, whether of the duty of confidence or the duty of mutual trust. The case law is fairly clear that where information relates to issues such as fraud, tax irregularities or corruption, or breach of health and safety regulations at work, it is in the public interest that it be disclosed. The public interest in such information being reported outweighs the duties the employee otherwise owes to be loyal to the enterprise, and to respect its confidence. However, not all issues that one might expect to be classed as worthy of disclosure have been accepted by the courts, and it is not clear that issues such as environmental damage short of environmental disaster or wrongdoing short of iniquity would always be accepted as needing disclosure in the public interest.[118]

Before deciding that the disclosure is indeed in the public interest, and so involves no breach of contract, the court will consider other relevant factors, the main one being that the disclosure should be to a suitable recipient. Internal disclosures and those to a regulatory body are more likely to be in the public interest even where the information is commercially highly sensitive. This will also be the case where evidence to support the allegation is vague, or where the information does not relate to an especially serious issue. Disclosure to the press, in contrast, is unlikely to be warranted unless it reveals a

---

[118] Contrast the statements in *Malone v Commissioner of Police* [1979] Ch 344 and *Beloff v Pressdram* [1973] 1 All ER 241 above at pp 126 and 127. Contrast also the position under the Public Interest Disclosure Act 1998, considered in Chapter 5, at pp 153–4.

current serious danger to health and safety or to liberty. In addition, a court may require that there is some evidence, beyond mere suspicion of the employee, that any such danger exists although even this may depend on the seriousness and imminence of the danger exposed.

In many cases, then, whistleblowers wishing to raise concerns and have them investigated may be able, without too much difficulty, to meet the requirements of the public interest concept as long as they raise their concerns via appropriate channels. Although it is always open to courts to take a restrictive view of the public interest, illustrated in some of the cases discussed above, and so find that there is a breach of contract on the facts, the law in relation to whistleblowing does, in the main, meet the requirements for free speech protection at work, set out in Chapter 2. There it was suggested that whistleblowers should be given employment protection because of the strength of the audience interests served by their speech. The fact that whistleblowing usually serves the public interest means that it should not involve a breach of the duties of confidence and mutual trust contained in the employment contract. It is therefore unlikely to be lawful for an employer to punish whistleblowing by imposing employment based sanctions such as dismissal. If the public interest is served by the whistleblowing, there is no legal justification for bringing the contract to an end. The employee will have a remedy for wrongful dismissal, unless contractual notice has been given of any dismissal. Although the fact that a dismissal is in breach of contract does not necessarily mean that the dismissal is unfair, the employee is also likely to have a remedy for unfair dismissal, under the Public Interest Disclosure Act 1998, discussed in Chapter 5 below.

POLITICAL SPEECH

The strong public and democratic interest in protecting political speech was established in Chapter 2. Enabling employees to participate in political discussion and debate both upholds the individual autonomy of the speaker, and improves the democratic process by creating a better informed electorate. In most cases the expression of political opinion will not involve disclosure of confidential information, nor will it breach the duty of mutual trust. The fact that an employee holds a particular political view, or participates in a political discussion, is unlikely to cause an interference with the interests of the employer. Such speech causes neither economic loss, disruption to the workplace nor does it have any impact on the reputation of the enterprise. In such cases, work based sanctions are unlikely, and if they were imposed, would probably involve the employer in a breach of the duty of mutual trust.

There will be some cases, however, where political speech by the employee does interfere with the rights of the employer, and thus causes a breach of either the duty of confidence or the duty of mutual trust or both. This might be because the information discussed is obtained as a result of the employment relationship. In such a case, the information could well be classed as confidential, even though it may also be known to the public at large, because it is obtained as a result of a trust based relationship.[119] Alternatively, the speech could cause distrust between the employee's colleagues which interferes with smooth workplace relations. Where the political speech is deeply unpopular, it could even bring the employer into disrepute for allowing the continued employment of a person with what are seen as unacceptable views.

In all these cases, the employer could have grounds to argue that the duty of mutual trust is breached by the employee's speech, and it is not entirely clear that courts would accept that the disclosure serves the public interest, despite the weight of the audience interests in protecting such speech. For example, an employee could disclose information that suggests the error of a political policy such as statistics suggesting that small classes do not improve pupil performance. This information could be classed as confidential because it is obtained as a result of employment, even though others could come to the same view using other independent sources. The information does not relate to an immediate danger or wrongdoing, and so it may not count as the type of information required to be disclosed in the public interest. Moreover, such information will only be useful to the public if widely disclosed, again militating against a finding that the public interest requires disclosure.

Discussion of this type of information could very easily be classed as political speech, however, as it directly relates to a political policy. If a disclosure of such political information did give rise to a finding of breach of confidence or breach of mutual trust, because of the subject matter and breadth of disclosure, it would represent a failure of the current law to provide adequate protection for free speech about work. Yet it appears from the common law on confidentiality that this is a very likely outcome, not least because of a restricted view of what can count as political speech, as demonstrated in the *British Steel* case.[120] The position may improve once the common law is interpreted to comply with the ECHR, as its case law demonstrates a greater recognition both of the importance of political speech and of the range of speech that can be classed as political. But unless this broader understanding of the public interest in political speech develops, the common law will continue to provide inadequate protection for employees' freedom of political speech.

PRINCIPLED DISSENT

Again, in many cases discussion of general work related matters outside the workplace will not involve breach of confidence, nor breach of the duty of mutual trust. NHS staff speaking in public about the provision of

[119] See the discussion of *Schering Chemicals v Falkman Ltd* [1982] QB 1 above at pp 118–19.
[120] *British Steel Corporation v Granada Television* [1981] AC 1097.

health care, railway staff speaking in public about the impact of rail privatisation, and teachers discussing standards in schools do not disclose any information not reasonably accessible to the public, and so their speech should not involve a breach of the duty of confidence. Even so, it is open to the courts under the law as it currently stands to find that confidence is breached because the information was learnt, and the understanding of the information was formed, by virtue of the employment relationship. Moreover, principled dissent is likely to breach the duty of mutual trust: the fact that the speech is termed dissent refers to the fact that it involves disagreement with, or criticism of, the employer's policies or practices. Publicly to voice such dissent is highly likely to amount to a breach of the implied duty of mutual trust, and the duty of fidelity and loyalty included within it.

Furthermore, in some cases, both the duty of trust and the duty of confidence will be breached, as a speaker may disclose information that is prima facie confidential in order to add weight to any dissent. For example, in discussing recent changes in the organisation of the NHS, a speaker may reveal current staffing levels, information that may be commercially sensitive for the employing NHS Trust. In such a case there will be competing public interests in disclosure and confidence, and the interest in disclosure is unlikely to prevail. In favour of maintaining confidence will be the fact that disclosure of staffing levels can give competitors a commercial advantage in future bidding rounds. Although general discussion of NHS staffing levels may be in the public interest in terms of aiding the democratic process through informing the electorate, it is unlikely that such a disclosure would be said to be in the public interest because it does not indicate misconduct or illegal behaviour. The other factors taken into consideration by the courts in determining the issue, such as the recipient of the information, will also weigh against a finding of public interest. The fact that the disclosure is of commercially sensitive information, that it will almost certainly be made publicly rather than through a regulator, and the fact that it will be hard to verify whether staffing levels are adequate in any event, may mean that disclosure would be found not to serve the public interest.

Yet dissent requires publicity if it is to serve any purpose beyond the personal autonomy of the speaker. Internal disclosure is therefore inappropriate. In order to gain proper protection for their speech, dissenters need courts to recognise more readily the wider public interest served by public debate on issues of public importance, and the public interest served by the participation of insiders in that debate. Until they do, the law will remain inadequate for the protection of this type of employee speech.

PERSONAL VIEWS AND GENERAL COMMENT

It will be rare for employees to be dismissed or disciplined for the mere expression of personal opinions, unless of course those opinions amount to some form of unlawful behaviour such as racial or sexual harassment in which case the penalties would be justified. However, cases can arise where the expression of opinion leads to workplace sanctions. The example used in Chapter 2 was of Glenn Hoddle, dismissed for expressing his views on the causes of disability.[121] The views expressed caused the employer embarrassment and threatened its own public reputation. Mutual trust between employer and employee was no longer present.

If such a case were to reach the courts for a decision on whether there was indeed a breach of contract, it is by no means clear on the precedent set by the common law that the public interest in upholding the right to individual freedom of speech would be sufficient to act as an exception to the duty of mutual trust. All the factors considered by the courts would point against a finding that the public interest is served by the speech: the public nature of the speech, the fact that it does not reveal any danger, wrongdoing or other urgent matter, and the fact that the view is a matter of opinion and cannot be proved to be true.

THE CONTRACT OF EMPLOYMENT: MODEL EMPLOYMENT PROTECTION?

In making proposals for proper protection of free speech for employees in Chapter 2, a range of factors were identified as affecting whether protection could be justified. Many of those factors mirror the factors considered by the courts in assessing whether or not a disclosure serves the public interest, indicating that there is some commonality between the current law on the contract of employment and the public interest, and that which has been proposed as a model for employment protection for free speech about work. To some extent, employment protection is warranted where speech serves the public interest; thus issues such as the type of speech, the subject matter of the speech and the identity of the person spoken to are important to both questions. Where these factors point towards a finding that the speech serves the public interest, then any action taken against the employee is likely to be in breach of contract. To this extent the protection available against dismissal at common law meets the requirements set out in Chapter 2 with regard to good employment protection for employee speech. However, some factors may also militate against employment protection for the speaker, even though the speech may serve the public interest. Speech made in public, using information obtained as a result of the employment relationship, and which does not relate to a matter of serious and urgent concern, may result in a breach of either the duty of mutual trust or the duty of confidence or both. Where the employee is in breach of contract this may give the employer grounds to dismiss. Dismissal or discipline imposed where the employee has

---

[121] See Chapter 1, p 8.

not breached the contract would instead involve the employer in breach of contract.

The extent to which employment protection is afforded to employees in such circumstances is the subject of Chapter 5 below. What is clear from this discussion of the contract of employment is that the wide public interest in upholding individual freedom of speech is not given sufficient recognition when it is weighed against the need to maintain mutual confidence and trust in the employment relationship. If free speech is to be granted adequate protection against work based sanctions, courts need to give greater recognition to the audience interests served by speech, in particular where its content relates to the discovery of the truth, and to the upholding of the democratic process.

5

Freedom of Speech and Dismissal

Employees who exercise the right to free speech about work may well find their employers less than pleased. The employer may perceive the employee's action to be disloyal as well as disliking any adverse publicity that results from the speech. In response, the employer may take disciplinary action against the employee, and may even dismiss. The legal position of any employee subjected to action of this type will depend in large measure on the subject matter of the speech. The Public Interest Disclosure Act 1998 extends the law on unfair dismissal to provide automatic protection for employees who raise matters of concern relating to designated types of wrongdoing or malpractice at work. Employees raising matters not covered by the Public Interest Disclosure Act will be dependent on the general law of unfair dismissal for any protection for speech. In addition, several statutes, such as the Sex Discrimination Act 1975, provide protection for employees who disclose that their standards are not being met. This chapter considers the extent to which these various provisions provide adequate employment protection for free speech.

WORKPLACE SANCTIONS FOR EXERCISING THE RIGHT TO FREE SPEECH

A number of different work based sanctions may be imposed on employees for exercising the right to free speech, including dismissal, demotion, denial of the opportunity to apply for promotion, the removal of benefits and the unjustified use of grievance or disciplinary proceedings. Although couched in terms of dismissal, the protection against unfair dismissal probably includes protection against any of these sanctions. For the purposes of unfair dismissal protection (which includes PIDA), the Employment Rights Act 1996 defines dismissal as including the termination of employment by the employer, expiry of a fixed term contract, or termination *by the employee* in circumstances where the conduct of the employer is such that the employee is entitled to terminate the contract.[1] It is this last form of dismissal, constructive dismissal, that is relevant where the sanction imposed by the employer takes a form other than outright dismissal by the employer, as the

---

[1] ERA 1996 s 95(1).

interaction between constructive dismissal and the implied duty of trust and confidence means that where an employer's actions are unjustified, there will often be grounds to find that the employee has been dismissed.

The working of constructive dismissal is strictly contractual, the question being whether the employer has breached the contract of employment sufficiently to entitle the employee to treat the relationship as ended. The question is very clearly not whether the employer has been so unreasonable as to entitle the employee to leave.[2] However, the implied duty on the employer to maintain a relationship of trust and confidence with the employee means that unjustified or unreasonable behaviour by the employer can, if bad enough, amount to a breach of contract, giving rise to a contractual entitlement on the employee to treat the contract as ended. As argued in Chapter 4 above, where the employee's exercise of the right to free speech does not involve a breach of contract, because its content or context means that it does not breach the duty of confidence or any other employment duty, the employer will have no contractual grounds for taking any step against the employee in response. Any detrimental action taken against the employee, such as bringing disciplinary action, may therefore amount to a breach of contract by the employer which, if the employee chooses, may allow him to treat the contract as ended and claim constructive dismissal.[3]

Once the employee can show that there has been a dismissal, then the various protections against unfair dismissal can be applied. Under the Employment Rights Act 1996 there are a number of grounds on which dismissal will be designated automatically unfair. Automatically unfair dismissal as created by the Public Interest Disclosure Act's amendment to the ERA 1996 is the form of employment protection most relevant to those who exercise their right to free speech in the public interest. The ERA 1996 contains a number of other heads of automatically unfair dismissal which may apply to speech relating to specific subjects such as health and safety at work. Others who fall outside these provisions will be dependent on the general rules of unfair dismissal.

Where the sanction imposed by the employer does not amount to dismissal, or where the employee chooses not to treat the contract of employment as at an end, the protection under the Public Interest Disclosure Act and the protection of health and safety representatives can still apply, as they give grounds for the employee to claim compensation for detrimental action short of dismissal. The basis and circumstances of such claims are identical to those for dismissal protection, although self evidently, the remedies of re-engagement or reinstatement do not arise. Protection against dismissal will be the focus of the discussion that follows, but it should be borne in mind that

---

[2] *Western Excavating (ECC) Ltd v Sharp* [1978] QB 761.
[3] In *Walker v Josiah Wedgwood and Sons Ltd* [1978] IRLR 105 it was pointed out that unjustified disciplinary warnings can give rise to constructive dismissal.

compensation can be available in cases where the sanction imposed for speech does not involve actual dismissal.

THE PUBLIC INTEREST DISCLOSURE
ACT 1998

The Public Interest Disclosure Act 1998 (PIDA) came into force on 2 July 1999, with the aim of providing employment protection to workers who make disclosures of information in the public interest. The need for such protection had become clear in a number of cases in the preceding decades, where staff had felt unable to raise public interest concerns for fear of retaliation at work, and where subsequent disaster had proved the validity of those concerns. Examples of such cases include the Clapham Junction train crash,[4] the explosion on the Piper Alpha oil platform,[5] the high mortality rates following heart surgery on young babies at the Bristol Royal Infirmary,[6] and doubts about the probity of the Bank of Credit and Commerce International (BCCI) before its collapse.[7]

The need for legislative protection had been increasingly recognised since the late 1980s. During the 1990s employment protection was provided for safety representatives who raise concerns about health and safety.[8] In the NHS, guidance was published by the NHS Executive confirming that employees' free speech can play a role in improving the health service, and requiring management to create systems to encourage the reporting of concerns.[9] In 1995 the Nolan Committee on Standards in Public Life made recommendations for the introduction of whistleblowing procedures for employees of various public bodies,[10] proposals that were accepted by the government.[11] The Labour Party, when in opposition, agreed to legislate as part of its Freedom of Information legislation after a ten minute rule bill and private members bill introduced before Parliament in 1995 and 1996 were unsuccessful.[12] However, in the event, action was taken earlier than expected when the Conservative MP Richard Shepherd used his place in the Private

---

[4] Investigation into the Clapham Junction Railway Accident, November 1989, HMSO Cm 820.

[5] The Public Inquiry into the Piper Alpha Disaster, November 1990, HMSO Cm 1310.

[6] *The Guardian*, 30 May 1998, concerns subsequently found to be correct: Secretary of State for Health HC Deb, 18 June 1998 cols 529–30.

[7] Inquiry into the Supervision of The Bank of Credit and Commerce International, 2 October 1992, HMSO, 198.

[8] ERA 1996, ss 44 and 100, introduced following the adoption of the EC Framework Directive 89/391.

[9] 'Guidance for Staff on Relations with the Public and the Media' (1993) NHS Executive.

[10] First Report of the Committee on Standards in Public Life, 1995, HMSO Cm 2850 I–II.

[11] Government Response to the First Report of the Committee on Standards in Public Life, 1995, HMSO Cm 2931.

[12] Tony Wright's 1995 Whistleblower Protection Bill, a ten minute rule bill and Don Touhig's 1996 Public Interest Disclosure Bill, a private members bill.

Members ballot to sponsor the Public Interest Disclosure Act. The Act received the support of the CBI and Institute of Directors as well as the TUC, and was passed virtually without opposition.

Although the Act is called the Public Interest Disclosure Act, its aim is in fact to prevent public disclosures where possible. Instead it aims to encourage the introduction of clear internal processes into workplaces through which concerns can be raised, thereby making external disclosure unnecessary. The Act gives internal disclosures virtually automatic protection, in order to encourage concerns to be reported internally. As long as the concerns raised are adequately dealt with this should prevent external disclosure. In contrast, external disclosures are given less protection. In order to qualify there must be a good reason to report a concern outside the organisation, such as fear of victimisation for reporting internally, fear that evidence of wrongdoing will be destroyed, or the fact that internal disclosure has already taken place (without an adequate response).[13] As a result, employees who publicise their concerns will not be protected by the Act if they work for an employer who encourages internal disclosure and responds to concerns raised. This creates an incentive to employers to set up effective internal processes through which disclosures can be made. The aim is to prevent some of the disasters of the past recurring because of management remaining unaware of, or ignoring, the concerns of their staff; it is not to provide a green light for employees to publicise grievances against their employers.

A second aim of the PIDA is also achieved by the encouragement of internal disclosure; that is, to introduce greater employer accountability for accidents or malpractice that occur.[14] If employers can be shown to have known about a concern relating to danger or malpractice, it is much easier for them to be held accountable for their failure to bring it to an end if the concern turns out to be well founded. Where employees have not raised concerns with employers, they can only be held accountable on the basis of constructive or implied knowledge of the danger, a much more problematic concept.[15] Increasing the level of employers' direct knowledge about matters throughout the workplace should improve accountability when accidents do occur, and more importantly, should help to prevent them occurring in the first place.

The PIDA is based on the existing legal protection against unfair dismissal and provides that dismissal for making a relevant disclosure is automatically unfair. Public interest disclosure dismissals are thus added to the existing heads of automatically unfair dismissal, such as dismissal for trade union

---

[13] Section 43G(2)(a)–(c). Section 43G(2)(c) provides that external disclosure may be protected if internal disclosure has already been made, but in assessing the reasonableness of such disclosures under s 43G(3)(e), any action that the employer has made in response to the report is considered.

[14] See G. Dehn, 'Commentary on the PIDA' in *Current Law Statutes Annotated* (1999) Sweet & Maxwell, London.

[15] See C. Wells, *Corporations and Criminal Liability* (1993) Oxford University Press, Oxford.

membership or activities, for pregnancy, and for asserting a statutory right.[16] As with other automatically unfair dismissals, employees enjoy the protection of the Act as soon as they start work, without the need for a qualifying period of employment. The remedies are reinstatement, re-engagement or compensation.[17] Extra features of the PIDA are that compensation is unlimited,[18] and protection extends to workers not usually covered by unfair dismissal legislation, so that self employed and agency workers are explicitly covered.[19] As with the protection for employees who take part in trade union activities, protection covers dismissal and other detrimental action short of dismissal. Thus a demotion, refusal of a pay rise, unjustified use of a disciplinary process, or any other sanction imposed in response to a protected disclosure will be actionable under the PIDA.[20]

As well as encouraging internal disclosure, a further task facing the drafters of the legislation was to maintain a fair balance between the rights of employees to protection for raising public interest concerns and the interests of employers in preserving legitimate loyalty and confidentiality, a balancing of interests that has been discussed at length in earlier chapters. The PIDA achieves this balance by closely defining the subject matters on which disclosures are allowed, and by setting out procedures by which disclosures must be made in order to qualify for protection.

THE SUBJECT MATTER OF THE DISCLOSURE

Employment protection is only provided by the Act where the disclosure relates to one of the matters listed in s 43B. The matters specified are concerns about:

(a) criminal offences,
(b) failure by a person to comply with a legal obligation,
(c) miscarriages of justice,
(d) danger to health and safety,

---

[16] Other automatically unfair dismissals include dismissal for refusing to work on a Sunday (certain retail employees only), for asserting a claim under the National Minimum Wage Act, and for acting as a health and safety representative. Some of these rights are discussed below.

[17] As for dismissals for trade union activity, interim relief is available for employees while awaiting a full hearing.

[18] In one of the early cases under the PIDA, *Fernandes v Netcom Consultants (UK) Ltd* (18/5/00, Case No 2200060/00), an employment tribunal awarded compensation of £293,441.

[19] The word 'worker' will be used in what follows to mean employees and other workers covered by the Act. Workers are defined in s 1(43K) of the Act as including those working under a contract for services, those working as agency workers, trainees and those who work for the NHS but who are not employees. For detail on forms of labour covered by other employment protection legislation, see S. Deakin and G. Morris, *Labour Law* (2001) Butterworths, London, at 148–81.

[20] ERA 1996 s 47A.

(e) danger to the environment, or

(f) a concern that information about one of these matters is being deliberately concealed.[21]

Concerns may be current, or relate to past or future incidents. The list is fairly comprehensive, and covers most of the public interest concerns that might be raised by a worker blowing the whistle on malpractice or wrongdoing at work. However, the effect of the list is to limit the protection of the Act to whistle-blowing speech. Other types of speech such as political speech or principled dissent are unlikely to come within the terms of the Act. Those who face work based sanctions for taking part in these other forms of speech will be reliant on the general law of unfair dismissal discussed below.

Where the employee, in exercise of the right to free speech, discloses information covered by this section in accordance with the procedures set out elsewhere in the PIDA, employment protection will be provided. In contrast to the position at common law, this is the case whether or not the information is confidential in nature, and regardless of whether the recipient of the information is already aware of it. In general the subject matters that are included in the list aim to cover the types of information that should, in the public interest, be disclosed. The list is widely drafted, and may well cover some issues that would not be said to be in the public interest at common law. Although the common law definition of the public interest goes beyond merely the disclosure of criminal conduct,[22] it is not clear that it would cover the disclosure of damage to the environment, as the PIDA does, nor the disclosure of a failure to fulfil any legal obligation, a heading that is extremely far reaching, as will be seen below.

It is interesting to note that there is no specific requirement in the PIDA that the matter disclosed would need to serve the public interest before being protected, although the list of subjects is not dissimilar to the types of information covered by the common law on the meaning of the public interest. For example, disclosure of serious damage to the environment would probably be covered by the common law definition of the public interest; but the PIDA lists just 'damage to the environment', not necessarily serious damage. Similarly, the failure to comply with a legal obligation may not be very serious of itself, but seriousness is not a requirement for the subject matter to be covered. This gives employees a degree of certainty in advance as to whether the disclosures they intend to make will be covered by the Act. If the disclosure is made externally, the seriousness of the issue may be relevant; but if disclosure is internal, or to a regulator, it will be protected virtually auto-

---

[21] In the following discussion, these issues will be referred to as 'malpractice', or 'relevant concerns'.

[22] For example *Lion Laboratories v Evans* [1985] QB 526 concerned the disclosure of concerns about the reliability of the breathalyser when it was first introduced. See Y. Cripps, *Legal Implications of Disclosure in the Public Interest* (2nd edn, 1994) Sweet and Maxwell, London, for further examples.

matically. This contrasts with the position in common law where the person disclosing information cannot know, purely from the subject matter of the disclosure, whether it will be found to serve the public interest. The major advantage of this greater level of certainty is that it should provide encouragement to employees to disclose information that is in the public interest.

Apart from the category 'failure to comply with a legal obligation' which is discussed further below, the subject matters covered by the PIDA are fairly self explanatory. The list of subject matters is exhaustive and there are no additional indeterminate requirements such as that the disclosure be 'in the public interest', or 'serious'. It should thus be clear to both employer and employee whether or not they are dealing with a qualifying disclosure in terms of its content. This certainty is of benefit to both employer and employee, but it comes at a price. The scope of the Act is, to an extent, restricted by its certainty, and as a result can be said to lack flexibility. It is possible that matters could be raised that are not covered in the definition, but which are still worthy of protection in the public interest. The list lacks a catch-all provision to allow the court or tribunal to use its discretion to decide that a disclosure should have been made even though it does not concern a listed matter. Whilst the list appears fairly comprehensive at present, it may be that in the future new concerns will be viewed as worthy of protection. The development of the common law on the meaning of the public interest demonstrates the way in which the meaning of the term has evolved, from disclosure only of criminal conduct,[23] to include much wider categories of disclosure.[24] Taking environmental danger as an example, this might not have been regarded as a subject worthy of protection in the past, but such concerns are now seen as serious enough to be listed in the PIDA. Other examples of issues not included in the PIDA but which might nonetheless be in the public interest to be disclosed can be drawn from similar protection in the USA. Their Whistleblower Protection Act 1989, which covers state employees, protects disclosures of 'gross mismanagement', 'gross waste of funds' and 'abuse of authority',[25] issues not explicitly covered by the PIDA.

The scope for the PIDA to provide comprehensive protection for the public interest would be improved if it included a list of matters automatically covered with an additional catch-all provision covering matters that, in the opinion of the court, are in the public interest. Although a catch-all provision of this type would result in the loss of complete certainty for employer and employee as to exactly what is covered by the Act, the benefits of the flexibility to cover other public interest issues would override this disadvantage. Additional issues would only be covered if there was a clear public interest in their disclosure. Certainty as regards the named issues would be retained.

---

[23] *Gartside v Outram* (1856) 26 LJ Ch 113.
[24] See for example *Lion Laboratories v Evans* [1985] QB 526 and *Woodward v Hutchins* [1977] 1 WLR 760 discussed above, Chapter 4, p 126.
[25] 5 USC 2302 (b)(8).

However, this limitation in the coverage of the PIDA may not be as serious as it at first appears, as most concerns that are in the public interest may in fact be protected, even though this is not clear on the face of the Act. In particular, the category of 'failure to comply with a legal obligation' has the potential to be interpreted very widely in accordance with the wide ranging nature of legal obligations. Taking the examples of mismanagement and abuse of authority given above, it is arguable that such conduct would involve a breach of a legal duty owed by employers and employees. Employees owe their employers a legal duty of trust and confidence; arguably mismanagement by a senior employee will be a breach of that obligation. Abuse of authority at work could, depending on the type of work, leave some employers open to a claim for judicial review; again a breach of a legal obligation (to act reasonably and to comply with natural justice) may be suspected. Other legal obligations to which employers are subject include obligations not to dismiss employees unfairly, or discriminate on grounds of sex, race or disability;[26] duties of care to consumers or customers; and contractual duties in relation to goods sold, or other contractual duties.[27] In addition, public authorities must comply with the ECHR.[28] Disclosure by employees of a concern that any of these multifarious obligations has not been met could therefore be covered by the PIDA. Future concerns that are not yet anticipated are also likely to be the subject of some legal obligation once their importance is recognised and so again they will be covered by this section of the Act. For example, with the increased recognition of environmental damage as a public interest matter have come increased legal obligations relating to the environment. In effect, the inclusion of 'breach of a legal obligation' as a protected subject acts as a *de facto* catch-all provision.

It remains unfortunate that the potential for this subsection to be used in this broad manner is not explicit in the Act. In some cases only those with legal training would be able to recognise all the legal obligations owed at work. A worker acting without legal advice who is considering whether a disclosure will be protected may well decide that it is not, even though, on close examination, a breach of a legal obligation can be established. Concerns that are in the public interest may thus not be raised. In contrast, although a catch-all phrase would be bound to generate a case based system of precedent unknown to those without the requisite training or experience, the very use of the wording in the Act would alert uninitiated readers to the existence of a residual category to be investigated, which might cover the concerns they wish to raise.

---

[26] Sex Discrimination Act 1975, Race Relations Act 1976, Disability Discrimination Act 1995.

[27] Although it is not clear that 'breach of a legal obligation' extends to breaches of contractual obligations, it is Dehn's view that breaches of statutory requirements, contractual obligations and common law obligations are all covered. See G. Dehn, 'Commentary on the PIDA' in *Current Law Statutes Annotated* (1999) Sweet & Maxwell, London. This view was confirmed by the EAT decision in *Parkins v Sodexho Ltd* (unreported) 18/10/01.

[28] The Human Rights Act 1998.

Notwithstanding its potential breadth, the 'breach of a legal obligation' provision is also unlikely to go so far as to cover the concerns of employees who voice personal opinions that relate to work, or who express principled dissent over an employer's policy. For example, a teacher who participates in debate on government education policy would not be protected by the Act. Although it is in the public interest that such debate be informed by those with everyday experience of the education system, disclosures made in the course of such debate would not be covered by the section, as no specific wrongdoing is alleged or suspected. Whilst this may weaken the protection of the Act, it cannot be the basis for fair criticism of the Act as it was only designed and intended to cover whistleblowers. Those who engage in other forms of speech such as personal comment, dissent, or political speech will need to rely instead on the general law on unfair dismissal for protection.

PROCEDURES FOR MAKING PROTECTED DISCLOSURES

Although the PIDA is sometimes known as the Whistleblower's Act, as already noted the aim is in fact to discourage public whistleblowing and instead to encourage internal disclosure and action in most cases. The main way in which the PIDA does this is by closely specifying the processes by which disclosures are made. Internal disclosures are granted fairly wide protection, but the circumstances in which external disclosure is protected under the Act are strictly limited.

INTERNAL DISCLOSURE

Where relevant concerns are raised internally, employee protection against victimisation is virtually automatic. All that is needed is for the worker to act in good faith and on the basis that he reasonably believes that the information disclosed tends to show that wrongdoing has occurred. No further requirements are imposed. The employee does not need to believe that the wrongdoing has definitely occurred, but does need to believe that the evidence suggests that it has. For example, an employee may believe that he has uncovered evidence of corruption at work. He may not have the power or ability to tell whether his suspicion is correct, but as long as he has a reasonable belief that the evidence suggests corruption, he will be protected if he takes the matter further by disclosing that evidence to someone internally within the organisation. That way the person who does have the power and resources to investigate the allegation can take the matter up. The reporting of mere rumours is not protected, but an employee is enabled to report genuine concerns or suspicions without needing to wait for proof of their validity.

The fact that an employee is protected under this part of the Act whether or not he believes that the wrongdoing has actually taken place is fairly generous to the employee. To a large extent this is because if the concern turns out to be unfounded, no damage is likely to have been done to the external reputation of the organisation as the matter will have remained internal to it. Of course, there will still be costs to the employer where concerns are raised which turn out to be unfounded, and it might be argued that the Act provides too much protection for those who wish to cause trouble by raising spurious concerns. After all, even though the information may remain internal to the organisation, internal reputations of individuals may be damaged, and time and resources will be used in investigating the concern. It might be argued that it would be better to make the Act's protection dependent on the employee's reasonable belief that the allegation is correct. However, such a change would mean that the employee would need to wait to gather more information so as to be sure that he has reasonable grounds for believing in the truth of the allegation. In the meantime, where the concern is correct, the criminal offences, risks to health and safety, environmental damage or other qualifying wrongdoings would continue. Employees, particularly lower ranking employees, are often not in a position to substantiate their suspicions. Allowing suspicions to be disclosed allows those with the power to investigate to do so. The balance between the wider public interest in preventing wrongdoing, and the employer's interest in protecting the internal reputation of staff and preventing the waste of staff time, is probably struck in the right place here. Protection is given to those with reasonable suspicions but not to those who just spread rumours.

Internal disclosure includes disclosure to the employer, or to a third party where the malpractice is caused by that third party or is his legal responsibility.[29] This means that where a person is employed to work on the premises of another party, for example an agency nurse in a care home, or an auditor working at a client's premises,[30] he can report the concern to the person for whom he is carrying out the work, and who is responsible for the matter being reported, rather than only to his actual employer.

Disclosure has to be made to 'the employer' to be protected under s 43C(1)(a). An employee in a large enterprise may not know who exactly will count as 'the employer' for these purposes. Would it be the chairman of the company, the chief executive, the board of directors, head of the department, or the immediate line manager? It is suggested that for the purposes of the Act to be achieved, any reports made higher up the management chain from the reporter should count as disclosure to the employer, but that disclosure to a colleague would not.[31] The point is not only that 'internal' disclosures do not breach confidence (as the information will not have gone outside the workplace if reported only to a colleague) but that it must be reported to someone who can take action over it. This interpretation would enable the Act to create more readily the greater accountability of employers that the Act seeks to achieve.

---

[29] ERA 1996 s 43C.   [30] Examples used by Dehn, n 27 above.   [31] Ibid.

In its provision of the widest protection to internal disclosures, the PIDA mirrors the common law on the public interest and the duty of confidence, in which courts have made clear that where disclosure is made to 'one with a proper interest to receive the information' no breach of confidence occurs.[32] Clearly, in relation to concerns about malpractice at work, the one with the most interest in the information is the employer. Thus disclosure to an employer gives rise to no breach of confidence vis-à-vis the employment relationship. Arguably such disclosures may already be protected under existing unfair dismissal law, as there may be no misconduct on which to base the dismissal where there is no breach of confidence. If such is the case, it could be said that the PIDA creates no extra protection beyond that already available in the law on unfair dismissal. However, even where there is no breach of confidence, there may be some other form of misconduct on which to base a potentially fair dismissal, and so the existing unfair dismissal legislation may not provide full protection. PIDA also creates much greater certainty for employees who raise concerns; it protects the worker against suffering any detriment at the hands of the employer; and provides protection to a wider group of staff, without the need for a qualifying period of employment.

Apart from disclosure to the employer, several other types of disclosure are given the same extensive protection as internal disclosure. Section 43C(2) provides that disclosure will count as internal disclosure if it is made in accordance with a whistleblowing procedure authorised by the employer. This covers the situation where an employer introduces a process for reporting concerns which allows reporting to an external person, such as a trade union official, a health and safety representative, or one of the whistleblowing hotlines run by some unions and professional bodies. Where an employee works for a government appointed body, such as an NHS Trust, disclosure to the relevant Minister of the Crown is also treated as an internal disclosure.[33] Even wider protection is available under the Act where disclosure is made in the course of obtaining legal advice.[34] In such a case, the worker is automatically protected. There is not even the need for the disclosure to be made in good faith, although the worker must reasonably believe that the malpractice has occurred.

During the debate on the Bill in the House of Lords, an attempt was made to include disclosure to trade union officials as a type of internal disclosure that would be given automatic protection. However, proposals to introduce amendments to this effect were unsuccessful. As a result, disclosure to a union legal adviser will be treated in the same way as any other disclosure in the course of obtaining legal advice; and where unions are recognised,

---

[32] Lord Denning in *Initial Services v Putterill* [1968] 1 QB 396 at 405.
[33] ERA 1996 s 43E.
[34] ERA 1996 s 43D. Public Concern at Work is designated a legal advice centre by the Bar Council so it will be covered by this section.

union officials may well play a part in the employer's internal procedures for disclosure. However, in other cases, disclosure to trade union officials will be treated as an external disclosure, albeit a potentially reasonable one.[35]

The virtually automatic protection available for internal disclosure is very welcome. Not only does such disclosure rarely involve breach of confidence, as it usually involves keeping information within the organisation, but it also allows a simple and quick way for concerns to be addressed. If concerns are made public, the response of those running the organisation is often to become defensive and deny that there is a problem. If matters are kept internal to the organisation, there is less incentive for the employer to go into denial over the issue raised, and therefore more likelihood that it will be tackled. Moreover, where concerns are raised and dealt with internally, there can be very little moral justification for an employer to impose penalties on the employee, and the introduction of legal protection can hardly be said to be contentious.

Having said that it is right to grant internal disclosure very broad protection because it causes no damage to the external reputation of the organisation, there are of course some costs that can arise where internal disclosures are made. As mentioned above, the internal reputation of staff can be adversely affected. Moreover, a great deal of staff time, and thus financial cost to the employer, can be used in investigating and dealing with allegations, some of which will be unfounded, or may even be made maliciously. Indeed, viewed in this light, the PIDA could be seen as a charter for troublemakers. It is also possible that internal disclosures will be very disruptive to the workforce. For example, if one member of staff alleges that another is committing a criminal offence, or is in breach of a legal obligation, this will cast serious doubt on the probity of the individual concerned. Where allegations are unfounded, but become known within the organisation, it is quite likely that tensions and difficulties will arise between staff members, which could be damaging to the organisation. These various costs could be used to argue against the introduction of the PIDA in the first place. However, given the benefit of uncovering those concerns that are valid, the costs are worth paying, particularly as only serious public interest issues are covered by the Act.

Moreover, there are a number of ways in which the costs to the employer of protecting those who raise concerns can be kept to a minimum. The first is the introduction of good internal procedures for raising concerns. Procedures need to ensure that allegations remain confidential even within the organisation whilst being investigated, and provide that where an employee is implicated and then exonerated, all those who know of the allegation are

---

[35] Lord Borrie QC, *Hansard* HL Vol 590, col 624. On reasonableness of external disclosure see discussion below.

made fully aware of the exoneration. Although it may be difficult to repair a reputation fully, some believing there to be 'no smoke without fire', the damage to individual reputations within the organisation should be minimal where reports are treated as confidential, and where allegations are investigated swiftly. The remaining costs of damage to internal reputations, disruption to the workplace, and the costs of the investigation are worth paying, because of the chance of uncovering serious misconduct, the discovery of which can prevent significant damage.

A second way in which the costs to the employer are limited is contained in PIDA itself, and is the requirement that any allegation be made in good faith.[36] The only exception to the requirement of good faith are disclosures made in the course of obtaining legal advice.[37] Such disclosures are themselves then confidential to the legal adviser, and are unlikely to lead to significant damage to the organisation itself, or to the reputations of those who work within it. Employees who act in bad faith will not be protected. Without the protection of the PIDA, the employee could be dismissed, probably fairly, for misconduct. Exactly what is meant by the requirement of good faith is not clear on the face of the Act, but it has been suggested that good faith probably requires the employee to act in the honest, even if unreasonable, belief that the concern raised is true.[38] An employee who raises a concern in the knowledge that it is false, or for an ulterior motive such as blackmail, revenge or malice against the employer or a fellow employee, or to protect himself against dismissal for some other reason, will not be acting in good faith. Of course, this does not remove all difficulties: some employees may act with mixed motives, perhaps to embarrass the employer or to negotiate a better position in disciplinary proceedings, as well as to raise a genuine concern, and in any event, proving good faith or lack of it may be difficult in practice. The PIDA does not give guidance on how employers or tribunals are to deal with such cases, nor does it specify where the burden of proving good faith lies, providing potential difficulties in the application of the Act in the courts. However, despite these difficulties, the good faith requirement does offer some safeguards to employers against malicious use of the Act, and should meet some of the objections to the Act as creating a charter for troublemakers. Moreover, although the good faith requirement may have its limitations, such as difficulties in proof, any alternatives would make the protection much more limited. For example, restricting protection to those who can *prove* that wrongdoing has taken place would result in loss of many of the benefits of the legislation in enabling danger and wrongdoing to be uncovered, as

---

[36] ERA 1996 ss 43C(1), 43D(b), 43F(1)(a), 43G(1)(a), 43H(1)(a). A similar requirement of good faith is contained in the protection against victimisation in SDA 1975 s 4, RRA 1976 s 2 and DDA 1995 s 55, discussed below at pp 193–5.

[37] ERA 1996 s 43D.

[38] J. Bowers, J. Mitchell and J. Lewis, *Whistleblowing: The New Law* (1999) Sweet and Maxwell, London, at 26.

employees would be discouraged from raising concerns in case they could not be substantiated.

By providing generous protection for those who raise serious public interest concerns internally within their organisation, the PIDA brings the law into line with the model for protection proposed in Chapter 2. There it was suggested that speech that remains internal to the business harms very few employer interests; if the matter is dealt with internally there will be only limited financial loss or loss of reputation, and there is no breach of confidence or loyalty. Even if some losses do arise, such as costs of investigation of false claims, where the subject matter of speech warrants it, it was suggested that protection of speech should be upheld. Given that it provides maximum protection for employees who raise relevant concerns internally, the PIDA can be said to make a significant contribution to meeting the requirements for good freedom of speech protection for employees set out in Chapter 2.

EXTERNAL DISCLOSURE

More contentious than the protection provided for internal disclosure is that for disclosure external to the organisation, as here the employer has more to lose. The protection is therefore much more limited, and is dependent, in essence, upon the employee having very good reason to disclose outside. There are two main limiting preconditions to the PIDA's protection for external disclosure. The Act sets out a limited number of good reasons for external disclosure, and imposes an obligation that the disclosure be reasonable in the circumstances.

Greater limitations on external disclosure are warranted, as the balance between employer and worker interests is more complex in these cases. If protection for internal disclosure can be viewed as a charter for troublemakers, how much more so protection for external disclosure. Employers clearly need to be protected against having confidential information discussed in public unless there is very good reason. If the worker is to be protected, then the public interest in external disclosure must be very clear. The PIDA addresses the complexity of this issue by providing various criteria which have to be met before protection is given. To an extent, these echo the factors considered at common law for determining whether disclosure is in the public interest. In addition, unlike internal disclosures which can be based on reasonable suspicion, external disclosure is only protected where the worker acts in the reasonable belief that the information disclosed and any allegations made are substantially true.[39] External disclosure of a bare suspicion would not be protected; the worker must believe that the allegation is actually true, and have reasonable grounds for that belief. Supporting evidence is probably necessary.

---

[39] ERA 1996 s 43G(1)(b).

Authorised Regulators

As part of the policy of discouraging unnecessary public disclosure of concerns, the PIDA provides greater protection to disclosure to regulatory bodies than to general external disclosure.[40] The PIDA makes provision for certain regulatory bodies to be prescribed by regulation, regulations that have been published in the Public Interest Disclosure (Prescribed Persons) Order 1999. Where a worker discloses a concern to a prescribed regulatory body, the disclosure is treated in much the same way as an internal disclosure, the only material difference being that the worker must believe that the allegation is true and cannot act on the basis only of suspicion. Under the 1999 Order, the Secretary of State has prescribed a number of regulatory bodies for the purposes of the Act, including the Financial Services Authority, the Health and Safety Executive, Director General of Fair Trading and the Commissioners of the Inland Revenue.[41] The 1999 Order prescribes both the regulatory bodies and the relevant concerns that can be reported to them. For example, the Treasury is prescribed for disclosure of concerns about the carrying on of insurance business.

Not all bodies that play a regulatory role appear in the list of prescribed bodies. For example, professional bodies such as the General Medical Council (GMC), and United Kingdom Central Council for Nursing, Midwifery and Health Visiting (UKCC), are not listed in the Order, even though they play a role in regulating the professional conduct of medical staff.[42] Moreover, the police do not count as a prescribed body, even though criminal behaviour ought to be reported to them. Any disclosure to an external body that is not prescribed under the 1999 Order would be treated as a general external disclosure, and would then be subject to the extra requirements that internal disclosure had been tried (or had not been tried for good reason) and that external disclosure is reasonable in the circumstances. However, where disclosure is made to an appropriate external body which is not in fact prescribed under the Order (for example, disclosure of concerns relating to nursing practice disclosed to the UKCC) it is likely that the reasonableness requirement will be met. Indeed in one of the early tribunal cases under the PIDA, the applicant disclosed concerns to his local authority's nursing home inspectorate and the Social Services Inspectorate, neither of which are prescribed by the 1999 Order. In the absence of an appropriate prescribed body, the employment tribunal found his external disclosures to these regulatory bodies to be reasonable.[43]

---

[40] ERA 1996 s 43F.

[41] The Public Interest Disclosure (Prescribed Persons) Order 1999 (SI 1999/1549).

[42] However, the Audit Commission is prescribed to receive concerns about fraud or value for money in the health service; and matters which may affect health and safety at work can be reported to the Health and Safety Executive. Disclosures can also be made directly to the Department of Health and are treated as internal disclosures.

[43] *Bladon v ALM Medical Services Ltd* (25/4/00 Case No 2405845/99).

The treatment of disclosures to authorised regulators closely parallels decisions at common law dealing with disclosure to relevant regulatory bodies. In such cases, courts have been more willing to find that disclosure serves the public interest, even where other factors might point to disclosure being unacceptable. In *Re a Company's Application*[44] there was no breach of confidence where an employee disclosed tax irregularities to the Inland Revenue and other financial irregularities to FIMBRA, even though the disclosure was motivated by malice, and it was not clear at the time of the hearing whether the facts reported were accurate or not.

As in the case of internal disclosure, the arguments in favour of generous protection for employees who report concerns to prescribed regulatory bodies are fairly incontrovertible. These bodies are specifically charged with regulating or investigating the relevant issues. To allow employers to penalise employees who help them would be to significantly impair their ability to fulfil this function. In Chapter 2 it was suggested that disclosure to a relevant regulatory body should be given the same protection as internal disclosure. Nonetheless, the PIDA in fact imposes on such disclosures the extra requirement that the employee reasonably believe that the allegation made is true, in contrast to the requirement for internal disclosure merely of a reasonable suspicion. Although this may be viewed as an unnecessary extra requirement (disclosures based on suspicion, backed by no reasonable belief in their truth, should be disposed of by the regulators fairly easily), it does reflect the aim of the PIDA to promote internal regulation as much as possible. It also reduces the chances of external regulators being inundated with spurious claims, which could be expensive to investigate, however well intentioned,[45] leaving them free to concentrate on those cases which have a reasonable factual basis.

OTHER EXTERNAL DISCLOSURES

The most obvious form of external disclosure is to the press, but this part of the Act is aimed at all disclosure external to the employing enterprise, such as to the police, MPs, a trade union or another person or external body with an interest in the concern. For example, a concern about abuse in a nursing home might be reported to Age Concern, and concerns about an individual patient in a home could be raised with a relative. Extra preconditions are set before protection is provided for these external disclosures, and they come in three stages. First, the worker has to make the allegations in good faith, and in the reasonable belief that they are true, and disclosure must not be made for the purposes of personal gain. Second, the worker must also have tried to raise the concern internally or with a prescribed regulatory body first, although protection will be granted without this if the worker reasonably

---

[44] [1989] Ch 477. See discussion in Chapter 4, p 141 above.
[45] Even internal disclosures must be made in good faith: s 43C(1).

believes that he will be victimised if he makes the disclosure internally, or he reasonably believes that evidence will be destroyed or concealed if raised internally, and there is no regulatory body with whom to raise the concern. Finally, in addition to meeting these requirements, one final condition is set, in that the disclosure must be reasonable in the circumstances.[46]

Preconditions to External Disclosure

Although it does not only apply to disclosure to the press, it is under this section that any such disclosure would need to be considered, and so, perhaps unsurprisingly, the restrictions on disclosure are far greater. This reflects the concern that disclosures on a wide scale should not be justified too readily, because they are more likely to be damaging to the employer's interests. The requirement for good faith and a reasonable belief in the truth of the allegation on the part of the person making the disclosure[47] is the same as for disclosures to prescribed regulatory bodies. In addition, for external disclosures the worker must not act for purposes of personal gain.

The denial of protection to those who make disclosure for personal gain[48] is understandable in this context. The provision is aimed at chequebook journalism and prevents disclosures made for payment, in cash, or in benefits in kind. Section 43L(2) provides an exception to the rule where a reward is payable under any enactment, preserving the right of organisations such as the Inland Revenue to continue to offer rewards for disclosure of relevant information.[49] Precisely what will be counted as disclosure for personal gain in other cases is, as yet, unclear. What does not appear to be covered is the worker who acts for mixed motives, and happens to make a personal gain as a result of his disclosure. For example, an employee may believe that a wrong should be reported but also think that he will be promoted as a result of the good citizenship displayed by his disclosure, thereby gaining financially. Presumably a court or tribunal would need to try to establish the 'primary' motive for disclosure and then limit protection in cases where the primary purpose is to make personal gain.

In considering in Chapter 2 the extent to which external disclosure should be provided with employment protection, it was suggested that in order for an employer's legitimate interest in confidentiality and its reputation to be properly protected there needs to be a good reason for the disclosure to be made outside the organisation. Again, the PIDA meets this requirement, by restricting protection for external disclosure to cases which have already been raised internally,[50] or where there is good reason to go outside immediately. The good reasons for direct external disclosure are where the worker reasonably fears victimisation for raising the concern either internally or with

---

[46] ERA 1996 s 43G.   [47] ERA 1996 s 43G(1)(a) and (b).
[48] ERA 1996 s 43G(1)(c).
[49] See proceedings of Standing Committee D, Hansard 11 March 1988.
[50] ERA 1996 s 43G(2)(c).

a prescribed regulator; and where there is no prescribed regulator and the worker reasonably believes that the evidence of wrongdoing or failure will be destroyed or concealed if it is raised internally.[51] Where either of these circumstances exist, it is obvious that protection should be given to those who choose to go outside the organisation with their concerns. Employers who deal with concerns sympathetically will not give reasonable grounds to workers to fear retaliation or a cover-up, and should thereby prevent external disclosure. Those who give reasonable cause to employees to fear retaliation or destruction of evidence will risk external disclosure; and any resulting sanction imposed by the employer may well qualify for unlimited compensation.

The good reasons for making a disclosure externally without prior internal disclosure are limited to fear of victimisation and of evidence being destroyed or concealed. One further good reason that is not included is the reasonable belief on the part of the worker that internal disclosure would serve no useful purpose. A 'no useful purpose' test would be not dissimilar to the test for exhaustion of domestic remedies in relation to applications to the ECtHR.[52] In such cases, applicants must satisfy the European Court that they have tried all domestic remedies, or, in the alternative, show that there was no point in claiming the domestic remedy as to do so would be futile. Similarly, it might be helpful for a worker to be able to claim that internal disclosure would serve no useful purpose, because he knew that the concern would not be taken seriously. Although the lack of a 'futility' justification for external disclosure may seem regrettable, a contrast can be drawn between the position of the ECHR and that under the PIDA. Under the PIDA, raising concerns internally should not take very long. If no evidence is destroyed, and no victimisation suffered, there can be little harm done by the short delay that may arise. In contrast, exhausting domestic legal proceedings in ECHR cases can take years. In those few cases under the PIDA where the delay caused by prior internal disclosure could cause significant harm to the public interest, it is likely that the issue will be very serious, and can then be dealt with under the separate section of the PIDA which deals with exceptionally serious issues and protects disclosure without any prior internal disclosure.

Where disclosure has already been made internally or to a prescribed regulator, this can give an alternative reason for external disclosure. In assessing the reasonableness of any subsequent external disclosure, the response of the employer will be considered.[53] Only where they do not deal with the matter adequately are they likely to become liable to compensate employees who are

---

[51] ERA 1996 s 43G(2)(a) and (b).

[52] D. Harris, M. O'Boyle and C. Warbrick, *The Law of the European Convention on Human Rights* (1995) Butterworths, London.

[53] ERA 1996 s 43G(3)(e).

penalised for going public. This allows employers a chance to avoid external disclosure and provides a clear incentive for them to deal with matters properly when raised internally.

Once the worker can show that the disclosure is made externally for a good reason, and that he is acting in good faith, not for purposes of personal gain, and has a reasonable belief in the truth of his allegation, the final question is whether, in all the circumstances, the decision to raise the matter externally is reasonable. The PIDA includes a list of factors that the court or tribunal should take into account in assessing reasonableness. These are based to an extent on the factors considered at common law on the question of whether disclosure serves the public interest. Although they arise in a slightly different context (the provision of employment protection as opposed to the decision on whether to allow publication at all) and so may operate a little differently, the close correlation between two sets of factors means that guidance on the expected interpretation of the PIDA can be taken from the case law on the duty of confidence that exists at common law, discussed in detail in Chapter 4.

Factors in Determining Reasonableness

The factors used to determine the reasonableness of a disclosure are the identity of the person to whom disclosure is made; the seriousness of the failure; whether the failure is continuing; whether disclosure is made in breach of a duty of confidence owed by the employer to another; where internal disclosure has been made, any action taken by the employer or the relevant regulatory body; and where there has been an initial internal disclosure, whether the worker had complied with internal whistleblowing procedures.[54]

The various factors listed interact with each other. For example, the more serious the issue, the more likely that wide external disclosure will be seen to be reasonable. This reflects the position at common law. For example, in *Lion Laboratories v Evans*,[55] concerning employees who disclosed to the press information casting doubt on the reliability of breathalyser machines, the Court considered that because of the serious nature of the information, the public interest was served by disclosure on such a wide scale. The information related to potential miscarriages of justice, and wide publicity was the best way for these to be avoided.

The third factor listed is whether the failure is continuing or not.[56] The suggestion here is that external disclosure is more likely to be reasonable if the failure or malpractice is current, or is likely to occur in the future. This has usually been the approach of the courts when considering the meaning of the public interest in disclosure at common law.[57] Using *Lion Laboratories* as the

---

[54]   ERA 1996 s 43G(3).   [55]   [1985] QB 526.   [56]   ERA 1996 s 43G(3)(c).
[57]   See discussion in Chapter 4, pp 135–7 above.

example again, the information about reliability of breathalysers could bring immediate benefit to any person facing criminal charges based on evidence from such machines, and so the court allowed its wide publication. Where a concern relates to a danger that may arise in the future, then again the courts have favoured disclosure.[58] Conversely, disclosures have been prevented on the ground that they relate to past wrongdoing. In *Schering Chemicals Ltd v Falkman Ltd*,[59] Shaw LJ referred to the fact that the drug 'Primodos' had been withdrawn from the market and that the immediate threat to health had therefore passed in deciding that the film about it should not be shown. However, there may well be times when it is reasonable to disclose past wrongdoing externally. After all, the fact that a risk is not current does not mean that public discussion serves no purpose. A disclosure of past wrongdoing may in some cases serve the public interest, and a worker who makes such a disclosure may deserve protection against victimisation. Clearly, whether the failure is continuing or impending is of relevance to the reasonableness of a disclosure, and so this factor is rightly included in the list of reasonableness factors in the Act. But its inclusion does not preclude a tribunal from finding that a disclosure of past malpractice is reasonable, and its presence as a reasonableness factor should not have the effect of deterring appropriate disclosures of past wrongdoing.

Where the need to disclose externally arises because internal mechanisms have been unsuccessful, the question of whether internal procedures for reporting have been complied with becomes relevant.[60] Where no other explanation for external disclosure is suggested, it is not unreasonable for the tribunal to consider whether internal procedures have been complied with. If they have not, this may provide an explanation for the adverse treatment of the worker. Conversely, and of more significance, if the employee has complied with an internal whistleblowing procedure, but the employer has not responded, it will be very likely that external disclosure will be reasonable. Alternatively, if the employer lacks a clear or fair policy, or has a policy that is not publicised within the workplace, so that the worker was, reasonably, unaware of it, this again will tend to show that external disclosure is reasonable.[61] The impact of this factor should be to provide employers with a strong incentive to respond to concerns and to institute fair internal procedures. If they wish to avoid the publicity of external disclosure, then internal mecha-

---

[58] See *Initial Services v Putterill* [1968] 1 QB 396, where Lord Denning held that the public interest exception to the duty of confidence should extend to 'crimes, frauds and misdeeds, both those actually committed as *well as those in contemplation*' (emphasis added); see also *Malone v Commissioner of Police* [1979] Ch 344 where Megarry V-C held that information relating to 'some apprehension of an impending chemical or other disaster' should, in the public interest, be disclosed.

[59] [1981] 2 WLR 848.   [60] ERA 1996 s 43G(3)(f).

[61] The lack of a whistleblowing policy was a factor in the decision by the employment tribunal that disclosure to an external body was reasonable in the ET decision in *Bladon v ALM Medical Services Ltd* (25/4/00 Case No 2405845/99).

nisms for reporting concerns need to be set up and publicised within the workplace; and employers need to take action on the concerns raised, or explain their reasons for not doing so.

One difficulty with the inclusion of this factor is that it can make the protection available appear to depend to a large degree on following correct procedures. A concern for procedural correctness can seem to overshadow the public interest in disclosure of the malpractice. On the other hand, a tribunal is not bound to decide that a disclosure is not protected merely because internal procedures were not followed. This is only one factor to be considered in deciding the matter.

Where a worker turns to external channels of disclosure after having tried internal disclosure or disclosure to a regulator, the court should of course consider the response of the employer or regulator.[62] An inadequate response will, in effect, make external disclosure more reasonable. The external disclosure must be of substantially the same information as that raised internally, in order for the initial internal disclosure to be able to give the employer a fair chance to respond appropriately. Section 43G(4), however, does allow the worker to include as part of a later external disclosure a comment on the failure or inadequacy of the response. This is clearly necessary if a worker is ever to be allowed to explain, externally, the reasons for choosing to raise the concern outside the organisation. Otherwise the additional comment, not having been made internally first, could give separate cause for victimisation. On the other hand, a good internal procedure should allow for a system of response and counter response to be given before the process is exhausted, and any employee reporting outside the organisation should comply with the full procedure first.[63]

The archetypal external disclosure, and that probably most feared by employers, is disclosure to newspapers or broadcasters, but it will be rare for it to be protected under PIDA. The fact that this is probably the form of disclosure most damaging to employers will mean that tribunals will need to be very clear that it was necessary before deciding that it is reasonable. The other reasonableness factors, such as the seriousness and urgency of the issue, will therefore need to point to wide disclosure. This will not unduly affect those who raise concerns about specific incidents of malpractice. They should be able to find some less public route to raise their concern, such as the police, MP or other interested body.

Those for whom this is a greater obstacle are workers engaged in political speech or principled dissent. In some cases of principled dissent or political speech, the subject matter will be covered by the PIDA. But even where the subject matter is protected, the method of disclosure (the media is likely to be

---

[62] ERA 1996 s 43G(3)(e).

[63] If exhaustion of the full procedure would cause unacceptable delays in disclosure, perhaps because it is unnecessarily long, then this may make disclosure reasonable in the circumstances, even though the full procedure had not been completed.

essential to their cause) makes it difficult to show that the disclosure is reasonable. For example, a member of nursing staff wanting to take part in a public debate on standards of care in the NHS is unlikely to be protected. Although in this case the subject matter may be covered, the health and safety of a person being endangered if standards are not adequate, it may be rare for the issue to be viewed as serious or urgent enough to be disclosed on such a wide basis.

The decision on the reasonableness of external disclosure is really the only area of the PIDA that is open to the discretion of the tribunal or court hearing the case. The list of criteria is not an exclusive one; it is just stated that the tribunal must consider those issues 'in particular'. Other issues such as vindictive motive, disruption caused at work, financial loss caused to the employer, and the status of the employer and the employee, matters discussed as relevant to the right to free speech about work and the employer's reasonableness defence in Chapter 2, could all be considered by a tribunal after it had given particular regard to the matters listed. Moreover, although the matters listed may be based on those considered at common law on the issue of the existence of a public interest in disclosure, it may well be that the list will operate somewhat differently in the context of the provision of employment protection.

It is only in relation to the reasonableness of an external disclosure that arguments about the importance of free speech can hold any sway, the other sections of the PIDA not really containing any element of discretion for the court or tribunal. Similarly, this is the main area of the PIDA with scope for judicial interpretation, interpretation that will have to develop in line with the case law of the ECHR, in accordance with the HRA 1998.[64] The protection available to freedom of speech, and the need for any restriction to be proportionate to its aim, will both have to inform the courts' thinking on whether any particular external disclosure is reasonable.

Using arguments based on the ECHR might give limited scope for some forms of speech other than pure whistleblowing to be protected under PIDA. If an issue can be said to come within the qualifying subject matters and as long as an attempt has been made to raise the issue internally first, it might be open to a court to find that it is reasonable for a speech with political overtones to be made in public, for example via the media. This is particularly the case because of the requirement for special protection for political speech (and the wide interpretation of that category of speech) under the jurisprudence of the ECHR. The argument is most likely to have an impact on speech relating to politically sensitive issues such as the state of the National Health Service. Taking the NHS as an example, it can be readily shown to relate to a qualifying subject matter, health of individuals being endangered. If the issue

---

[64] See discussion in Chapter 3, pp 69–78 above.

is raised internally, and receives what the worker believes to be an inadequate response, he may wish to raise and comment on the matter in public. If that speech has political implications, for example it refers to central health care policies, then it might be open to a court to find that the speech is reasonable, taking into account the requirements of the ECHR to give special protection to political speech, even though at first sight it does not appear to meet the reasonableness criteria set out in s 43G(3). However, the approach of the ECtHR to the protection of freedom of speech at work has not been particularly extensive,[65] and regard to its jurisprudence on this issue will certainly not guarantee acceptance of such an interpretation by the courts.

EXCEPTIONALLY SERIOUS MALPRACTICE

Where the matter disclosed is of an exceptionally serious nature, the PIDA removes most of the preconditions to protection, in recognition that the public interest can override most other interests.[66] Prior internal disclosure is not needed, nor is a belief in victimisation or destruction of evidence necessary to explain that lack of internal disclosure. Protection is automatic where the worker acts in good faith, reasonably believes in the truth of the allegation, does not act for personal gain and it is reasonable to make the disclosure.

In Committee stage the Act was amended to make the need for reasonableness of disclosure a precondition to protection. It was introduced because of fears that the section may otherwise be open to abuse, where a worker with a serious concern could be protected even when acting unreasonably, such as by disclosing to the press without trying first to use less damaging ways to raise the concern. The section now requires that the disclosure be reasonable in the circumstances, and states that in determining reasonableness regard shall be given to the identity of the person to whom the disclosure is made. The tribunal is not required to consider the other factors of reasonableness relevant to external disclosures. It is arguable that this provision really serves no purpose, other than to appease those concerned that the overall balance of the Act was too favourable to workers. In practice, it is hard to imagine when external disclosure would be unreasonable, assuming that the concern was serious enough. Presumably if a tribunal thought that the manner of disclosure was inappropriate, it may in fact not think the matter exceptionally serious in the first place.

This leads on to the main difficulty in relation to the disclosure of exceptionally serious concerns. It is obvious that an exception to the fairly strict rules on external disclosure is needed in cases of great seriousness but it is not at all obvious when a concern will be classed as 'exceptionally serious'. Only one example of an exceptionally serious matter is given by Public Concern at

---

[65] See Chapter 3.   [66] ERA 1996 s 43H.

Work in their consultation paper on PIDA and that is sexual abuse of a child.[67] However, guidance is not given about what type of external disclosure would be reasonable in such a case. Is disclosure to the media envisaged, or disclosure to the police or an organisation such as the NSPCC? Given the rather different preconditions that exist for protection of external disclosure in general and external disclosure of exceptionally serious matters, it might be helpful to have more guidance on the face of the Act on what will be viewed as *exceptionally* serious, as opposed to just serious. Any guidance will now need to come from the tribunals before whom cases appear.

REMOVAL OF GAGGING CLAUSES

In addition to protecting from dismissal or other detriment for making protected disclosures, the PIDA provides that agreements to prevent employees from making disclosures which would be covered by the Act ('gagging clauses') are void.[68] The restriction on contractual agreements only applies to disclosures that would be covered by the PIDA. Thus an employer could make a valid contractual requirement on an employee not to disclose to the media, even though a requirement not to contact a regulator would be void, disclosure to the media being unlikely to be reasonable except in the most serious of cases.

This provision is important. Gagging clauses are often included in settlement and severance agreements, so that the employee receives compensation, but is prohibited from raising his concern, even with a regulator. Staff are prevented from speaking even after the end of their employment. Those anxious to gain some compensation for their dismissal have had little option but to sign such clauses. Now they are illegal. In effect, employers can no longer prevent staff from raising public interest matters during employment by penalising them for doing so, nor can they impose contractual obligations to prevent disclosures which serve the public interest after the end of their employment.

CONCLUSION

The Public Interest Disclosure Bill, when before the House of Lords, was praised by Lord Nolan as 'skilfully achieving the essential but delicate balance . . . between the public interest and the interests of employers'[69] and there is no doubt that the provision of clear employment protection for workers who blow the whistle on wrongdoing or malpractice at work can only improve the rights to free speech about work. As far as whistleblowing speech is concerned, the PIDA meets with most of the requirements suggested in Chapter 2 for free speech employment protection. It provides extensive

---

[67] Consultation Paper on Richard Shepherd's Public Interest Disclosure Bill (1997) Public Concern at Work, London.
[68] Section 43J.   [69] Hansard, HL Vol 590, col 614.

protection for those whose speech serves clear audience interests by disclosing public interest matters, while protecting the legitimate interests of employers by imposing the requirement of good faith and fairly strict procedural requirements in all but the most serious of cases.

However, a number of matters leave the ultimate success of the Act in question. First, the different procedural requirements for different types of disclosure, whilst necessary to achieve a fair balance between the interests of employers and employees, mean that the drafting of the Act is very complex, with a strong emphasis on procedure. The danger is that, without fairly specialised legal advice, workers could remain unsure of whether they are protected. They may then be deterred from raising a legitimate concern for fear that they may not use the correct procedure.

Secondly, the Act does not explicitly address the fact that cases may fail because of a failure to prove a causal link between disclosure and dismissal or detriment suffered. The evidential burden of proving that there was a fair reason for the dismissal will fall on the employer, once the employee has adduced evidence showing that there was an automatically unfair reason for the dismissal.[70] Although the burden of proof is favourable to employees, it will not be of great help if employers are too easily able to establish an alternative reason for the dismissal other than the protected disclosure. This is most likely to be the case if tribunals or courts accept too readily that the reason for dismissal was the manner and circumstances of a disclosure rather than the fact of disclosure itself. Experience in relation to other types of automatically unfair dismissal suggests that proving a causal link between dismissal and the protected action can be difficult, despite the fact that the burden of proof is the same for all automatically unfair dismissals. *Shillito v Van Leer (UK) Ltd*[71] involved the protection against dismissal or action short of dismissal for health and safety representatives who carry out their duties.[72] Shillito, a trade union shop steward and safety representative, had been disciplined after he had raised a concern, in a belligerent manner, about safety on one of the production lines at his workplace. His claim under the provisions providing employment protection for health and safety representatives was unsuccessful. One of the reasons for finding the dismissal fair was that Shillito was the safety representative for 'line 8' and the safety problem with which he became involved was on 'line 6'. He was not therefore disciplined for acting as a safety representative.[73] Similar difficulties have been

---

[70] Confirmed in the ET case *Fernandes v Netcom Consultants (UK) Ltd* (18/5/00, Case No 2200060/00).

[71] [1997] IRLR 495.   [72] Now under ERA 1996 ss 100 and 44.

[73] One should not read too much into this case, in the light of the comments in the EAT judgment that Shillito was not genuinely pursuing a health and safety matter, but was rather acting in bad faith, with the intention of embarrassing the company. Nonetheless, this was not the only reason for the decision in the case, the other reason being that he was not acting as a safety representative.

experienced by those who raise concerns about race or sex discrimination.[74] Applicants have been unsuccessful where employers have shown that the reason for dismissal was not the raising of a concern *per se*, but the manner in which it was raised.[75]

If the causal link between a protected act and dismissal can be broken too easily, by pointing to other reasons for dismissal, this will undermine the potential for the legislation to provide adequate protection to employees. It is to be hoped that courts will not take a narrow approach to causation when using the PIDA. Under the PIDA, a dismissal is automatically unfair where the making of a protected disclosure is its reason, or its principal reason.[76] The situation might be improved if it had been expressly provided that a dismissal would be unfair as long as the protected disclosure was *one* of the reasons for the dismissal. Alternatively, the example of the USA could have been followed. The Whistleblower Protection Act 1989[77] requires only that the employee show that the whistleblowing was a *contributing factor* to the dismissal. This can be shown by pointing to circumstantial evidence, such as that dismissal followed swiftly after disclosure and that the employer knew of the disclosure. The burden of proof then shifts to the employer who can only avoid liability by showing, by *clear and convincing evidence*, that the dismissal would have taken place even without the whistleblowing. Although the experience in the USA indicates that proving causation remains a major hurdle for employees even after changes to the burden of proof,[78] such an approach might at least have gone some way to improve the ability of employees to prove their cases under the Act.

Some of the difficulties in showing causation may be overcome if courts and tribunals are willing to draw inferences about causation in the same way as they are able in cases under the Sex Discrimination Act 1975 and Race Relations Act 1976. In discrimination cases it is recognised that the discriminator is very unlikely to admit the discrimination. In *Baker v Cornwall County Council*[79] the Court of Appeal pointed out that if alternative explanations for the discriminator's behaviour are accepted too readily, then it will often be very difficult to prove the complainant's case. Instead, the Court suggested that tribunals should be prepared to draw the inference that there has been discrimination in cases where the circumstances are consistent with discrimination, unless the alleged discriminator can show otherwise. In *Owen and Briggs v James*,[80] the Court of Appeal held that a finding that a racial consideration was an important factor in a decision is sufficient to found a case

---

[74] Protected under the Sex Discrimination Act s 4, and the Race Relations Act s 2.

[75] *British Airways Engine Overhaul Ltd v Francis* [1981] IRLR 9 EAT and *Re York Truck Equipment Ltd*, Industrial Relations Legal Information Bulletin 20 February 1990, p 11.

[76] ERA 1996 s 103A.   [77] 5 USC 2320.

[78] See 'Whistleblower Protection: Determining whether reprisal occurred remains difficult', October 1992, US General Accounting Office.

[79] [1990] IRLR 194.   [80] [1982] IRLR 503.

of discrimination. A similar approach in whistleblowing cases would assist employees to succeed in their claims under PIDA. Clearly, tribunals must allow defences to succeed where appropriate, but the ease with which an alternative explanation can be given also needs to be recognised. In one of the early cases heard under PIDA, the Employment Tribunal drew this analogy with discrimination cases and stressed the need for tribunals to be willing to draw inferences from the evidence. Where an employee has made a protected disclosure which has been followed by dismissal, tribunals should be willing to infer that the reason for the dismissal was the disclosure, unless the employer can give an explanation that stands up to close scrutiny.[81]

The third limitation with the PIDA is that it does not protect the worker whose disclosure involves the commission of an offence.[82] This excludes from its protection those who breach the Official Secrets Act 1989 (OSA). Given the wide ambit of information covered by the OSA, this may be a significant limitation. Clearly, employment protection is not deserved where the disclosure made threatens national security, but that does not warrant the exclusion of all information covered by the OSA from the PIDA. The OSA prohibits the disclosure of information relating to a variety of issues such as security and intelligence, defence and international relations.[83] Disclosures relating to security and intelligence are prohibited regardless of whether they are damaging, whereas disclosures about defence and international relations must be damaging before they are prohibited. In those cases which require damage, one could argue that a disclosure that is in the public interest and otherwise covered by PIDA cannot be damaging in any sense, as a disclosure which serves the public interest cannot also damage the state.[84] However, the definition of damage in the OSA varies according to the type of information disclosed,[85] and it is not at all clear that such an argument would be successful. This is likely to remain the case even after the legislation is interpreted in the light of the ECHR, because of the wide margin of appreciation granted to states in cases with national security implications.[86]

Whilst the exclusion of workers who commit an offence limits the reach of PIDA, its impact should not be overstated. It should be noted that those who raise matters covered by the OSA internally within Whitehall or with the Civil Service Commissioner[87] will not commit an offence under the OSA, and so

---

[81] *Fernandes v Netcom Consultants (UK) Ltd* (18/5/00, Case No 2200060/00).

[82] ERA 1996 s 43B(3).

[83] Other types of information covered are: information obtained in confidence from other states or from international organisations; information likely to result in an offence or other related consequences; and special investigations under statutory warrant. OSA 1989 ss 1–6.

[84] On the meaning of the state see *R v Ponting* [1985] Crim LR 318.

[85] The definitions of when a disclosure is damaging contained in the Official Secrets Act s 1(4) (security and intelligence information), s 2(2) (defence information), and s 3(2) (information about international relations) are all different.

[86] See Chapter 3.   [87] Under the Civil Service Code, para 12.

will be protected by the almost automatic protection that PIDA provides for internal disclosures. Moreover, before the restriction applies, it must be shown either that the whistleblower has been convicted under the OSA, or that an offence under the OSA has been committed. Where criminal proceedings are in progress or are expected, a tribunal should await the outcome before deciding a case under PIDA. Where no criminal proceedings are expected, the tribunal itself should use the high standard of proof required by the criminal courts to assess whether an offence has been committed.[88] If it seems that no offence has been committed under the OSA, for example because one of the limited defences available under the OSA[89] might apply to the employee's case, tribunals should not exclude the protection offered by PIDA. In effect, unless the employer can show, using the criminal standard of proof, that an offence under the OSA has been committed, it seems that the PIDA will continue to apply.

In addition to the restrictions where offences are committed, staff who work for the security services face an absolute restriction on their use of the PIDA, as those whose work involves national security and intelligence are not covered.[90] This exclusion applies regardless of the type of information disclosed, and of any damage it could cause. This could mean, for example, that the internal disclosure of corruption in the awarding of a cleaning contract made by the security services would be excluded from the coverage of the PIDA, despite the fact that there are no national security implications involved. It might have been preferable to exclude these exceptions in the PIDA, and in their place add to the factors affecting reasonableness the question of whether or not a disclosure breaches the criminal law. Any disclosure that threatened national security would clearly not be reasonable and therefore would not be protected.

One final restriction on the protection provided by the PIDA is that it only protects workers against dismissal or other detriments imposed at work. There is no protection for those who are refused work because they are known to have made protected disclosures in the past.[91] If a worker raises a concern which then attracts a large amount of publicity, finding new employment may be very difficult, as new employers may be reluctant to employ someone who is known to have made disclosures previously. Even where the particular case has not gained general publicity, notoriety may be gained in the particular sector in which the whistleblower works which may cause him difficulties in finding new work, for example workers in the NHS and in the education sector. An example of such a case is Dr Stephen Bolsin, the anaes-

---

[88] This is the view of Guy Dehn in his commentary in *Current Law Statutes Annotated* where he cites the view of the government spokesman Lord Haskell (Hansard HL 5 June 1998 col 616).

[89] E.g. the defence under s 7. See further Chapter 6 below.

[90] ERA 1996 s 193.

[91] D. Lewis, 'The Public Interest Disclosure Act 1998' (1998) 27 ILJ 325.

thetist who raised questions about the high mortality rates of child heart patients at the Bristol Royal Infirmary.[92] After raising the concerns he found himself shunned by the medical community and went to work abroad.[93] The concerns were found to be well founded in the public inquiry which followed, but his difficulty in getting new work preceded the wide publicity over the affair. If the PIDA had included a remedy against prospective employers refusing to employ someone who had made a qualifying disclosure, it would have provided protection for cases such as Dr Bolsin's in the future.

Despite the fact that the PIDA does have these limitations, it should not be viewed too pessimistically. In particular, the strong message sent to workers and employers by the very existence of the Act is that free speech should not end at the factory gate or office door, and that workers can make a significant contribution to the public interest if they exercise their rights within the ambit of the Act. Although the PIDA does not protect employee speech by creating a right to speak, limited only where the employer can show that dismissal is proportionate, as suggested in Chapter 2 above, the overall effect of the Act is very similar. One of the advantages of the creation of such a right was that it would give certainty to the employee, avoiding the uncertainty inherent in a more general balancing approach. By providing that those who meet the subject matter specification and the procedural requirements will be automatically protected against dismissal, the PIDA creates this level of certainty. As acknowledged in Chapter 2, it is impossible to avoid all balancing of interests, and the PIDA contains an implicit balance in the test of reasonableness in s 43G(3). However, this will need to be interpreted taking into account the jurisprudence of the ECHR under the HRA 1998, and accordingly issues of proportionality may be introduced into the assessment of reasonableness. Moreover, the central thrust of PIDA is that those who report concerns internally, or, with good reason, externally, will be protected. With this reassurance, more employees should feel safe to raise legitimate concerns that affect the public interest.

The PIDA is directed only at whistleblowing, although it is possible that in some circumstances employees might be able to make use of the protection for other forms of speech. However, in general, those employees whose exercise of free speech does not come within the scope of the PIDA will be dependent for employment protection on the general law on unfair dismissal, discussed in the next section of this chapter.

FREE SPEECH AND UNFAIR DISMISSAL

The general law on unfair dismissal, not having been designed for public interest dismissals, is far less helpful in terms of providing protection for the right to free speech than the PIDA. In the first place, the qualifying

---

[92] See discussion in Chapter 1, pp 5–6 above.   [93] *The Guardian*, 30 May 1998.

conditions are more onerous. The protection only applies to employees[94] who must have worked for a year before being granted protection.[95] Secondly, there is no automatic assumption of unfairness, the issue being determined by the Employment Tribunal. Thirdly, the protection only applies to dismissal and not to other detriment short of dismissal. Finally, the remedies for unfair dismissal are more limited. Reinstatement and re-engagement are possible remedies but are rarely granted,[96] and interim relief is not available. Compensation is limited and although the financial limit has been lifted to £50,000 and is index linked,[97] this may still not allow for full compensation to be made, particularly where employees are highly paid. The PIDA is thus clearly the best avenue of protection for those who can come within its terms, principally those who blow the whistle on wrongdoing at work.

The general unfair dismissal law is only likely to be used by those whose actions fall outside the scope of the PIDA, in particular those whose speech is classified as principled dissent, political speech or general comment, all forms of speech which may not come within the specified subjects listed in the Act. Because of its limited application to free speech, a full analysis of the operation of the law on unfair dismissal will not be undertaken in this chapter, and only those parts of the law which may be used by employees exercising the right to free speech outside the bounds of the PIDA will be considered. An assumption will be made that free speech has been exercised in a way that the employer finds unacceptable, for example because it involves a criticism of employer practices or policy. Clearly there will be cases where employee speech will not serve the public interest, and may interfere with the financial or managerial interests of the employer sufficiently for dismissal to be proportionate according to the criteria discussed in Chapter 2. However, the focus of this chapter is on the protection available under unfair dismissal legislation for speech that serves wider audience interests.

The statutory protection against unfair dismissal operates on a separate basis from the common law. A dismissal can be fair even though it involves a breach of contract by the employer; conversely, a dismissal can be unfair even when the employee acts in breach of contract. Thus, where an employee is dismissed for exercising the right to free speech, deciding whether or not the

---

[94] See S. Deakin and G. Morris, *Labour Law* (2001) Butterworths, London, at 148–168 on identifying who is an employee.

[95] The qualifying period was reduced from two years to one year in June 1999. The Unfair Dismissal and Statement of Reasons (Variation of Qualifying Period) Order 1999, SI 1999/1476.

[96] Reinstatement and re-engagement have been ordered in less than 5% of cases. However, Dickens et al argue that reinstatement or re-engagement could be ordered more often and that the assumption that employees do not favour these remedies may be false. L. Dickens, M. Jones, B. Weekes and M. Hart, *Dismissed: A Study of Unfair Dismissal and the Industrial Tribunal System* (1985) Blackwell, Oxford.

[97] Employment Relations Act 1999 s 34. This section was brought into force on 14 October 1999 (The Employment Relations Act 1999 (Commencement No 2 and Transitional and Savings Provisions) Order 1999).

speech amounted to a breach of contract will not resolve the issue of fairness. The question may be relevant, however, to deciding whether there was a fair reason for the dismissal in the first place.

Where an employee brings a claim for unfair dismissal, it must first be shown that there has been a dismissal. The onus then shifts to the employer to show that there was a fair reason to dismiss. The potentially fair reasons are limited to those listed in ERA 1996 s 98, namely the capability or qualification of the employee, the conduct of the employee, the fact that the employee is redundant, that the continued employment of the employee is illegal, or some other substantial reason that justifies the dismissal of a person holding the position that the employee held.[98] This last reason acts as a catch-all provision that can be used to cover almost any reason for dismissal, and together with 'the conduct of the employee' is the most applicable reason in the context of freedom of speech and work. Where the employer can show that the dismissal was for one of the fair reasons, then the tribunal decides whether the dismissal was fair or unfair, having regard to the reasons shown by the employer and looking at whether, in the circumstances (including the size and administrative resources of the employer's undertaking), the employer acted reasonably or unreasonably in treating the reason as sufficient reason for dismissing the employee, and this is determined in accordance with the equity and substantial merits of the case.[99]

The test of fairness contained in the legislation is of key importance in assessing the extent to which a dismissal for exercising the right to free speech will be fair or unfair. The intention was to make the test neutral as between the parties and so it is worded to ensure that the burden of proving fairness does not rest on either party. However, when the decisions of tribunals are examined it is clear that the neutrality of the legislation is somewhat elusive. The fairness or unfairness of the decision to treat the reason as sufficient to dismiss is a question of fact;[100] it is not the job of the tribunal to substitute its own judgment for that of the employer. It has long been accepted that there may be a range of employer responses that are reasonable and fair and that as long as the employer's decision to dismiss does not fall outside that range the decision will be fair.[101] In effect the benchmark against which the fairness of an employer's response has been tested is that of other employers. Where it has been shown that many employers react in a certain manner to particular types of conduct the tribunal does not have to find the reaction unfair, even though the decision may be harsh.[102] Given that it is

---

[98] ERA s 98(1) and (2).   [99] ERA s 98 (4).   [100] *UCATT v Brain* [1981] IRLR 224.
[101] *Rolls Royce Ltd v Walpole* [1980] IRLR 343. *Richmond Precision Engineering Ltd v Pearce* [1985] IRLR 179.
[102] See *Saunders v Scottish National Camps* [1980] IRLR 174 and *Mathewson v R.B. Dental Laboratories* [1988] IRLR 512. See also, H. Collins, *Justice in Dismissal* (1992) Clarendon Press, Oxford, Chapter 1. In *Haddon v Van Den Bergh Foods Ltd* [1999] IRLR 672 the employment tribunal found the decision to be 'harsh in the extreme', but still found it fair.

likely that most employers will not react well to employees who use the right of free speech to speak against employer practices or policies, dismissal may well be viewed as within the range of reasonable responses for an average employer.

The 'range of reasonable responses' test of fairness adopted in *Iceland Frozen Foods v Jones*[103] has been criticised for merely reflecting current employer standards, rather than setting good standards.[104] Employment tribunal members are prohibited from assessing whether they think that the employer acted correctly. Instead they must decide whether the employer's actions can be fair, according to the standard of the reasonable employer. If the tribunal substitutes its own view of fairness for that of the employer, the decision will be open to appeal, and tribunal findings can be overruled on this basis. The job of the tribunal is only to assess the employer's actions in the light of current management and industrial practice.[105] Moreover, by accepting that there may be a 'range' of reasonable responses, tribunals effectively accept that fairness may be of varying standards, and that practices which fall below, and even well below, the standards of best practice can still be fair. It is open to employers to argue that although their actions were not ideal, when one takes into account commercial or other factors, they were within the range of responses that can be expected of reasonable employers.[106]

The difficulties presented to employees by this interpretation of the test of fairness have long been recognised,[107] and were recently challenged by the Employment Appeal Tribunal in *Haddon v Van Den Bergh Foods Ltd*.[108] However, the challenge was short lived, and after a year of uncertainty, the original 'range of reasonable responses test' was confirmed by the Court of Appeal.[109] In attempting to change the test of fairness for unfair dismissal, Mr Justice Morison pointed out that in practice the test allows only perverse employment decisions to be found unfair. As fairly extreme views of reasonableness are taken as being within the range it becomes very difficult to show that a dismissal was unfair. In effect, the position had been reached whereby a dismissal is fair unless no reasonable employer could decide to dismiss in the circumstances in question. This amounted, in his view, to a test of perversity, and was a long way from the wording of the statute with its reference to the equity and substantial merits of the case. This judgment was followed in a number of other cases,[110] suggesting that many in the employment tribunals

---

[103] [1982] IRLR 439.

[104] 'the concept of fairness . . . becomes norm-reflecting rather than norm-setting'. P. Elias, 'Fairness in Unfair Dismissal: Trends and Tensions' (1981) 10 ILJ 201 at 213.

[105] *Iceland Frozen Foods v Jones* [1982] IRLR 439.

[106] H. Collins, *Justice in Dismissal* (1992) Clarendon Press, Oxford, at 38.

[107] See, for example, P. Elias, 'Fairness in Unfair Dismissal: Trends and Tensions' (1981) 10 ILJ 201, and Collins, *Justice in Dismissal*.

[108] [1999] IRLR 672.

[109] *Post Office v Foley, HSBC Bank (formerly Midland Bank) v Madden* [2000] IRLR 827 CA.

[110] *Midland Bank v Madden* (2000) IRLR 288 and *Wilson v Ethicon* (2000) IRLR 4.

are unhappy with the range of reasonable responses test, because it sets too low a standard of review in employment cases.

In *Post Office v Foley, HSBC Bank (formerly Midland Bank) v Madden*[111] the Court of Appeal set aside these rulings in the interests of certainty, and re-asserted the range of reasonable responses test. In doing so, they asserted that the test does not amount to a test of perversity. However, it is difficult to see how the range of reasonable responses test differs much from a test of perversity. Decisions to dismiss are fair unless they are outside the range of reasonable employer responses. In effect, unless no reasonable employer would dismiss, the dismissal will be fair. Despite clear evidence that the test is operating in effect as a perversity test, with tribunals ruling that dismissals can be harsh, but still fair, the Court of Appeal pointed out that the range of reasonable responses test has a long pedigree, and Parliament has never chosen to amend it, despite ample opportunity to do so. It seems that the reasonable response test with all its faults is here to stay for some time.

Even though the test of fairness used is favourable to the employer, the un-fair dismissal legislation nonetheless does provide a degree of protection for employees, and may well be of some use for employees dismissed for exercis-ing the right to free speech at work. The legislation has curbed unfair em-ployer behaviour by requiring that there be a reason for the dismissal that can, in principal, be fair, before the fairness of the actual dismissal is assessed. Those that are most appropriate in the context of freedom of speech are the conduct and the catch-all 'some other substantial reason justifying the dis-missal'. These two reasons, and the way in which the test of fairness operates in relation to each, will be considered in turn.

CONDUCT AND FAIR DISMISSAL

The reason for dismissal is not limited to misconduct, but is phrased 'the con-duct of the employee', and so can include conduct which is not technically misconduct nor a breach of contract. In most cases, however, dismissals under this heading will involve some form of misconduct, although the ulti-mate fairness of any dismissal will await application of the test of fairness to all the circumstances of the case. There is a substantial overlap between mis-conduct and breach of the employment contract. Most breaches of contract will amount to misconduct, although some may be too minor to warrant the term: and the implied duty of trust and confidence owed by the employee to the employer means that most cases of misconduct at work will amount to a breach of contract.

Although most employment contracts do not include express terms on freedom of speech, the implied duty of trust and confidence owed to the em-ployer may involve some restrictions on the employee's freedom of speech.

---

[111] [2000] IRLR 827 CA.

For example, it is likely that if the employee publicly criticises the employer, this will be viewed as a breach of the duty of trust and confidence by the employee. However, whether or not it is termed misconduct, or even a breach of contract, this behaviour may amount to conduct of the employee that gives rise to a valid reason for dismissal.

Moreover, even where the exercise of speech takes place outside the workplace and outside working hours, it could still give grounds for a potentially fair dismissal based on conduct. There is nothing in the legislation that limits the fair reasons to matters that take place at work. A comparison can be drawn with cases where a criminal offence, unconnected with work, has given rise to a dismissal. Such dismissals can be fair.[112] The ACAS Code of Practice on Disciplinary and Grievance Procedures makes clear that such dismissals are not to be treated as automatically fair, although the code points out that dismissal may be appropriate in cases where an offence makes the individual unsuitable for his or her type of work.[113] Although this refers to criminal conduct outside the workplace, the same approach may well be taken in relation to other external conduct which the employer considers to have an impact inside the workplace. Speech that bears no relation to the workplace and which takes place outside working hours is unlikely to give rise to an adverse employer reaction. But if the speech relates to work, or if the speech has an impact on other employees, perhaps leading to disruption of the workplace due to the unpopularity of the views expressed, this may give rise to a potentially fair reason for dismissal based on the conduct of the employee, even though that conduct did not take place on work premises or in working time.

As was noted in Chapter 4, where the exercise of free speech serves the public interest, no breach of the implied contractual duties will have taken place. In fact, leaving aside the issue of breach of contract, it will be hard to argue that speech that serves the public interest amounts to misconduct, or to conduct which justifies dismissal. In such a case, there may be no potentially fair reason for dismissal. However, in cases of free speech that do not involve whistleblowing, and which are not covered by the PIDA, it is less likely that a court or tribunal will find that the speech serves the public interest, even though the argument can be made at a philosophical level.[114] In such cases, the conduct of taking part in the speech will mean that the dismissal will be potentially fair. However, the Employment Tribunal will still need to assess the fairness of the dismissal in the circumstances, and it may well be that issues such as the public interest in the speech can be considered again at this stage of the process.

When it comes to assessing the fairness of conduct dismissals, the main issues are lack of a fair procedure and inconsistency on the part of the employer in treating the conduct as a reason to dismiss. Particular problems can arise where the employer believes there to have been misconduct at the time of dis-

---

[112] *Mathewson v R.B. Dental Laboratories* [1988] IRLR 512.
[113] ACAS Code of Practice on Disciplinary and Grievance Procedures para 26 (2000).
[114] See Chapter 2.

missal yet it is subsequently discovered that there was in fact no misconduct, perhaps because of the later discovery that the public interest was served by the disclosure.

Fair Procedure

The test of fairness is usually interpreted to require that dismissals are carried out using a fair procedure.[115] This will be so even though the public interest is not served by the disclosure and the whistleblowing involves a breach of contract. Even where there is no contractual right to a particular form of hearing, a fair dismissal will need to be preceded by a system of warnings before the final sanction of dismissal is imposed. However, in cases of dismissal for gross misconduct there is no need for warnings to be given, and summary dismissal without notice can be fair.

Consistency

There are two elements to the need for consistency: the employer must act consistently as between different employees in similar situations, and there must be consistency between the reason given for dismissal and the treatment of the employee. In *Post Office v Fennell*,[116] the employee's dismissal for assault of a fellow employee was held to be unfair as the employers had not dismissed other employees for similar conduct in the past. This rule applies regardless of the 'human agency' through which the employer acts, and so the fact that different decisions are taken by different individual managers will not excuse the employer.[117]

The employer also needs to be consistent in relation to any disciplinary action taken. An employer who chooses to ignore an incident of speech and then takes severe action such as dismissal on a later occasion may have difficulty showing that the dismissal is fair. If no formal warning or other action is taken at first, it is hard to argue that subsequent outright dismissal is appropriate;[118] if disclosure is so serious that it warrants dismissal, the employer needs to explain the lack of action on the first incident. On the other hand, if an employer reacts to a first incident with immediate dismissal, a tribunal may feel that the action is unfair, for lack of a fair system of warnings. Employers must therefore act as consistently as possible as between different employees and in relation to different incidents of speech if they are to avoid findings of unfair dismissal, even where the speech gives grounds for dismissal on the basis of conduct.

Employer's Belief in Misconduct

Where it is unclear whether there has been misconduct in a particular case, an employer can dismiss fairly as long as there are reasonable grounds for the belief that there has been misconduct. Where an employer suspects that the

---

[115] See, for example, *Lovie Ltd v Anderson* [1999] IRLR 164.
[116] [1981] IRLR 221.   [117] *Cain v Leeds Western HA* [1990] IRLR 168.
[118] See *F.S. Investment Services v Lawson* [1991] IRLIB 426, 12–13.

employee is guilty of misconduct such as theft from the workplace, the dismissal can be fair if it was based on a genuine and reasonable belief that the employee dismissed was the culprit, even though the truth of the matter, proved after the dismissal, is that the employee was not.[119]

The reasonableness of the employer's belief is judged according to the facts known to the employer *at the time the decision to dismiss was taken*. It is not open to an employer to rely on information acquired after the event to demonstrate that the dismissal was fair.[120] This can work to the employee's advantage where the employer subsequently discovers additional misconduct that could have given rise to a fair reason to dismiss had it been known at the time. However, the rule can also work harshly on the employee, who cannot rely on later information to show that the dismissal was unfair. If the employer reasonably believed that the employee was guilty of misconduct at the time of the dismissal, the fairness of the dismissal is judged on the assumption that the employer's belief was correct, even though it later transpires that there was no misconduct.

This is likely to cause significant problems in free speech cases where the public interest in speech is difficult to determine. The question of whether speech was justified or not, and therefore whether there was misconduct or not, cannot easily be determined without a court hearing in which all aspects of the case are weighed and considered, and it can be hard to predict the outcome of the balancing exercise involved. However, the employer is faced with a situation which may need to be dealt with immediately. If, at the time when the decision to dismiss is made, the employer believes that it is not in the public interest to speak in the way that the employee has done, the dismissal, based on a genuine belief that there has been misconduct, will probably be found to be fair. This will be the case, even though it is later decided that the public interest was served by the disclosure.

'SOME OTHER SUBSTANTIAL REASON' AND FAIRNESS

The catch-all provision contained in the ERA, 'some other substantial reason that justifies the dismissal', in effect, allows any reason that is sufficiently substantial to be subjected to the test of fairness. It has been used to provide a potentially fair reason for dismissal in many cases which do not fall easily into the other categories, for example the refusal to accept changes in the terms and conditions of employment which were necessary for business reasons.[121]

The wide ambit of 'some other substantial reason' means that it could be used in freedom of speech cases where there is no misconduct, so that the

---

[119] *BHS v Burchell* [1980] ICR 303. This part of the decision is unaffected by the later decision in *Boys and Girls Welfare Society v McDonald* [1996] IRLR 129.

[120] *W Devis and Sons Ltd v Atkins* [1977] AC 931.

[121] *RS Components v Irwin* [1970] 1 All ER 41, where a dismissal for refusal to accept the introduction of a restrictive covenant in the contract of employment was fair.

fairness of a dismissal could be determined without reference to the question of whether the disclosure is in the public interest. For example, a particular disclosure may or may not serve the public interest and so may or may not involve misconduct. Nevertheless, the employer could argue that the resulting bad relationship between the parties is itself a separate and substantial reason that justifies ending the employment relationship. In deciding whether such a reason for dismissal is a potentially fair reason, the tribunal would not need to consider contractual questions of confidentiality and loyalty, and so the public interest in the speech would not be legally relevant.[122]

Another 'substantial' reason that an employer might rely on is that the working relationships between employees have been adversely affected by the employee's speech. Again issues of confidentiality and the public interest are avoided. Tribunals have even been willing to accept the employer's genuinely mistaken belief that a fair reason existed as 'some other substantial reason justifying the dismissal'.[123] Thus, even though there may in fact be no conduct justifying dismissal because disclosure was in the public interest, an employer could possibly argue that the mistaken belief that there had been such conduct was sufficient reason to dismiss.[124] Some substantial reasons that may lead to a decision to dismiss are worthy of specific discussion: pressure to dismiss brought by colleagues of the employee who has spoken out; and pressure brought by those external to the organisation such as customers of the business.

Internal Pressure

If an employee's speech criticises fellow employees, either explicitly or implicitly, those employees could create pressure on the employer to dismiss the speaker. Although ERA s 107 requires the tribunal to ignore any pressure exercised on the employer by way of industrial action when deciding on the reason for dismissal, pressure to dismiss may take forms other than industrial action. For example, where employees are very unhappy about working with a particular colleague it could affect their work, amounting to a commercial pressure on the employer to dismiss (see below). Alternatively, a personality clash between staff can provide a potentially fair reason for dismissal, as it creates a substantial reason justifying the dismissal. A personality clash between colleagues can severely interrupt the work of those involved, and is highly likely to occur where one employee criticises another. However,

---

[122]   One would hope that it would be relevant once s 98(4) was being applied, but see below on the tendency for the application of s 98(4) to be merged with the question of whether the reason for dismissal was substantial.

[123]   *Bouchaala v Trust House Forte Hotels Ltd* [1980] IRLR 382. Here the employer mistakenly believed that continued employment of the employee was illegal.

[124]   Such an argument should not be necessary, given the rule in *W Devis and Sons Ltd v Atkins* [1977] AC 931 and *Polkey v A. E. Dayton Services Ltd* [1988] ICR 143, that the employer is judged according to the facts as he believed them to be, discussed above.

dismissal for this reason is only potentially fair, and will not be found to be fair unless sufficient attempts are made by the employer to improve the relationship before dismissal.[125] This may be by talking to the individuals involved, or by moving them so that they do not need to work closely together. Where these options are unsuccessful, or are inappropriate because of the size of the workplace or nature of the work, dismissal could be fair.

Internal pressure to dismiss can operate indirectly. It may be that colleagues continue to work with the employee who has spoken, but ostracise him so that he feels he has no option but to leave. The position of the employer where there are poor working relationships between colleagues is unclear. On the one hand, employers who fail to protect an employee from harassment may themselves be in breach of contract;[126] on the other, tribunals are reluctant to require employers to employ workers where trust and confidence have broken down.[127] In *Wigan Borough Council v Davies*[128] the employer's failure to provide support to an employee to enable her to carry out her job without harassment from colleagues was found to be a breach of contract entitling the employee to claim constructive dismissal. In such circumstances, it is difficult for an employer to show that dismissal was fair. Yet, despite the employer's duty to protect employees from harassment by fellow employees, it may not be practicable to require people to work together when relationships have clearly broken down between them, hence the fact that a personality clash between staff can be a fair reason for dismissal. This is especially so where the work involves a high degree of trust and cooperation between colleagues. In such a case, it may be possible for the employer to succeed in arguing that a dismissal that results from colleagues' hostility is fair, as the employer cannot be required to continue to employ someone who is adversely affecting a team's ability to work together.

External Pressure

Additional problems arise when employers face pressure to dismiss from those outside the organisation, such as customers. The employer may feel that the commercial interests of the business will be best served by yielding to the pressure and that this is a substantial reason justifying the dismissal. Tribunals have varied in their approach to this issue. In *Scott Packing and Warehousing Co Ltd v Paterson*[129] a major customer of the employer demanded an employee's dismissal in return for its continued custom. The dismissal, in compliance with the demand, was held to be fair. The EAT held that 'an employer cannot be held to have acted unreasonably if he bows to the demands

---

[125] *Turner v Vestric Ltd* [1981] IRLR 23.

[126] See discussion of the duty of trust and confidence in Chapter 4 at pp 122–4 above.

[127] See B. Napier, 'AIDS, Discrimination and Employment Law' (1989) 18 ILJ 84 and R. Watt, 'HIV, Discrimination, Unfair Dismissal and Pressure to Dismiss' (1992) 21 ILJ 280.

[128] [1979] IRLR 127.

[129] *Scott Packing and Warehousing Co Ltd v Paterson* [1978] IRLR 166.

of his best customer . . . even if the customer's motive for seeking the removal of the employee was suspect'.

This reasoning, especially that referring to the motive of the customer, has been disapproved in later cases,[130] and it has been pointed out that although the demands of a customer may be a substantial reason justifying the dismissal, the reason must still be subjected to the fairness test, so that a resulting dismissal cannot be assumed to be fair. In *Wadley v Eager Electrical Ltd*,[131] the employee was dismissed following his wife's arrest and conviction for theft (his wife also worked for the company). The employer believed Wadley's continued employment would lead customers to lose confidence in the company. Although the EAT accepted that concern about customers' loss of confidence could amount to a substantial reason justifying the dismissal, when all the circumstances of the case were considered, such as the fact that the employee had 17 years' service and had been dismissed without notice, it was not reasonable for the employer to treat the reason as a fair reason to dismiss. The dismissal was thus unfair.[132]

This scenario may become more common in future as a result of the trend towards increased contracting out of services, with the result that the service providers are dependent on a small number of clients, perhaps only one. Problems could arise if the employee of a subcontractor criticises the practices or policies of the main contractor. The subcontractor may feel it necessary to dismiss its employee in order to continue to hold the contract for the service. The fairness of the dismissal then turns on the reasonableness of the employer's action in dismissing the employee in order not to jeopardise the continued custom of a major client. The content of the speech and whether or not it served the public interest are not of direct relevance to that issue.

Even though 'some other substantial reason' for dismissal is capable of broad interpretation, it should always be remembered that such dismissals are not automatically fair. The employer must still comply separately with the test of fairness: that it be fair to treat the substantial reason as a reason to dismiss in this case. For example, the employer should give notice or warning of any dismissal. In cases of dismissal after pressure exerted by customers, the employer may need to see whether the employee can be moved to work that does not involve that customer, before the use of dismissal will be considered to be fair.

It has been suggested that the 'some other substantial reason' category of fair reasons for dismissal is sometimes interpreted such that the fairness test becomes redundant, the enquiry into the substantiality of the reason being merged with that of the fairness of the reason.[133] Any such merging has great

---

[130] See *Grootcon (UK) Ltd v Keld* [1984] IRLR 302.
[131] [1986] IRLR 93.
[132] See also *Dobie v Burns International Security Services (UK) Ltd* [1984] IRLR 329.
[133] J. Bowers and A. Clarke, 'Unfair Dismissal and Managerial Prerogative: A Study of "Other Substantial Reason"' (1981) 10 ILJ 4.

disadvantages for the employee as substantial reasons are then assumed to be fair, without sufficient emphasis on the fair procedures required in relation to other dismissals. This danger was recognised in *Wadley v Eager Electrical Ltd*[134] where it was made clear that not only must any dismissal under this heading be for a substantial reason, but its fairness must also be separately assessed. The temptation to merge the fairness and substance of a reason to dismiss gives rise to a second danger; where dismissal seems fair, or at least within a range of reasonable responses of an employer, the dismissal may be held to be fair without sufficient investigation of whether the reason was substantial in itself. Yet the requirement that the reason for dismissal be substantial is the only requirement that the tribunal can judge objectively when assessing the fairness of the decision to dismiss under the 'some other substantial reason' heading. If the tribunal determines whether the reason for dismissal was substantial by reference to the standards of the average employer then, in effect, the question of whether there was a fair dismissal becomes a single question ('was the dismissal fair?'), rather than remaining twofold as it is for the other fair reasons, where the tribunal decides first whether the reason is made out (was there a substantial reason for the dismissal, judged objectively); and then applies the test of fairness applying the standard of the average employer. Where the dismissal is only judged according to the standards of the average employer, issues such as the public interest served by the employee's action are very unlikely to receive the attention they deserve in the determination of whether there was an unfair dismissal in the circumstances.

FAIRNESS AND THE PUBLIC INTEREST

The limited number of reported cases involving dismissal for speaking out at work would now be dealt with under the PIDA, but they do give some guidance on how tribunals have viewed issues such as the public interest and the right to free speech. The cases suggest that some of the factors that determine whether or not a disclosure is in the public interest, such as the channel of communication used, may influence the decision on the fairness of a dismissal. For example, in *Thornley v ARA Ltd*,[135] the plaintiff raised matters of concern about aircraft design internally at first. It was only when he disclosed confidential information to the press (following what he believed was an unsatisfactory response by the employer) that he was dismissed. It is clear from the reasoning of the Industrial Tribunal (IT) and the Employment Appeal Tribunal (EAT) that it was the disclosure to the press that formed the grounds for dismissal. As the EAT said: 'the real gravamen of the employer's complaint . . . was that by sending the letter to [the press] he was in breach of trust to his employers'.[136] The assumption can be made that

---

[134] [1986] IRLR 93; see also *Grootcon (UK) Ltd v Keld* [1984] IRLR 302.
[135] 14 September 1976, 539/11 and 11 May 1977 EAT 669/76.   [136] Ibid, at 8.

had disclosure remained internal (a factor that would also affect whether there was a breach of confidence), then the dismissal might have been said to be unfair.

In *Cornelius v London Borough of Hackney*,[137] an employee disclosed confidential documents, revealing corrupt practices by council staff, to a local councillor and to his union. His dismissal was found to be unfair, and an earlier order reducing his compensation by 50% on the basis that he had contributed to his dismissal by failing to use the proper channels of communication with management was overturned. The EAT held that communication to a councillor and to the union was a proper means of communication; it was also pointed out that Mr Cornelius was acting from good motives. Again, these factors, which would affect the classification of a disclosure as a breach of contract at common law, affected the tribunal's assessment of the fairness of the dismissal.

However, tribunals are not *required* to take such matters into account when assessing the fairness of a dismissal by anything in the ERA 1996. The question is whether the dismissal itself was a reasonable response by the employer at the time of dismissal, not whether the action by the employee that led to dismissal was reasonable or, indeed, in the public interest. For example, in *Byford v Film Finances Ltd*,[138] the employee gave information about her employer to the opposing side in a shareholders' dispute because she believed that the employer was involved in illegal conduct. In finding the dismissal to be fair, the EAT were concerned with the reasonableness of the employer's actions at the time of the dismissal and gave short shrift to arguments based on the reasonableness of the *employee's* actions.

This accords with the test of fairness within the statute, which provides that it is the fairness of the employer's actions which is judged, not the fairness or justice of the outcome from the employee's perspective. This interpretation of the fairness test was confirmed in *Polkey v A.E. Dayton Ltd*[139] where it was said in the House of Lords that '[t]he choice . . . is between looking at the reasonableness of the employer or justice to the employee . . . the correct test is the reasonableness of the employer'. The requirement that the fairness be assessed in accordance with the 'equity and substantial merits of the case' has not been used by tribunals to broaden the issue to include the fairness of the outcome from the employee's point of view.[140] In fact the limited enquiry undertaken by Employment Tribunals in assessing fairness, and the restriction of the question to whether it was within a range of reasonable

---

[137] EAT/1061/94, reversing the IT decision COIT 4376/92/LS.

[138] EAT/804/86 (Lexis Transcript).

[139] [1988] ICR 143, where Lord Mackay adopted the statement by Browne-Wilkinson J in *Sillifant v Powell Duffryn Timber Ltd* [1983] IRLR 91.

[140] In *Haddon v Van Den Bergh Foods Ltd* [1999] IRLR 672, it was suggested that the fairness of the outcome from the employee's point of view should be considered, as part of the review of the equity and substantial merits of the case.

employer responses, has given rise to the main limitation of the protection under the ERA 1996.

The 'range of reasonable responses' standard, discussed above, works particularly badly in the case of public interest dismissals. Judged by the standards of ordinary employers, dismissals for exercising the right to free speech in a way that does not please the employer will be fair, as many employers will view the conduct as disloyal, and will dismiss. Of course if the speech interferes substantially with the financial or managerial interests of the employer and its subject matter does not serve the public interest sufficiently to warrant protection dismissal may indeed be proportionate. However, a finding that the dismissal is fair will inevitably be the result even where speech serves the wider general interest, as the public interest is not considered in the fairness equation. The only way in which the employee will stand a chance of success in such cases will be where the employer makes a procedural 'error' in the course of the dismissal. And yet the whole point of protecting the public interest is that the interests of the many are thereby protected, instead of the 'private' concerns of the main actors, the employers. The 'range of reasonable employer responses' test is thus incompatible with the protection of the public interest.

In contrast to the standard reflecting test used in unfair dismissal cases, the basis on which freedom of speech and other fundamental human rights are protected in international law is by a mechanism of standard setting. The ECHR sets standards with which the members of the Council of Europe must comply in the protection of human rights, and these are based on irreducible rights, not on the standards of reasonableness. Although a margin of appreciation is allowed in the enforcement of these standards, decisions of the ECHR are not challengeable on the basis that the Court indulged in standard setting. The whole point of the Convention is to set international standards and to protect rights on the basis of their status as fundamental human rights, regardless of the prevalence with which they are protected by states, and regardless of their popularity or convenience.[141]

Where the dismissal of an employee interferes with a fundamental human right, protected by international treaty, it would therefore be appropriate for tribunals to play a greater role in setting standards of behaviour for employers in respecting those rights, instead of allowing the low level of protection for human rights at work in the business and industrial community to undermine those rights. The case has been made in an earlier chapter for employment protection for free speech, due to the chilling effect on speech of a lack of adequate protection at work. The justifiable limits of any such protection were also discussed in detail, in order for any protection to give proper respect for employer prerogative in operating and managing the enterprise. For example, the right to free speech would not justify disclosure of confidential

---

[141]   See discussion of the ECHR in Chapter 3 above.

financial information to the press. But where free speech by an employee is justifiable in the public interest, for example, the voicing of criticism about the impact of government policy on workplace practice, a resulting dismissal should not be lawful.[142] Yet the standard of fairness by which dismissals have been judged means that such a dismissal could well be fair.

Changing the standard of fairness used in unfair dismissal cases is quite simple. As was pointed out in *Haddon*, the traditional interpretation of the test of fairness is not the only possible interpretation of the test of fairness in ERA 1996 s 98(4). There is nothing in the Act itself requiring that the standard be that of a reasonable employer: the statute only requires the tribunal to decide if it was fair or not to dismiss for the reason given, and that question has to be decided in accordance with equity and the substantial merits of the case. The 'range of reasonable responses' test is a gloss on the statute produced by the case law.[143] In order for the law of unfair dismissal to provide better protection in free speech cases, all that is needed is for the test of fairness to be interpreted in a broader fashion; no legislative change is required.

Although the Court of Appeal in *Post Office v Foley, HSBC Bank (formerly Midland Bank) v Madden*[144] clearly stamped out the attempt to change the range of reasonable responses test, the case did not refer to the HRA 1998. It is possible that in unfair dismissal cases that raise human rights issues, the range of reasonable responses may need to be abandoned to meet the HRA's requirement that courts interpret legislation *so far as it is possible* to comply with the ECHR.[145] It is arguable that, in cases involving freedom of speech of the employee, ERA 1996 s 98(4) will have to be interpreted to give adequate weight to the right to free speech. This can be done by allowing the tribunal to assess fairness of dismissal not by reference only to current employer standards, but with due regard for the right to free speech as exercised by the employee. A reinterpretation of the test of fairness, in the light of the jurisprudence of the ECHR, could significantly enhance the ability of the law on unfair dismissal to protect freedom of speech. The fairness of dismissals could then be assessed taking into account the public interest in the speech and issues such as the proportionality of the employer's response.[146]

---

[142] Where the relationship of trust and confidence between the parties has broken down, re-engagement or reinstatement may not be suitable. However, compensation would be appropriate.

[143] See *Haddon v Van Den Bergh Foods Ltd* [1999] IRLR 672 for a history of the range of responses test.

[144] [2000] IRLR 827 CA.   [145] HRA 1998 s 3(1).

[146] See H. Collins, 'Market Power, Bureaucratic Power and the Contract of Employment' (1986) 15 ILJ 1, H. Collins, 'Commentary on *Midland Bank v Madden*' (2000) 29 ILJ 293, H. Collins, K. Ewing and A. McColgan, *Labour Law* (2001) Hart Publishing, Oxford, at 575 and S. Fredman and S. Lee, 'Natural Justice for Employees: The Unacceptable Faith of Proceduralism' (1986) 15 ILJ 15 for a debate on the extent to which the introduction of public law concepts such as proportionality and legitimate expectation would improve the law on unfair dismissal.

CONCLUSION

As the law is currently interpreted, the employment protection for employees who exercise the right to free speech about work, but who do not come within the terms of the Public Interest Disclosure Act 1998, is sparse. Where the legitimate interests of the employer such as financial interests or the interest in effective management of the enterprise are harmed by employee speech, dismissal may well be a proportionate response, and such cases are highly likely to be found to be fair. Whether or not the exercise of free speech to the detriment of the employer's interests is technically misconduct or breach of contract, it can in any event be termed 'conduct' of the employee warranting dismissal. As long as any other similar cases have been treated consistently and that appropriate procedures are used, any claim of unfair dismissal will probably fail. The law is thus broadly equitable when relating to speech that does not serve the public interest. However, where speech serves wider audience interests, there is little scope for this fact to be taken into account under the law as it currently operates, and dismissal for these types of speech is also liable to be found to be fair. The main reason for the paucity of protection for public interest speech is the 'range of reasonable responses' test used to assess fairness. A change in that test, for public interest dismissals in particular, would greatly improve the protection available. Any such change is now dependent on the interpretation given by the courts to the HRA. The case for increased protection in the workplace both for whistleblowing and for other forms of speech was made earlier in Chapter 2. The scope of protection in cases which do not involve whistleblowing should, as was argued in that chapter, be limited to ensure adequate protection for employer interests, but nonetheless protection could be significantly increased beyond current levels and still meet those limits. The HRA 1998 has the potential to improve the protection available under current legislation. We shall have to wait and see whether it will fulfil that potential.

ADDITIONAL STATUTORY PROTECTION

In addition to the protection against unfair dismissal in the ERA 1998, and protection under the PIDA, various statutes provide special protection for employees who speak out about the fact that their provisions are not being met. For example, the Sex Discrimination Act 1975 (SDA), Race Relations Act 1976 (RRA) and Disability Discrimination Act 1995 (DDA) protect those who raise concerns about equal pay, sex, race or disability discrimination and ERA 1996 s 100 provides protection for those who take action on health and safety matters at work. Where the exercise of free speech amounts to trade union activity, any retaliatory action will be unlawful under the TULR(C)A 1992. Protection for those who raise concerns is also available under the Pensions Act 1995 and dismissal for asserting any other statutory right is automatically unfair under the ERA 1996.

To an extent these varied statutory provisions have been overtaken by the more recent legislation, as employees who come within their terms will often also be able to claim protection under the PIDA. Health and safety concerns are specifically included in the list of protected subject matters in the PIDA, and the other subjects will be covered by the 'catch-all' heading of failure to comply with a legal obligation. The various provisions will therefore only be considered in brief.

PROTECTION UNDER THE SDA, RRA, AND DDA

The anti-discrimination statutes provide protection not only against acts of direct and indirect discrimination but also to those who suffer victimisation for making use of their provisions. Where victimisation has taken place, unlimited compensation is available. Victimisation occurs where a person is treated less favourably for bringing proceedings or giving evidence under the Act, alleging that acts of discrimination have occurred and for doing 'anything under or by reference to [the Acts] in relation to the discriminator or any other person'.[147] This final heading is very broad, and would clearly cover any sanctions imposed for speaking publicly about discrimination issues.[148] Protection is only lost if an allegation is neither true nor made in good faith.[149]

Despite the breadth of the provisions of the discrimination legislation, successive restrictive interpretations by the courts[150] have had the effect of rendering the protection virtually unusable for many employees, especially because of the difficulties in establishing a causal link between their actions and the victimisation. These hurdles to using the provisions have only recently begun to be removed. In one of the earlier cases, *Aziz v Trinity Street Taxis Ltd*,[151] the Court of Appeal held that a causal link must be shown between the action of the applicant and the reaction of the discriminator. Aziz had been expelled from a taxi company for making secret recordings of conversations in order to prove that the company was operating in a racist manner. The Court of Appeal accepted the argument that the decision to expel him was made because the making of secret recordings was felt by members to be underhand and a breach of trust, thus breaking any chain of

---

[147] RRA s 2, SDA s 4. The wording of DDA s 55 is not identical, but it is assumed that, in this area at least, the provisions of the Disability Discrimination Act 1995 will be interpreted in the same way as those in the SDA and RRA.

[148] In *Kirby v Manpower Services Commission* [1980] 1 WLR 725 the EAT held that an employee who reported a concern about race discrimination to a local Council for Community Relations was doing something under or by reference to the Act (although the case failed on other grounds).

[149] RRA 1976 s 2(2) and SDA 1975 s 4(2). Disability Discrimination Act s 55(4) has a similar provision.

[150] The restrictive interpretation in *Kirby v Manpower Services Commission* [1980] 1 WLR 725 EAT was later overruled but replaced by an equally restrictive alternative in *Aziz v Trinity Street Taxis Ltd* [1988] IRLR 204.

[151] [1988] IRLR 204.

causation between the complaint of discrimination and the expulsion from the company.[152] Allowing a breach of trust arising from the speech to break the causal link between the retaliation and the protected speech makes the protection of the SDA and RRA extremely difficult to use. This is especially the case where an employee speaks out about concerns at work, as employers are likely to be able to present this as evidence of disloyalty.

The restrictive effect of *Aziz* has been partially removed by more recent cases. In *Nagarajan v London Regional Transport*[153] the House of Lords found that if the employer was even unconsciously motivated to victimise the employee because he had brought claims under the RRA 1976, then the employer was liable for discrimination by victimisation. There is thus now no need for the employer to make a conscious link between his treatment of the employee and the employee's conduct in relation to the Act. The victimisation provisions of the SDA and RRA should be more effective in protecting staff who raise concerns about discrimination issues after this more generous interpretation of the causation issue. Yet the difficulties in showing causation may remain. Although the decision in *Nagarajan* clarifies the issues of motive, it does not overrule the decision in *Aziz*. In *Aziz*, the causal link was broken because of the breach of trust involved in making the secret recordings. Clearly, in some cases there will be a completely separate cause of the detrimental conduct, with no connection with discrimination, and in such cases victimisation should not be made out. However, it will be unfortunate if that 'separate cause' can be the manner in which a claim is raised, as this may still allow an employer to deny a link between detrimental treatment and a claim of discrimination.

There is a degree of overlap between the protection available under the anti-discrimination legislation and that available under the PIDA where employees suffer adverse treatment for speaking out about matters relating to unlawful discrimination. Employers are required to comply with the anti-discrimination statutes, so a worker who discloses that an employer is not complying will be disclosing that it is not complying with a legal obligation. To this extent then, the provisions overlap. It may make little difference which route an employee chooses to use to seek redress for any detriment suffered for speaking out about discrimination matters. However, it may be that the provisions of the SDA, RRA and DDA are more generous, as they do not include strict procedural requirements: there is no need for employees to raise the matter internally in order to be protected. Where this is an issue, it would seem that the protection under the anti-discrimination legislation can still serve a separate purpose in freedom of speech cases after the introduction of the PIDA.

---

[152] See also *British Airways Engine Overhaul Ltd v Francis* [1981] IRLR 9 EAT, and *Re York Truck Equipment Ltd* [1990] IRLIB 20 February 1990, p 11.
[153] [1999] ICR 877.

TRADE UNION ACTIVITIES

The Trade Union and Labour Relations (Consolidation) Act (TULR(C)A) 1992 provides protection against dismissal and action short of dismissal for taking part in the activities of a trade union at an appropriate time.[154] Where the exercise of freedom of speech takes place as part of trade union activities an employee will be able to rely on this protection. For example, in *Bass Taverns Ltd v Burgess*[155] the Court of Appeal held that a dismissal for making critical remarks about the company at a union recruitment meeting was a dismissal for trade union activities. The protection is, however, limited to actions that are endorsed by the trade union and can therefore be said to be an activity of the trade union; a unilateral decision by an employee to speak will not be protected merely because the employee is a trade unionist.[156] Moreover, even where the exercise of free speech is a trade union activity, the protection only applies where the 'reason' for dismissal[157] or 'purpose' of action short of dismissal[158] is to penalise the individual for taking part in the trade union activity. This imposes restrictions on the operation of the section similar to the causal requirement in relation to the protection provided by the SDA and RRA.

The circumstances in which the protection provided by TULR(C)A 1992 ss 146 and 152 can be used to protect freedom of speech will be fairly rare. The speech would need to be part of recognised trade union activity and the penalty would need to have been imposed because it was trade union activity rather than because of any perceived disloyalty involved. The limited protection provided for freedom of speech is hardly surprising. The sections were designed to provide support for individual workers seeking to further their collective interests. Although public interest speech can be seen as the pursuit of collective interests it tends to be carried out by individualist means, and is not one of the core activities that the legislation aims to protect.

PROTECTION FOR HEALTH and SAFETY MATTERS

Under ERA 1996 s 100 it is automatically unfair to dismiss a safety representative for raising concerns about health and safety in the workplace.[159] Where there is no safety representative or safety committee, or it is not

---

[154] TULR(C)A 1992 ss 146 and 152. Employee representatives are also provided with protection, even if not part of a union, where they perform their functions as employee representatives for the purposes of collective redundancies (TULR(C)A 1992 s 188) or transfers of undertakings (under the TUPE Regulations 1981).

[155] [1995] IRLR 596.

[156] *Chant v Aquaboats Ltd* [1978] ICR 643 where an employee acted as a spokesman for a group of employees in raising safety concerns with management. The action was not an action of the union just because he was a trade unionist.

[157] TULR(C)A 1992 s 152.   [158] TULR(C)A 1992 s 146.

[159] Remedies include a special award and interim relief: ERA ss 125 and 128.

practicable to use those means, the protection extends to cover any employee who raises such concerns.[160] Section 44 ERA provides parallel protection for employees who suffer any other detriment for raising health and safety concerns.[161]

The protection under ss 100 and 44 focuses on safety representatives and the additional remedies of interim relief and the special award are only available to these employees.[162] Other employees are protected only when there is no safety representative or committee, or, if they do exist, when it is not reasonably practicable to use them as the channel through which to communicate concerns.[163] The protection also only covers those who raise concerns about health and safety *in the workplace*, rather than, for example, concerns about the safety of consumers of the goods once they have left the workplace.[164] The only possible exception to this is where appropriate action is taken to protect the employee *or other persons* from serious and imminent danger.[165] In these circumstances, protection might be available even though the health and safety concerns do not relate to the workplace. If, for example, an employee were to raise a concern about a serious health hazard presented to the public by a product manufactured by the employer, it might be that the employee could come within this section, even if the individual were not a designated safety representative. The risk would need to be serious and imminent, and the disclosure would need to be viewed as an appropriate step taken to avoid the danger.

The protection under the PIDA is probably much stronger than that under ERA ss 100 and 44. One of the subject matters specifically covered by the PIDA is danger to the health and safety of an individual. Moreover, the full protection of the PIDA applies to all staff, not just safety representatives. It also applies to disclosures about health and safety of any person, whether or not in the workplace, without the need for serious and imminent danger. To a large extent then, ERA ss 100 and 44 are redundant following the introduction of the PIDA, although they remain in place.

---

[160] The dismissal of employees who leave their place of work (or refuse to return to it) in circumstances of serious and imminent danger is also covered.

[161] The measures were introduced into UK law following the adoption of EC Framework Directive 89/391. Employees were already under a duty to inform their employer of concerns about health and safety under Health and Safety at Work Act 1974 s 7, SI 1977/500 Safety Representatives and Safety Committees (SRSC) Regulations 1977 and SI 1992/2051 Management of Health and Safety at Work (MHSW) Regulations 1992, Regulation 12.

[162] ERA ss 118(3) and 128.　　[163] Section 100(1)(c).

[164] In *Brendon v BNFL Flurochemicals Ltd* COIT Case No 59163/94, an employee was unsuccessful in claiming the protection of s 100 in relation to his dismissal for his reluctance to sell a particular chemical to customers abroad as he believed that they might sell the product on illegally. The tribunal commented that 'the protection given by the subsection extends only to matters concerned with the health and safety at work or in the workplace and not to matters which are . . . not connected with the safety of the products but are in reality ethical considerations regarding [the] possible end user [of the product]'.

[165] Sections 100(1)(e) and 44(1)(e).

PENSIONS ACT 1995

Some legislation imposes a duty to blow the whistle on certain concerns. Section 48 of the Pensions Act 1995 imposes a duty on auditors and actuaries to report cases to the Occupational Pensions Regulatory Authority where they have reason to believe that any duty imposed by law is not being complied with, and where that failure will prevent the Authority from carrying out its functions. Failure to make a report can lead to the auditor being disqualified by the Authority. The Pensions Act 1995 states that compliance with this duty will not constitute a contravention of any other duty owed by the auditor, so that it cannot amount to a breach of confidence or breach of contract on the part of the auditor. Auditors in other financial sectors are under a similar duty to report concerns to their respective regulators.[166] No specific employment protection is provided by the Pensions Act and other similar regulations. However, employees dismissed or disciplined for reporting such issues would be protected under the PIDA.[167]

ASSERTING A STATUTORY RIGHT AND OTHER AUTOMATICALLY
UNFAIR REASONS FOR DISMISSAL

Where the subject matter of speech involves one of the issues which is given automatic protection against dismissal, then it will be open to the worker to argue that dismissal for the speech is automatically unfair. For example, a dismissal for claiming maternity leave rights would be automatically unfair.[168] Moreover, some statutory protection includes specific protection against dismissal for alleging that the employer is in breach. So, after the introduction of the Working Time Regulations 1998, employees must not be dismissed or suffer a detriment for claiming that the employer is infringing their terms.[169] Equally, in such cases, the subject matter of the speech will also be that the employer is in breach of a legal obligation, and so the speech will also be protected under the PIDA.

CONCLUSION

In conclusion, it is fair to say that freedom of expression does receive at least partial protection in the workplace. The adequacy of the protection available depends to a large degree upon the subject matter of the speech, that relating to wrongdoing receiving the greatest protection. Returning to the classifications made in Chapter 2, speech which is worthy of protection on grounds of its content, such as whistleblowing, is now afforded good protection under

---

[166] For example, Auditors (Insurance Companies Act 1982) Regulations 1994 SI 1994/449; Auditors (Financial Services Act 1986) Rules 1994 SI 1994/526; Accountants (Banking Act 1987) Regulations 1994 SI 1994/524; Building Societies (Auditors) Order 1994 SI 1994/525.

[167] Dismissal for acting as a trustee of an occupational pension scheme is automatically unfair under ERA 1996 s 102.

[168] ERA 1996 s 104.   [169] ERA 1996 ss 45A and 101A.

the PIDA. Speech which deserves protection only on the basis of its role in upholding the autonomy of the speaker, such as personal comment or dissent, is provided with virtually no protection within the workplace. To this extent, the autonomy of the individual is not afforded protection under the current employment protection provisions.

In respect of the protection of speech on the basis of content, the Public Interest Disclosure Act 1998 provides a similar level of protection for the reporting of wrongdoing and malpractice at work to that advocated in Chapter 2, with its almost automatic protection for internal disclosure, and more limited protection for external disclosure. For speech not covered by the PIDA, the protection is less extensive, and is dependent to a large extent on the view of the fairness of dismissal taken by the tribunal in any given case.

The main limitation on protection for free expression in cases covered by the PIDA is the difficulty over the issue of causation. The PIDA's ability to protect free speech will, to an extent, depend on a broad approach being taken to this issue. If the tribunals allow employers to argue that dismissal was not for raising a concern, but for the disciplinary offence of failing to follow the correct internal procedure in doing so, then the power of the Act will be much undermined. The precedents on this issue on the interpretation of similar legislation are mixed. The cases under health and safety legislation are not particularly encouraging, allowing, as they have, employers to argue that the reason for dismissal was the incorrect method of raising the concern, rather than the subject matter *per se*.[170] In contrast, the case of *Nagarajan v London Regional Transport*[171] shows that a broader interpretation can be given to these sections by allowing subconscious motivation to be taken into account. The indications from the early tribunal cases on PIDA, allowing inferences about causation to be drawn from the employer's conduct, should also help overcome some of these difficulties.[172]

If the PIDA is to be successful in protecting free speech at work a broad approach to interpreting its provisions needs to be maintained. Dismissal which follows disclosure should be assumed to be caused by the disclosure, unless the contrary can be shown; and although internal procedures may not have been used properly, this should not be allowed to give separate grounds for dismissal in cases where information remains internal to the organisation. The requirement under the HRA that the PIDA be interpreted as far as possible to comply with the ECHR should give strong backing for such a purposive approach to causation, given the ECHR's protection for freedom of expression as a fundamental right.

---

[170] *Shillito v Van Leer (UK) Ltd* [1997] IRLR 495, *British Airways Engine Overhaul Ltd v Francis* [1981] IRLR 9 EAT, and *ReYork Truck Equipment Ltd* [1990] IRLIB 20 February 1990, p 11.

[171] [1999] ICR 877.

[172] *Fernandes v Netcom Consultants (UK) Ltd* (18/5/00, Case No 2200060/00).

Speech such as political speech and principled dissent which falls outside the parameters of the PIDA is afforded much more limited protection in the workplace. Increased protection for these types of speech will depend on the interpretation of the test of fairness found in the unfair dismissal legislation. As long as the test of fairness is interpreted to mean, in effect, that dismissal is fair unless no reasonable employer would dismiss in the circumstances, the unfair dismissal legislation can provide virtually no protection to freedom of expression, as many reasonable employers will dismiss for voicing dissent or political views. If the equity and substantial merits of the case can be properly considered, the right to free speech will be afforded a much greater chance of protection. Despite the clear indication by the Court of Appeal that the range of reasonable responses test is here to stay, it is possible that in freedom of speech cases this view will need to be revisited. The HRA requires that legislation be interpreted to comply with the ECHR. The question of fairness of a dismissal should therefore be assessed with reference to the jurisprudence of the ECHR. As seen in Chapter 3 above, the ECtHR does not give absolute protection to the right to freedom of expression, particularly where it is exercised at work, but is nonetheless committed to freedom of expression as an essential foundation of democratic society.[173] If the test of fairness can be interpreted in the light of the jurisprudence of the ECHR, this could significantly improve the protection, in domestic law, for those who are dismissed for their exercise of the right to freedom of expression.

---

[173] *Handyside v UK* (1981) 1 EHRR 737.

6

Freedom of Speech and Public Sector Employment: The Civil Service, Local Government, and The NHS

In a number of areas of public sector work, employees face additional restrictions on speech above and beyond those imposed by general employment law and the duty of confidence. The freedom of speech of those employed in the civil service and local government is governed by the provisions of the Official Secrets Acts 1911–1989 and the Local Government and Housing Act 1989. Staff in these sectors are also governed by sector specific codes of conduct which impact on their freedom of speech. The legal provisions governing the speech of these employees will be examined in this chapter, and an assessment made of the extent to which the restrictions on speech are justified.

The chapter will also consider the position of staff in the National Health Service in relation to freedom of speech. The NHS is the largest employer in the country, and as the provider of health care for the vast majority of the population, it has special political significance. The NHS was one of the first areas to be highlighted by the Nolan Committee as needing to introduce whistleblowing procedures for employees,[1] and it serves as a good illustration both of the difficulties in balancing the competing rights at play in freedom of speech cases, and of the development of increased recognition of the value that free speech can have in improving the public service.[2] As well as considering the additional restrictions on the free speech of staff in these areas of the public sector, the Freedom of Information Act 2000 and its interaction with the freedom of speech of public sector staff will be briefly considered.[3]

---

[1] First Report of the Committee on Standards in Public Life, 1995, HMSO Cm 2850 I–II.
[2] For details on whistleblowing in other areas of work such as education see D. Lewis (ed), *Whistleblowing at Work* (2001) Athlone Press, London.
[3] For detailed consideration of the Freedom of Information Act 2001, which is beyond the scope of this book, see P. Birkinshaw, *Freedom Of Information: The Law, the Practice and the Ideal* (2001) Butterworths, London.

THE FREEDOM OF INFORMATION ACT 2000

The Freedom of Information Act 2000 applies across the public sector, and in all three areas considered in this chapter.[4] The full impact of the Act is as yet unknown, but it should certainly result in an increased amount of hitherto unknown information entering the public domain. It might therefore be thought that the role of employees in bringing public interest information to light will be reduced as the information becomes readily available to anyone who wishes to see it. However, as suggested earlier[5] the creation of the Freedom of Information Act in 2000 does not reduce the need for protection for the free speech of employees in the public sector, as freedom of information and freedom of speech serve connected but complementary roles in informing the public. Both increase the amount of information to which the public can have access, and both can play a part in keeping the public informed.

Moreover, limitations on one method of informing the public places a greater burden on the other method to fulfil its informative function. Restrictions on free speech increase the importance for the democratic process of freedom of information rights, and vice versa. The weaknesses of the Freedom of Information Act 2000, in particular the wide ranging exemptions that apply, mean that the protection of free speech is all the more important for the subjects of this chapter, workers in the civil service, local government and NHS.

The Act creates a right for individuals to have access to information held by public authorities.[6] Part II of the Act creates a series of exemptions where the right of access does not apply. Some exemptions are absolute exemptions such as those that apply to information relating to security matters.[7] Other exemptions operate where disclosure of the information would, or would be likely to, prejudice a specified interest, and where the public interest in maintaining the exemption outweighs the public interest in disclosure.[8] For example, information which would be likely to prejudice the economic interests of the country could be exempt. Where information is exempt, the individual has no right to discover whether the information requested even exists.

Information that relates to the formulation of government policy is exempt without need to show prejudice to any other interest, and thus without the need to assess the public interest in disclosure of the information.[9] Although the exemption does not apply to statistical information, once a decision of policy has been taken this exemption from the need to provide information is very wide. Staff who wish to contribute to debate on areas of government policy relating to the sectors in which they work

---

[4] Freedom of Information Act 2000 Schedule 1.   [5] Chapter 2, pp 26–7.
[6] Freedom of Information Act 2000 s 1.   [7] Ibid., s 23.
[8] Ibid., s 2.   [9] Ibid., s 35.

would need to rely on free speech protection to be able to do so, rather than relying on the right to freedom of information to be used to inform the debate. The existence of the Freedom of Information Act 2000 thus does not reduce the importance of free speech for workers in the public sector.

FREEDOM OF SPEECH IN THE CIVIL SERVICE

The freedom of speech of servants of the Crown deserves particular consideration because the public interests in both disclosure and confidentiality are especially strong. As discussed in Chapter 2, the audience interests in information relating to the public sector are much greater than those that operate in relation to the private sector. Set against this is the fact that the close relationship between government and the civil service means that a high degree of confidence over information has traditionally been required.

There are a number of arguments in favour of allowing special protection to the right to free speech of civil servants. First, the public expects that government work should be carried out with the highest levels of probity and integrity, and civil servants are well placed to ensure that high standards are maintained, or to report cases where they are not. Where a civil servant discovers that these standards are not being met, it may be in the public interest that it be disclosed. There is a second way in which granting freedom of expression to civil servants can serve the public interest. As Schauer points out in *Free Speech: A Philosophical Enquiry*,[10] governments have enormous power, and with it the ability to make enormous errors. This power is wielded in a context in which the issues are complicated and where answers are rarely clear cut. It is therefore important that they are debated and discussed widely in order that the chance of error is minimised. Speech which informs public debate on matters that relate in any way to government policy should, on this argument, be given the very widest protection. Information about how a government policy is working or how government funding policies affect the public sector is necessary if the electorate is to participate fully in the political process.

However, against this has to be balanced the fact that governments need to be able to conduct their business and develop policies with a degree of confidentiality. Although there may be a public interest in full debate of policy, there is also a public interest in allowing governments to govern, and to put their policies into practice. The smooth running of government also requires that civil servants be prepared to serve any duly constituted government, regardless of the political views of the individual. Thus impartiality of

[10] F. Schauer, *Free Speech: A Philosophical Enquiry* (1982) Cambridge University Press, Cambridge.

staff is needed. Moreover, in the course of their work, Crown employees may have access to particularly sensitive and confidential information. Often some of this information is of great interest to the public, such as information about proposed policy initiatives, legislative reforms, and even information relating to the personal views of members of the government hidden from the public by the convention of cabinet collective responsibility. Despite the fact that the public might be interested in it, routinely to disclose such information would not be in the public interest. As with any private business, the government needs privacy within which to develop its ideas, and to conduct its day to day business, and civil servants need to respect the confidential nature of much of their work, in the same way as private sector employees. The need to maintain impartiality, together with the particularly sensitive nature of much of the information civil servants deal with, puts them in a special position vis-à-vis their freedom to raise issues of concern and to participate in public debate.

Despite the strength of both these competing arguments, the need for confidentiality in the civil service has usually trumped the need to serve the public interest by disclosure of information. Yet the traditional silence of those who work for the government is being increasingly challenged as those who have left government service write memoirs of their time in office. Stella Rimmington, formerly the head of MI5, is the latest member of security services staff to publish memoirs that may reveal what is traditionally viewed as confidential information.[11] After the introduction of the HRA, with its guarantee of freedom of expression, the limits of the traditional rules on confidentiality of the civil service are likely to be thoroughly tested. Moreover, the introduction of the Freedom of Information Act 2000 may also contribute to the creation of a less secretive culture for the civil service than has hitherto been the case.

As well as being subject to the provisions of the Official Secrets Act 1989 (discussed below), civil servants owe strong duties of loyalty and confidence to the government. Their duties are governed by two codes of practice, the Civil Service Management Code (CSMC)[12] and the Civil Service Code.[13] The CSMC covers all staff duties including the duty of confidentiality as well as terms relating to pay, discipline, equal opportunities, recruitment, grad-

---

[11] S. Rimmington, *Open Secret* (2001) Hutchinson, London.

[12] The Civil Service Management Code is issued under the Civil Service Order in Council 1995 under the Civil Service (Management of Functions) Act 1992. The regulations do not amount themselves to terms and conditions of employment, but a breach of them would probably be a disciplinary offence. The CSMC was updated in 1999 to reflect the changes brought about by devolution in Scotland and the creation of the National Assembly in Wales.

[13] The Civil Service Code contains a procedure whereby civil servants' concerns can be raised with the Civil Service Commissioners. It is incorporated into the terms and conditions of employment of civil servants via para 4.1.1. of the Civil Service Management Code. It was updated in 1999 to reflect the changes brought about by devolution in Scotland and the creation of the National Assembly in Wales.

ing, etc. The Civil Service Code, on the other hand, augments the provisions of the CSMC and covers duties and responsibilities of civil servants in relation to ministers. Both Codes set out internal processes by which staff can raise concerns about wrongdoing. Civil servants are also covered by the Public Interest Disclosure Act 1998 (unless a disclosure breaches the Official Secrets Acts). Disclosures made outside of the processes set out in the Codes may give grounds for fair dismissal unless they are reasonable according to the standards of the PIDA.[14]

The CSMC states that civil servants owe a duty of loyal service to the Crown as represented by the 'duly constituted Government'.[15] This is a change from the earlier statement regarding civil servants' duties of loyalty which said that the duty was owed to 'the Government of the day'.[16] It is not clear how the difference in wording works in practice, as the duly constituted Government is presumably also the Government of the day; however, the new wording does perhaps make clearer that the civil servant serves the interests of the Government without regard to any party political considerations that might also be operative. The duties of civil servants as set out in the CSMC make clear that civil servants are to be, and are to be seen to be, honest and impartial in the exercise of their duties.[17] Part of this duty involves maintaining confidentiality with respect to information communicated in confidence, and refraining from improper or premature disclosure of information to which access is given as part of the job.[18] The importance given to the duty of confidence within the Code emphasises its centrality to the operation of the civil service. In this regard, it is noteworthy that the duty of confidence extends even after the civil servant has left his or her employment.[19]

Despite the emphasis in the CSMC on confidentiality, the provisions of the Civil Service Code, setting out the duties and responsibilities of civil servants in relation to ministers, make equally clear that circumstances may arise in which a civil servant feels bound in conscience to raise certain concerns. The Code sets out the types of issue that a civil servant may raise, and sets out a procedure by which this should be done.[20] These matters include where they believe that they are being required to act in a way that is illegal, improper or unethical; is in breach of constitutional convention or a professional code; may involve possible maladministration; is otherwise inconsistent with the Code; or which raises a fundamental issue of conscience. The emphasis is on reporting occasions on which they, as civil servants, have been required to act improperly in the course of their employment. Other matters that can be reported include evidence of

---

[14] For more detail see Chapter 5.   [15] CSMC para 4.1.1.
[16] The Armstrong Memorandum (1985). The Armstrong Memorandum no longer forms part of the CSMC following the introduction of the Civil Service Code.
[17] CSMC para 4.1.3.   [18] CSMC para 4.1.3.a.
[19] CSMC para 4.2.3.   [20] Civil Service Code para 11.

criminal or other unlawful conduct by others and breaches of other provisions of the Code.

Guidance on what might be termed 'maladministration' can be gained from the examples given by the Parliamentary Commissioner's 1993 Annual Report. These headings are given in the context of the work of the Parliamentary Commissioner or Ombudsman who investigates complaints from the public of injustice arising out of maladministration. They include refusal to answer reasonable questions; neglecting to inform a complainant on request of his or her rights or entitlements; knowingly giving advice which is misleading or inadequate; showing bias; and faulty procedures. This definition is fairly wide, and is based on concepts of justice and fair treatment. The examples of maladministration that may arise in the context of a civil servant's work may differ from those given above, but the essence will remain the same. If a civil servant were required as part of his job to take a step that he believed would result in injustice being done to members of the public, he should report it under the procedure set out in the Code.

The Code gives clear guidance to civil servants on their duties if conflicts arise between them and their minister. However, it does not cover all concerns that a civil servant might have as it mainly applies where the civil servant himself is required to act improperly. It does not explicitly apply where the civil servant discovers improper conduct by a third party, unless that conduct amounts to unlawful behaviour. In particular, it does not clearly cover the disclosure of abuse of power or maladministration by another. 'Other breaches of the Code' are mentioned as matters that the civil servant might wish to raise,[21] but in the context in which this arises it is unclear whether this includes breaches of the Code by others. It may instead refer to a requirement on the individual civil servant to participate in 'other breaches of the Code'. If so, it would appear that the Code will not cover disclosure of general wrongdoing by civil servants. It is to be hoped that this more restrictive meaning is not what is intended, and that in fact civil servants are being advised to report breaches of the Code by others.

A two-fold procedure for raising concerns is set out in the Civil Service Code. First matters should be raised according to any departmental guidance or rules of conduct. In effect, this will usually require that matters are raised internally with the civil servant's line manager. If this is inappropriate, an alternative line of reporting is provided. If the civil servant feels that the response is not a reasonable response to the concerns, then the matter can be reported to the Civil Service Commissioners.[22] The Civil Service Commissioners are appointed by the Queen and are independent from the government. This will mean that concerns are examined afresh, by someone outside of the particular department involved. The Civil Service Code

---

[21] Civil Service Code para 11.   [22] Civil Service Code para 12.

does not seem to countenance external disclosure beyond the Civil Service Commissioners. The assumption is made that they will deal adequately with any concerns. However, elsewhere in the Code[23] civil servants are reminded of their legal obligations to maintain confidence, both statutory (Official Secrets Acts 1911–1989) and under the common law duty of confidence.

The Civil Service Code together with the CSMC make clear a commitment within the civil service to encourage staff to raise concerns internally. The Civil Service Commissioners report annually and give anonymised details of the concerns that have been raised under the procedure set out in the Civil Service Code. The process has been in operation since 1996 and in the first three years of operation only three matters worthy of their investigation were raised. The two in which details are given involved the misuse of statistical information to misleadingly represent that performance targets had been met. In each case the concerns were raised internally at first. They were then investigated, and recommendations were made to ensure that the concerns were addressed. The Commissioners report in the following year that the recommendations had been followed up and checks made to ensure that no victimisation had taken place.[24] The process of internal reporting coupled with an independent review does seem to give good protection and encouragement for civil servants to raise internally matters of concern about the conduct of their work. Their freedom to participate in the whistleblowing type of speech is well protected, as long as it is exercised internally to the organisation.

Civil service staff are also subject to the protection of the PIDA. This adds useful protection for staff, although in many ways civil service staff already enjoy the type of protection it introduces. The existing line management reporting system together with the provision for independent review mean that civil servants already enjoy the sort of internal whistleblowing procedures envisaged by the drafters of the PIDA. In fact in some respects the provisions of the Codes are wider than the PIDA. Although the PIDA protects disclosure about a wider range of subjects, for example, concerns about the environment, which are not explicitly referred to in the two Codes, the Codes, in turn, cover types of concern not dealt with by the PIDA, such as maladministration, and matters of personal conscience.

As with other internal reporting mechanisms, the processes in the two Codes allow any wrongdoing to be put right without unnecessary or damaging publicity, and may avoid feelings of frustration on the part of staff which can sometimes lead to information being leaked unofficially. The fact that the Code states that staff 'should' raise concerns internally if they have them

---

[23] Civil Service Code para 10.
[24] See the Annual Report of the Civil Service Commissioners 1996–7 and 1997–8.

suggests an obligation, not just a permission, to disclose. If matters of concern are raised externally by civil servants, they will only gain the protection of the PIDA if they can show that this course was reasonable. In this context they will need to show that they feared that the wrongdoing would be covered up, or that they would face retaliation for raising the concern internally. Alternatively, they would need to show good reason not to have raised the concern under the procedures set out in the Codes. Both Codes meet the main requirements of fairness (in that they call for independent enquiry into the claims made) so it will be difficult to show that there was good reason not to try them in the first instance.

The difficulty for civil servants is that the restriction on raising concerns externally can have a significant impact on their freedom of speech in a wider sense. Concerns about specific instances of wrongdoing can be raised, but not more generalised concerns. Similar restrictions on the speech apply for all workers, public sector or not, as the PIDA does not protect those who engage in personal comment, principled dissent or political speech. So a civil servant who anticipates a serious detrimental impact of a particular policy would be in breach of contract to voice that concern publicly. Once a policy has been decided it is the duty of the civil servant to carry it out, whether or not he agrees with it; he cannot frustrate government policy by disclosing information to the public.[25]

Civil servants are also prevented from making any public statement which draws upon experience gained in their official capacity (without prior approval of their department),[26] and from taking part in political activities.[27] Political activities are defined widely, and include speaking in public, or writing to the press, on matters of national or local political controversy.[28] Again, this restriction denies to the public the benefit of the experience and knowledge of those in the best place to comment, and to an extent, is a waste of a valuable resource that could improve the level of public knowledge in important areas of policy.

The restriction on personal participation in the political process could also be viewed as a fairly serious encroachment on the personal autonomy rights of the individual civil servant. However, such restrictions are justified on the basis that governments need an impartial bureaucracy to implement policy.[29] Moreover, the CSMC provides fairly generous reinstatement options for those who wish to resign in order to pursue political office. Those who do so are able to return to their jobs if unsuccessful, or even if initially successful,

---

[25] CSMC para 4.2.6.   [26] CSMC para 4.2.4.

[27] CSMC para 4.4. Civil servants above a certain grade may not run for political office, hold office in a political party (although mere membership is acceptable), or take part in political activities without permission. Civil servants in industrial and non-office grades are 'politically free' (para 4.4.2.).

[28] Para 4.4.1.a and b.

[29] The need to restrict political activity by local and central government staff was accepted by the ECHR in *Ahmed v UK* [2000] 29 EHRR 1.

once their term of office ends.[30] This fairly generous concession to the strong restrictions on political activity probably counteracts the claim that the personal rights of staff are unduly limited.

Under the Human Rights Act 1998, the government will need to act in accordance with the European Convention on Human Rights and so the Codes will need to be interpreted to comply with Article 10 guaranteeing the right to freedom of expression.[31] However, despite strong statements in favour of allowing special protection to freedom of political speech,[32] and fairly broad definitions of political speech, the European Court of Human Rights does allow restrictions on the speech of workers, in particular the speech of civil servants.[33] The margin of appreciation given to governments in the interpretation of Convention rights means that restrictions on speech of government employees are likely to remain lawful under the Convention, despite public interest arguments to the contrary.[34]

Clearly, many of the restrictions on the free speech of civil servants are necessary. The government operates with a permanent civil service, and those civil servants cannot personally agree with all the policies of the differing governments which they may be required to implement. Moreover, the employer interests identified in Chapter 2 in being free to exercise managerial prerogative in the running of an enterprise, and in the efficient provision of services, apply as much within government service as to other employers. It will thus often be in the public interest to allow some restriction on civil servants' speech. However, the restrictions contained in the two Codes are drafted in very broad terms, with no mention of a public interest exception, even though the public interest could be well served by allowing greater participation in debate by public servants, given their experience and expertise in many areas of public importance. Moreover, when the restrictions imposed by the Official Secrets Acts are added to those mentioned in the Codes, the potential breadth of restrictions on the speech of civil servants becomes apparent.

RESTRICTIONS ON SPEECH UNDER THE OFFICIAL SECRETS ACTS 1911–1989

Alongside the restrictions on speech imposed by the general duty of confidence, the Civil Service Code and CSMC, additional restrictions on the speech of those employed by the Crown can be found in the criminal law. The Official Secrets Acts 1911–1989 impose criminal liability on those disclosing certain classes of confidential information. Where a disclosure of information breaches the Official Secrets Acts, the civil servant will not be covered by the PIDA, and can be liable to be dismissed, even if criminal proceedings are not brought. The Official Secrets Acts could inhibit staff from raising concerns

---

[30] CSMC s 4.4.   [31] See discussion in Chapter 3, pp 71–3 above.
[32] *Lingens v Austria* (1986) 8 EHRR 407.   [33] *B v UK* (1986) 45 D&R 41.
[34] *Ahmed v UK* [2000] 29 EHRR 1. Although the case relates to local government, the reasoning could equally be applied to central government service.

about wrongdoing, although they should not inhibit internal disclosure. Disclosure within the civil service or to the Civil Service Commissioner would not count as a breach of the Acts, and could still be protected by the PIDA.

Some sections of the Acts only apply to civil servants, but to these are added provisions that apply to those to whom information is disclosed, making it an offence to publish or pass on the information. These provisions, although rarely used in practice, have a significant impact on the freedom of speech of civil servants and the extent to which they are able to raise public interest concerns about matters relating to their work. On entering the civil service, those who will have access to confidential information are required to sign a declaration that they will abide by the provisions of the Acts. They are thus aware of the criminal sanctions that can be attached to a prohibited disclosure from the very beginning of their civil service careers.

The precursor to the Official Secrets Act 1989 was s 2 of the Official Secrets Act (OSA) 1911, an extremely widely drafted provision that covered a huge range of information, by no means all of it confidential in nature.[35] Understandably the Act covered the disclosure of information relating to prohibited places, so that it could prevent military information from being revealed. It also covered information disclosed in confidence, again understandable given the sensitive nature of much government work. However, it extended far beyond these acceptable limits, to cover any information obtained, or to which the civil servant had access, owing to his position as a civil servant.[36] Thus anything that civil servants knew by virtue of their jobs in the civil service was, technically, covered by the Act, leading to the observation that it could, technically, cover such trivial information as the number of cups of tea served in a department.[37] There was no requirement to show that any damage was caused by the revelation before liability could be imposed. Communication of the information was forbidden except where it was to 'a person to whom [the civil servant] is authorised to communicate it, or a person to whom it is in the interest of the State his duty to communicate it'.

The criminal offence created by OSA 1911 s 2 required no *mens rea* other than the intention to communicate the information: no knowledge of the status of the information was needed. Knowingly to disclose information covered by the Act was to commit the offence. The fact that a disclosure was made in good faith and in the belief that it served the public interest

---

[35] The 1911 Act was drafted in haste to deal with feared German espionage operations in 1911. See D. Feldman, *Civil Liberties and Human Rights in England and Wales* (1993) Oxford University Press, Oxford, at 638.

[36] Either during or after he has held that job, or to which he has access because he is employed by a civil servant. OSA 1911 s 2.

[37] Feldman, n 35 above at 639.

was no defence, unless the defendant could claim that the public interest in the information created a duty to disclose the information 'in the interests of the State'. This always was a very limited defence, but once the 'interests of the State' was interpreted to refer to the interests of the government of the day by McCowan J in the *Ponting* case,[38] it became virtually unusable. In Ponting's case, initial disclosure of an internal memo relating to the sinking of the *General Belgrano* ship during the Falklands war was made to an opposition MP, Mr Tam Dalyell. If this did not serve the interests of the State, it is impossible to imagine that disclosure to the press could ever do so.[39] As a result, the provision came in for sustained and serious criticism as being too stringent a restriction on the rights of civil servants to raise public interest issues.[40] Although prosecution for disclosure of trivial information was not a practical problem, the blanket coverage of the Act meant that it lost its moral authority in relation to serious disclosures as well.

The Official Secrets Act 1989 was the government response to these concerns.[41] It was said to be a liberalising measure; however, in a number of important respects this is not an accurate description. The 1989 Act does limit the categories of information subject to restriction, and requires damage to be caused by the disclosure in respect of some types of information. Thus the breadth of the old s 2 offence, and its catch-all effect, is gone. However, the absence of any public interest defence, even of the limited nature available under s 2, undermines any claim that the 1989 Act represents a liberalisation of the UK's secrecy laws, and the freedom of speech of civil servants remains significantly restricted as a result.

The categories of information covered by the 1989 Act are: security and intelligence matters; defence; international relations; and law enforcement matters. Disclosures by Crown servants are covered as are disclosures by those to whom that information is disclosed.[42] Although some disclosures must be damaging before they are covered by the Act, this is not the case for all categories of information. For example, members of the security services

---

[38] *R v Ponting* [1985] Crim LR 318. See further, C. Ponting, *The Right to Know: The Inside Story of the Belgrano Affair* (1985) Phere, London.

[39] Sarah Tisdall pleaded guilty to an offence under s 2 because she believed she had no defence after her disclosure to the *Guardian* newspaper of an internal memo concerning ministerial tactics to be used in statements regarding the installation of nuclear weapons at an RAF base in the UK. *R v Tisdall*, unreported, 23 March 1984, and her appeal, *R v Tisdall* 9 April 1994 (CA Crim Div).

[40] For criticism of the Act see Feldman, n 35 above; Y. Cripps, *Legal Implications of Disclosure in the Public Interest* (2nd edn, 1994) Sweet & Maxwell, London; D. Hooper, *Official Secrets; Use and Abuse of the Act* (1988) Coronet, London; and R. Thomas, *Espionage and Secrecy: The Official Secrets Acts 1911–1989 of the United Kingdom* (1991) Routledge, London.

[41] The White Paper was called *Reform of Section 2 of the Official Secrets Act 1911*. Cm 408 (1988). See S. Palmer, 'In the Interests of the State: The Government's Proposals for reforming Section 2 of the Official Secrets Act 1911' (1988) PL 523.

[42] Sections 1–5.

are bound not to disclose any information relating to their work, damaging or not. This is a lifelong duty, remaining in force even after the individual has left the service. It applies to any disclosure, regardless of motive or other circumstances. It makes criminal both the disclosure for financial gain of information that breaches national security, and the disclosure of serious wrongdoing motivated by a concern for the public interest.[43] Similarly, any disclosure of information which was gathered under the Interception of Communications Act 1995 (telephone tapping) would also be an offence under the Act, regardless of damage.[44] Thus although in 1985, following Ponting's acquittal, Catherine Massiter was not prosecuted under s 2 of the 1911 Act for her disclosures of telephone tapping activities by MI5,[45] her actions would be clear breaches of the 1989 Act. It would even be a breach of the Act to disclose merely that telephone tapping had taken place, regardless of the possible public interest in that fact, due for example to the identity of the person under surveillance. The failure to distinguish between serious and damaging disclosures and trivial, harmless ones, together with the failure to provide a public interest defence even for the most deserving of cases, causes the OSA 1989, like s 2 of the 1911 Act, to lose its moral authority.

Moreover, even where damage is required for a disclosure to be unlawful under the Act, its definition is wide. For example, a disclosure relating to defence is assumed to be damaging if it 'endangers the interests of the United Kingdom abroad, seriously obstructs the promotion or the protection by the United Kingdom of those interests or endangers the safety of British citizens abroad'.[46] Clearly some of these results would be seriously damaging, but others, arguably, could be less so, for example, obstructing the promotion of UK interests abroad. Disclosure of a concern about the safety of a defence system could seriously damage the promotion of British commercial interests abroad, even though it may be in the public interest to make the disclosure.[47] Although OSA 1989 s 2(3) provides a defence where the defendant did not know, and had no reason to know, that the disclosure would be damaging, the burden of proving this defence is on the defendant; and in any event, one may well know that information disclosed would cause damage to British commercial interests, but still believe that it was in the wider public interest to make the disclosure.

Other broad provisions of the 1989 Act include s 3, covering disclosure of information obtained in confidence from another state or an international

---

[43]   Section 1.   [44]   Section 4(3).

[45]   *The Times*, 28 February 1985, and see Y. Cripps, *Legal Implications of Disclosure in the Public Interest* (2nd edn, 1994) Sweet & Maxwell, London, at 157.

[46]   Section 2(2)(b).

[47]   Cf Stephen Thornley who was dismissed for disclosing to the *Guardian* his concerns about the capabilities of the new aircraft on which he was working. See *Thornley v Aircraft Research Association Ltd* 11 May 1977 EAT.

organisation. This will be assumed to be damaging if it endangers the interests of the UK abroad, and is not limited to matters of national security. Under s 3(3), the fact that the information is confidential may be sufficient to establish damage. This provision could cover disclosure of information communicated by a foreign government concerning public health and safety.[48] Information from a foreign government relating to the safety of products exported by the UK could be very damaging to British interests abroad, even though there may be immense public interest in disclosure of the information. However, the 1989 Act contains no public interest defence: the defendant only has a defence if he can prove that he did not know of the damage.

There is, however, one slight possibility of a defence under the Acts. OSA 1989 s 7 provides a defence where the disclosure is made with lawful authority because it is part of the civil servant's official duty to make the disclosure. Moreover, as long as the civil servant has reason to believe that he had lawful authority, he can use the defence.[49] Thus it may be possible for a civil servant to claim that, because of the public interest in the information, it was (or he believed that it was) his official duty to make the disclosure.[50] Furthermore, it may be arguable in some cases that the public interest in information means that it is not confidential at all. In such a case, any assumption that the disclosure of confidential information is damaging would not apply, and the disclosure may therefore not be caught by the Act.[51]

This limited public interest defence, if capable of being used in practice at all, is not explicit on the face of the Acts, and the lack of a clear public interest defence remains a major illiberal aspect of the 1989 Act. It was because of the lack of such a defence that the French courts refused to allow the extradition of David Shayler to the UK in 1998 to face charges under the Act for breaching the lifelong ban on speech imposed on members of the security services. Shayler claimed that his disclosures showed malpractice and incompetence in the security services, claims that one might think it in the public interest to disclose.[52]

The lack of a public interest defence also results in a certain illogicality as such a defence does exist in the civil law relating to breach of confidence. Thus, although the courts may allow publication of the information because of the public interest, the person making the disclosure could still be guilty of a criminal offence for disclosing it. For example, where information relates to an urgent health and safety matter, its disclosure could be criminal because the information was received in confidence from

---

[48] S. Palmer, 'Tightening the Secrecy Law: The Official Secrets Act 1989' [1990] PL 243.
[49] OSA 1989 s 7(4).   [50] See Cripps, n 45 above, at 161.
[51] In any event, s 3(3) only states that information that is confidential *may* be sufficient to show that its disclosure is damaging.
[52] *The Guardian*, 19 November 1998.

an international organisation,[53] even though a civil court would not prevent its disclosure because it is in the public interest that its contents be revealed. Similarly, a disclosure of information by a former member of the security services may not be in breach of confidence because it is already widely publicised.[54] Any application to the courts to restrain its publication would therefore be unsuccessful. However, under s 1 of the 1989 Act it will still constitute a criminal offence. There is no need to show damage in relation to such disclosures, and the public interest which is served by the disclosure serves as no defence to the crime. In an age of easy transnational communication via the internet, where information can lose its confidentiality by communication abroad which is easily and legally accessible in the UK, it is increasingly likely that information can lose its confidentiality in this way. Where the information does not significantly harm national security, it is surely unnecessary to hold the person who discloses it criminally liable. The contradiction involved in allowing a disclosure to be made in the public interest, whilst holding the person who discloses it criminally liable, brings the whole of the Official Secrets legislation into disrepute, and aids the conclusion that the Official Secrets Acts impose unnecessary restrictions on freedom of speech.

As currently understood, the Official Secrets Acts significantly limit the speech of civil servants. Yet it is possible that these limitations will need to be lessened in future to ensure compliance with the ECHR, under the HRA 1998. HRA 1998 s 3 requires that legislation be interpreted to comply with the Convention where possible. The Official Secrets Acts will therefore need to be interpreted to comply with Article 10, guaranteeing the right to freedom of expression. This means that the existence of possible defences where disclosure is in the public interest may be able to be exploited in future cases. Although Article 10(2) explicitly allows restrictions on speech on matters of national security, any restrictions still need to be proportionate and necessary in a democratic society. It may be that, if it is recognised that the democratic process is served by freedom of speech on political and other public interest matters, the possible defence under OSA 1989 s 7 will be able to be read widely to create a form of public interest defence to the offences created under the Act. However, the margin of appreciation granted by the ECtHR to member states on matters relating to national security has traditionally been wide. Even interpreted in the light of the requirements of Article 10, the restrictions on speech contained in the 1989 Act may well remain lawful.

---

[53] Section 3(1)(b) and s 3(3).
[54] *Attorney-General v Guardian Newspapers (Spycatcher) (No 2)* [1990] 1 AC 109; *Attorney-General v Times Newspapers* [2001] 1 WLR 885.

CONCLUSION

Even though the Official Secrets Acts and codes of practice contain restrictions on the freedom of speech of staff within the civil service, those who wish to act as whistleblowers internally to raise concerns about wrongdoing at work remain as well protected as those in any other employment sector. Disclosures made in accordance with the procedures of the Civil Service Code or the CSMC will not count as disclosures under the Official Secrets Acts, and so will not risk prosecution. As long as they are made in good faith, such disclosures will also usually fall within the virtually automatic protection of the PIDA as the Codes set out clear internal disclosure procedures.

In contrast, other types of speech, such as political speech, principled dissent or general comment, are not given much protection at all. Public disclosure is not covered by the two Codes, is unlikely to be protected by the PIDA and in some cases may risk breaching the OSA, in which case staff will usually prefer not to risk prosecution for disclosure. As a result, the contribution that civil service staff might be able to make to better informed public debate on matters that are in the public interest is lost. Clearly, the requirements of political neutrality, the impartiality in the civil service, and the need for efficient running of services are all important, and would be impossible to achieve if staff could speak openly about government policy and practice at all times and in all places, and it is not suggested that unlimited freedom be allowed to the civil service. As the ECtHR rightly asserts,[55] some sectors of employment carry with them extra responsibilities of confidentiality, and the civil service is one such sector. However, unquestioning acceptance of absolute duties of confidence for the civil service may be a mistake. While it would be naïve to suggest that civil servants should enjoy exactly the same rights to free speech at work as all other employees, suggesting that civil servants should be given a degree of wider freedom does have some judicial backing, albeit not always in British courts. The French courts clearly thought that there should be a public interest defence to the OSA when they refused, on this ground, to allow the extradition of David Shayler to the UK on charges of breaching his lifelong ban on speech.[56] It was also suggested by the dissenting judges in *Ahmed v UK* that all members of society should be allowed to participate in public discussion of public issues, whether or not they were employed in government service.[57] Civil service staff have great potential to serve the public interest by exercising freedom of speech because of their close knowledge of the working of government. The imposition of a duty of confidence on such staff, without scope for a public interest defence, may mean that some information that ought to be

[55] *B v UK* (1986) 45 D&R 41.   [56] *The Guardian*, 19 November 1998.
[57] [2000] 29 EHRR 1, dissenting opinion, at para 5.

disclosed will remain secret. As a result, the public interest is likely to be badly served.

FREEDOM OF SPEECH IN
LOCAL GOVERNMENT

Local government staff, the core of the public sector, are another category of staff whose speech requires special protection. As in all areas of employment, there are reasons for restricting the free speech of staff. Local authorities are responsible for a wide range of public services, and there is a clear need for them to be run efficiently to as high a standard as possible. At times this may mean imposing restrictions on employee speech and a curtailing of debate on policy issues. There is clearly a public interest in allowing local authorities to deliver public services, and constant debate on policy may at times hinder this. Moreover, as with any employer, local authorities need to know that confidential information will retain its confidence, and that they can manage their employees with a degree of freedom and privacy without every decision being debated in public.

However, despite these reasons for restricting speech of local government staff, there are also very strong reasons for allowing them a greater degree of freedom of speech. Local government is responsible for a large area of public administration and public spending. Many essential public services are run by local councils including education and social services. Local councils also administer state benefits such as housing benefit, as well as being responsible for environmental and planning matters. Although many services traditionally provided by local authorities are now contracted out to private providers, local government retains overall responsibility for those services. The range of essential public services for which local government is responsible provides strong audience interests in allowing free speech for the staff who are likely to know first hand about many of the problems involved in their delivery. Moreover, local government staff are in a strong position to ensure that high standards of probity are maintained in this important area of the public service. In order to run the many types of public service for which they are responsible, local authorities control huge budgets made up of public money. The potential for fraud and corruption as well as maladministration and abuse of power is therefore huge, and employees can play an important role as whistleblowers in uncovering any wrongdoing.[58]

In addition to their potential role in uncovering wrongdoing, the speech of local government staff may also serve a democratic purpose. As suggested in Chapter 2, speech which informs public debate on matters that relate to

---

[58] For examples of fraud committed by local government employees, see *Local Government: Blowing the whistle on fraud and corruption* (1994) Public Concern at Work, London.

government policy should be given a high level of protection, so that the electorate can participate knowledgeably in the political process. This argument applies as much to local as to central government. Local government has undergone huge organisational change in recent years, and this process is continuing, with the move to compulsory competitive tendering in the 1980s and the current move to replace this with 'best value'.[59] These changes themselves, while not as high on the public agenda as issues such as education and health, are nonetheless of significance to the delivery of those more high profile services. It is thus equally important that the impact of the changes is monitored. Those who work in local government are likely to have first hand knowledge of the impact of the changes, and there are therefore strong audience interests in their views being aired.

Apart from any specific knowledge about the impact of changes in local government, many local government employees gain significant experience and knowledge about matters of political policy and practice through their work. They may therefore have a valid contribution to make to the local and national political process if allowed to contribute to public debate on matters of general interest. However, when considering the legal position in relation to their speech, it tends to be the case that the interests in confidentiality, impartiality and efficiency in local government prevail over the right of individual staff members to exercise full freedom of speech.

PROTECTION FOR WHISTLEBLOWING

If local government employees wish to raise concerns about matters at work, they are subject to the same legal constraints as most other employees. Many will have express confidentiality clauses that cover disclosures of information to outside bodies. They will also be covered by implied duties of confidence, and so will be subject to the exception to the duty of confidence where disclosure is in the public interest. In addition, the protection of the PIDA extends to local government staff if they raise concerns about relevant issues according to the procedures set out in the Act.

Moreover, as well as the provisions that apply to all employees, there are additional provisions that apply to local government staff which provide further routes for raising concerns about workplace matters. A voluntary code of conduct, produced by the former Local Government Management Board (LGMB),[60] imposes a positive obligation on staff to raise concerns about any deficiency in the provision of service, or any concern about impropriety. Under the Local Government Act 2000,[61] there is to be a new statutory code of conduct for council employees, in addition to the creation of standards committees and ethical officers to oversee the behaviour of local council

---

[59] Local Government Act 1985 and Local Government Act 1999.
[60] Replaced in April 1999 by the Employers' Organisation for Local Government and the Improvement and Development Agency.
[61] Local Government Act 2000 s 50.

members.[62] The code of conduct will set out the conduct expected of staff on a number of issues, and is likely to include a duty to raise matters of concern about improper conduct. It will not set up its own enforcement mechanism, but will be implemented via existing disciplinary arrangements and employment law.[63]

In addition to the code of practice governing many aspects of the ethical standards that apply to local government employees, the LGMB has produced a model whistleblowing procedure, which is also expected to form part of the new statutory code of conduct. It calls whistleblowing 'confidential reporting', a term which may be preferable to whistleblowing, with its emphasis on confidentiality rather than publicity. The Code emphasises the need to disclose internally, although it does allow that in some circumstances staff may want to raise concerns externally. The Code provides a clear mechanism for internal reporting, and also includes information on how the council will respond to concerns. This will help staff to be clear about how concerns have been addressed, which should in turn enable them easily to judge whether a satisfactory outcome has been achieved.

The types of information covered by the Code include those set out in the PIDA, but to these are added the unauthorised use of public funds and possible fraud and corruption. In both cases such conduct would probably be covered in any event by provisions of the PIDA[64] but their specific inclusion adds clarity to the Code and avoids any doubts that could arise, particularly where staff are operating without the advantage of legal advice. In addition to a list of subject matters of concern, staff are given guidance about the types and levels of concern that are appropriate for reporting. These include reporting that the member of staff feels uncomfortable about a failure to meet known standards of conduct, concerns about behaviour that falls below established standards of conduct or practice, or behaviour that amounts to improper conduct. The Code thus makes clear that it is not only concerns about legal wrongdoing that the employer wants to be reported, but any breach of accepted standards of conduct at work. The wide range of concerns listed in the Code suggests a wish by management that the Code be used to uncover wrongdoing at any level, and makes the assurances about the lack of reprisals for reporting more credible.

Another positive aspect of the Code is that it carries an introduction setting out the purpose of the Code, and making a clear commitment to take concerns seriously and avoid victimisation. Staff reading the Code should as a result be given as much assurance as is possible in this type of document that they will be safe to raise concerns. It is to be hoped that the new statutory

---

[62] Local Government Act 2000 ss 53–56.

[63] See the White Paper, 'Modern Local Government: In Touch With The People', published in July 1998.

[64] They would amount to criminal offences, or to breaches of a legal obligation.

code of practice will follow the positive aspects of the current voluntary code.

The overall effect of the PIDA and the code of conduct is that local government employees should be protected if they face retaliation for raising concerns about illegal conduct at work. Even if concerns are raised externally to the organisation, they should be protected if the member of staff has complied with the provisions of the PIDA. The statutory protection, together with a fairly thorough code of practice and internal procedures, means that as much as possible has been done via the mechanism of formal and informal written procedures to make staff feel safe to raise such concerns. Whether or not staff do feel safe in practice will depend on the spirit in which the procedures are operated on the ground. The words of the local government employers, contained in their code of conduct, speak clearly in terms of protection for staff. The reality of the protection will depend on whether the actions of individual managers speak as loudly as those words. Nonetheless, the legal and extra-legal protection available for staff who blow the whistle on public interest concerns are about as strong as it is realistic to expect, and the protection for whistleblowers in local government does seem to meet the standards set out in Chapter 2 for model protection for this type of speech at work. This can be contrasted with the poor protection available for other types of speech such as political speech.

RESTRICTIONS ON OTHER FORMS OF SPEECH

Apart from cases where serious wrongdoing is revealed, where the public interest is clearly served by disclosure, the extent to which local government employees may exercise the right to free speech is limited. In particular, statutory restrictions are imposed on the right to free political speech for certain local government employees. As with the civil service, an employee with a career in local government will not agree with all policies followed by the range of political parties who may control the local council, but owes a duty of loyalty in any event to implement those policies. The implied public interest exception to which the duty of loyalty is subject does not reach as far as to allow employees to participate in general public debate on policy issues, even though they may have considerable experience and expertise in the area under debate.

The Local Government and Housing Act 1989 (the LGHA) contains provisions that have a significant impact on the wider freedom of speech of local government employees. The LGHA was introduced in the face of what was seen as an abuse of political power by some local authorities in taking part in party political campaigns.[65] They are drafted widely and have potentially

---

[65] See G. Ganz, 'The Depoliticisation Of Local Authorities: The Local Government And Housing Act 1989 Part I' [1988] PL 225.

far-reaching consequences for local authority employees who wish to participate in political activity,[66] as well as potentially affecting those who wish to
participate in more general public debate. The aim of the LGHA was to
reduce the extent to which politically active council employees could be in a
position to give policy advice to a council.[67] Prior to its introduction, a number of councils were run by councillors who were employed by neighbouring
councils, a practice known as twin-tracking.[68] For example, Derek Hatton,
the deputy leader of Liverpool city council, was also a community development officer employed by Knowsley borough council. It was felt that this was
inappropriate because of the political impact it could have on the councillor's
paid work, particularly where it involved giving policy advice, or implementing party political policies. There were also concerns about divided loyalties,
as well as a fear that council employees were taking too much paid time off to
devote to their work as councillors in neighbouring areas.[69] However, the response contained in the LGHA goes far beyond restricting twin-tracking,
and impacts upon the freedom of some employees to take part in lobbying
and pressure group work, and on their freedom to participate in debate on
matters of public importance which have political overtones.

The LGHA prevents particular categories of local authority employees
from holding any political post, or from participating in political activity.[70]
One of the matters of concern in the Act is the wide range of employees
prevented from taking part in political activities.[71] The restrictions[72] apply
to local government employees who are involved in a job which involves the
formulation of policy, such as the chief officers of environmental health,
transport, housing, etc,[73] any employee who earns over a certain level
(pegged to the pay grade of employees of certain seniority),[74] and any
employee whose job entails giving advice to the authority or speaking on a
regular basis on behalf of the authority to journalists and broadcasters.[75]
The provisions do not apply to teachers.[76] Staff who are covered by the regulations by virtue of their salary or because of the nature of their duties can
apply to an 'independent adjudicator' to be exempted from the provisions of
the Act.[77] Although the proportion of staff affected by the regulations is only
2% of total local government staff, the numbers are high, an estimated
47,000 people.[78]

---

[66] See G. Morris, 'Political Activities of Public Servants and Freedom of Expression' in
I. Loveland, *Importing the First Amendment* (1998) Hart Publishing, Oxford.
[67] The LGHA 1989 introduced the proposals of the Widdicombe Committee, 'The Conduct
of Local Authority Business', Cmnd 9797 (1986).
[68] See Ganz, n 65 above.
[69] The extent to which this was a real problem is discussed in Ganz, n 65 above.
[70] LGHA 1989 ss 1–2.
[71] For detail on the restrictions, see Morris, 'Political Activities of Public Servants and
Freedom of Expression', n 66 above.
[72] Sections 1 and 2.   [73] Non-statutory officers, s 2(1)(e).   [74] Section 2(2)(a).
[75] Section 2(3).   [76] Section 2(10).
[77] Section 3.   [78] Government figures provided in the *Ahmed* case, see below.

Employees who are covered by the regulations are barred from any political activity as prescribed by regulation of the Secretary of State.[79] Current regulations[80] prohibit standing as a candidate for election in local, national or European elections, canvassing in such elections, holding office or committee membership of a political party (although mere membership of a party is allowed). Qualifying staff are also prevented from participating in political activity including speaking to a section of the public, or publishing work with the aim of gaining public support for a political party. This can cover voicing support for a political party or for a cause that is identifiable with one particular party. Given the variety of issues that may be associated with one particular party, this could have a significant impact on the speech of employees who wish to participate in debate on matters of public importance, as such activity could be classed as political. In other contexts, such as the political activities of charities and trade unions, campaigning for a change in the law or in government policy is classed as political.[81] So the employee who engages in public debate about policy changes on matters such as health or education, whether or not using experience or expertise gained through her job, could be said to be engaging in political activity. Where this is the case, relevant local government employees could find that participation in public debate runs the risk of breaching the provisions of the LGHA. Although no such use of the restrictions has been made thus far, they may still inhibit the participation of such employees in important public debate.

The restrictions on local authority employees from partaking in political activity clearly have significant impact upon the freedom of expression of those employees who are subject to them, and their validity has been challenged on this basis. A test case, *Ahmed v UK*,[82] was heard in 1998 at the ECtHR on the basis that the regulations are a breach of Article 10 ECHR. The case was brought by four local authority employees who came within the restricted groups of employees, and who had been prevented from participating in political activity as a result. The impact of the restrictions on the individual applicants varied. One applicant, a council solicitor who gave advice on the Housing Benefits Review Board and a Housing Development Sub-Committee, had to withdraw as a candidate for election, two other local government officers had to resign from office in their local branches of the Labour Party. The final applicant was a Head of Committee Services, which involved contact with and advice to council members. He had to resign

---

[79] Section 1(5).
[80] The Local Government Officers (Political Restrictions) Regulations 1990 SI 1990/851. Updated in 1998 and 1999 to reflect devolution in Scotland and Wales.
[81] In the trade union context, *Mercury Communications Ltd v Scott-Garner and the POEU* [1983] IRLR 494, *Associated British Ports v TGWU* [1989] IRLR 291 and *London Borough of Wandsworth v NAS/UWT* [1993] IRLR 344. For charities, see *National Anti-Vivisection Society v IRC* [1948] AC 31, *Baldry v Feintuck* [1972] 1 WLR 552 and *McGovern v Attorney-General* [1982] Ch 321. See also *R v Radio Authority ex parte Bull* [1997] 2 All ER 561.
[82] (2000) 29 EHRR 1.

his position in the Labour Party and was unable to speak at public meetings on matters such as health and housing. This last applicant's case is perhaps the most significant for the purposes of the discussion on freedom of speech, as he was prevented from taking part in discussion on matters of public importance by virtue of his job, which involved giving advice on other issues.

Under Article 10(2), restrictions on freedom of speech are allowed where they protect the rights of others, and are necessary in a democratic society. The needs of the democracy will be of particular significance when considering the speech of members of a particular level of government within that democracy, and it may well be that some restrictions are necessary. However, it was suggested by the applicants that the restrictions in the LGHA did not meet the requirements of Article 10(2). Not only was it not clear which 'rights of others' were protected by the regulations, but the regulations were too broad, applying to staff who had an insignificant role in policy advice. The types of advice given by some of the applicants were purely technical, and could not be influenced by political affiliation. Moreover, the restrictions were said to be unduly restrictive of the right to free speech, in particular the right to participate in public debate. The applicants argued that the participation in political activity of the staff was not such as to threaten the constitutional or democratic order of the state, and that they were not necessary to democratic society.

Despite the seeming strength of these arguments, the ECtHR held that the restrictions on the political activities of local government staff were not in breach of Article 10 ECHR. They identified a right to an effective political democracy which needed protection, and found that the regulations were necessary in a democratic society to uphold this right. Moreover, the Court was of the view that the fact that the regulations did not cover all staff, and that most employees who were covered could apply to be exempted, meant that the restrictions were proportionate to their aim, and therefore came within the margin of appreciation allowed to states.

The Court focused on the rights of others to an effective political democracy, a hitherto unidentified right, and seemed mainly concerned with restrictions on local government staff in participating in elections either as candidates themselves or as canvassers for others. They did not distinguish between these cases and those where the employee is restricted from participation in more general public debate on issues that may be unrelated to the areas in which he works in an advice-giving capacity. The failure to draw such a distinction is disappointing, particularly as one applicant had had to desist from speaking about national health issues on the radio by virtue of his job as a planning manager with a local council. It is unclear why a job relating to planning, even at a policy level, should disentitle someone from participating in debates on health care, and yet this issue was not addressed by the Court. In effect, they gave little weight to general freedom of speech principles, such as the need to protect audience interests, and the role of free speech in up-holding the democratic process.

The decision of the Court is discouraging for those wishing to see greater freedom of speech for local government staff, particularly as a number of issues that would support a different decision seem to have been disregarded. The decision was not unanimous; three judges dissented from the view of the majority.[83] The views of this minority are worth considering, as they identify most of those points disregarded by the majority of the Court in coming to their decision. Whilst accepting that a level of neutrality is undoubtedly necessary in local government, the three dissenting judges felt that the regulations were more restrictive than was necessary to achieve this. For example, other European states with effective democratic systems do not find it necessary to impose such restrictions on their public servants. Instead, individual staff are left to act as they feel appropriate, with action being taken after the event if necessary, through disciplinary measures. The difficulty with the restrictions in the LGHA is that they apply in a blanket fashion to the expression of all opinion that could be associated with a political party. This covers an unduly wide range of issues with the result that the staff involved operated under almost permanent self censorship. The dissenting judges also noted that public servants should not be expected to be silent members of society and should have the right to participate in public discussion of public issues. This was particularly the case because of the large numbers of staff involved, approximately 47,000 staff. Although only a small proportion of the total number of employees, the numbers are high, and suggest that the coverage of the regulations may be too broad.

The views of the minority of the Court give much greater emphasis to the wide scope and coverage of the restrictions, and the effect this has of restricting free speech on a wide range of issues, some of which may have political overtones. In contrast, the majority of the Court in *Ahmed* concentrated on restrictions on local government staff in participating in elections, and did not distinguish between these cases and those where the employee is restricted from participation in more general public debate. By treating all types of speech in the same way, and failing to identify when free speech for local government staff might be appropriate, they failed to provide adequate protection for all staff to exercise their freedom of speech even where a democratic purpose might be served by the speech.

Moreover, it seems that, after *Ahmed*, the LGHA regulations are here to stay. In their decision the Court referred to the fact that the new Labour government in 1997 had undertaken a review of the regulations, and had concluded that they were still necessary. The decision not to revise the regulations is confirmed in *Modern Local Government: In Touch With The People*, the 1998 White Paper that preceded the Local Government Act 2000. The

---

[83] Judges Spielmann, Pekkanen and Van Dijk.

intention is to continue with the existing framework and merely revise the earnings threshold upwards to ensure that only the correct level of staff is covered.

The decisions of the ECtHR in *Ahmed*, and of the government to maintain the current regulations, mean that the right to free speech for local government staff is not adequately protected. It is reasonable for there to be some restrictions on speech. As identified in Chapter 2, some staff, by virtue of their jobs, will need to limit their freedom of speech. More senior employees are bound by a greater degree of loyalty towards their employer than others, and this is no less the case in relation to local government. Such restrictions are recognised in the jurisprudence of the ECHR,[84] and by the ILO in its Convention No 111 which protects against discrimination on grounds of political opinion.[85] However, the LGHA regulations restrict the fundamental right to freedom of speech of a large number of individuals, and limits are placed on all political activity and speech, even in areas not directly related to the areas of policy in which the staff member gives advice. To this extent, they are unduly restrictive of free speech, and may breach the requirements of the ILO. Staff are prohibited from full participation in the democratic process, with a consequent loss not only to their own personal autonomy, but to the very democratic process that the restrictions were said to uphold. The refusal to allow this large group of public servants to voice their opinions on a range of public issues denies the public a chance to hear what they may have to say, and the democratic process is the poorer as a result.

FREEDOM OF SPEECH IN THE NATIONAL HEALTH SERVICE

Freedom of speech in the NHS is of particular interest because of the range of competing forces that impact upon it. The NHS operates in a highly political context, with the state of the health service a high priority for much of the electorate. There are thus strong audience interests in having accurate information on how it is performing. The freedom of speech of staff could play a valuable role in serving these interests. Yet NHS staff also work in a field in which the protection of confidentiality is especially important. The dual public interests in disclosure of information and in confidentiality are therefore thrown into sharp relief.

After the high profile disasters such as the explosion on the Piper Alpha oil rig and the capsize of the *Herald of Free Enterprise*, the NHS has perhaps been the most important source of pressure towards recognising the value of protecting free speech at work during the 1990s. A number of individual

---

[84]   *E v Switzerland* (1984) 38 D&R; *B v UK* (1986) 45 D&R 41.
[85]   See discussion in Chapter 3.

cases raised awareness both of the difficulties facing staff who wished to raise concerns, and of the potential value of allowing them to do so. Helen Zeitlin mentioned nursing shortages at a public meeting. Although she was ultimately successful in gaining reinstatement after an appeal to the Secretary of State for Health, she did not return to her job.[86] Graham Pink published in *The Guardian* a series of letters he had written to hospital managers, his MP, the Chief Executive of the NHS, the Secretary of State for Health and the Prime Minister. In these he raised concerns about staffing levels on the ward in which he worked. He also spoke to the local press about his concerns. He was dismissed for gross misconduct.[87] Stephen Bolsin left the NHS after finding it impossible to continue work after he had raised concerns about high mortality rates following heart surgery on young babies at the Bristol Royal Infirmary. He was proved correct at the subsequent inquiry into the conduct of the surgeons concerned, but did not return to his old job.[88]

The importance of free speech and the need for whistleblowing procedures in the NHS has now been officially recognised on a number of occasions. The NHS Executive was one of the first bodies to take action on the issue of whistleblowing, publishing its *Guidance for Staff on Relations with the Public and the Media* in 1993 in the wake of the Zeitlin and Pink cases. This was followed by the First Report of the Nolan Committee on Standards in Public Life[89] which made recommendations for the introduction of whistleblowing procedures for employees of various public bodies, including the NHS. In 1997 in a letter to Chairs of NHS trusts, the Minister of State for Health emphasised the importance of free speech for the NHS and requested the removal of gagging clauses from the employment contracts of staff. The original NHS Executive *Guidance* was updated in August 1999[90] to reflect the entry into force of the PIDA. It was followed in April 2000 by the publication of a whistleblowing policy by the newly constituted Commission for Health Improvement. These various moves suggest that, as with local government, the issue of whistleblowing and freedom of speech within the NHS is being taken seriously at least at a policy level. Whether these policies are followed through in practice is, of course, a more difficult question to assess. Yet, even at the level of policy, these moves are valuable, as they recognise, at governmental level, the importance of freedom of speech in relation to the NHS.

[86]   *The Independent*, 10 September 1993.
[87]   *The Guardian*, 11 April 1990, *Stockport Express Advertiser*, 25 July 1990. See G. Pink, 'Whistleblowing: for whom the truth hurts' (1992) *The Guardian* and *Charter 88*, London.
[88]   *The Guardian*, 30 May 1998, confirmed by the Secretary of State for Health HC Deb, 18 June 1998 cols 529–30.
[89]   London, HMSO 1995.
[90]   'The Public Interest Disclosure Act 1998: Whistleblowing in the NHS', NHS Executive, HSC 1999/198, 27 August 1999.

Freedom of speech in the NHS is important, as mentioned above, because of the strong public interests served by allowing staff freedom of speech. The arguments in favour of freedom of speech based on the democratic value of speech are particularly strong in the case of public sector employment, and the arguments against allowing speech are correspondingly weaker as the economic interests in restricting speech are limited in respect of public sector employers. In the case of the NHS, the audience interests of speech are particularly strong because of the political significance of the NHS as a national institution. The principle of good quality health care, free at the point of delivery, is very important to the public and if they are to do well at the ballot box, governments need to be seen to uphold it. Full public debate on standards of care within the health service is therefore immensely important. In addition, the NHS has undergone massive organisational change in the last few decades,[91] at times without support from the medical profession.[92] Moreover, more change is due with proposals to introduce increased private sector funding into the NHS in the face of strong public sector union opposition.[93] As a result, the debate on standards of care has become highly politically sensitive. As discussed in Chapter 2 above, in relation to speech with a political dimension, the arguments for employment protection are particularly strong. In addition to serving the personal autonomy of the speaker, freedom of political speech upholds the democratic process, by allowing the fullest possible discussion of political matters. The participation of those who are knowledgeable about the subject, often employees, is needed if this discussion is to be sufficiently well informed. Additional arguments in favour of free speech in this context can be found in Mill's argument based on truth,[94] that debate and discussion of practice in the NHS may lead to improvements in the service offered.

The argument in favour of protecting free speech within the health service is complicated, however, because of the competing interests that exist. Set against the strong reasons for protecting speech are equally strong interests in preserving confidence. Patient confidentiality is a fundamental right in the context of health care, and is most famously traced to the Hippocratic Oath. It binds all those who work within the NHS, and is set out in its modern form in the codes of practice of the GMC and UKCC, the bodies that govern the professional conduct of the nursing and medical professions. Thus the traditional duty of confidence that is owed by all employees to their employers is augmented in the NHS by additional ethical obligations to patients. In terms

[91] The National Health Service and Community Care Act 1990 created new NHS hospital trusts. It introduced an internal market to the NHS. The internal market is now being dismantled after the change of government in 1997.

[92] The British Medical Association campaigned against the 1990 changes.

[93] *The Guardian*, 17 July 2001.

[94] See J. S. Mill, 'On Liberty' in S. Collini (ed), *On Liberty and Other Writings* (1989) Cambridge University Press, Cambridge. See Chapter 2 above.

of individual autonomy, the right to freedom of expression does not fare well when competing with the rights of patients.

In Chapter 2 it was argued that the democratic interest in political speech would often outweigh the financial and managerial interests of employers in preserving confidence. However, in the case of health service staff, the interest in confidence is not just financial or managerial: it is also ethical. This powerful interest in patient confidentiality introduces additional complications into the equation. There are two main reasons for upholding patient confidence. First, information relating to health is very often of a personal and private nature. Confidence should be upheld out of respect for patient autonomy, privacy and human integrity. Secondly, patient confidence needs to be upheld for the more practical reason that patients should not be deterred from seeking medical treatment for fear that confidence will be breached. Encouraging patients to come forward for treatment is essential not only for the individual's health but for general public health too. If infectious diseases or certain mental illnesses are left untreated, this can represent a risk to public health or safety. A fear that confidence will be breached could deter patients with such conditions from seeking the medical attention they both need and deserve. For both these reasons, based on individual autonomy and wider public interests, confidentiality in respect of patient information is, rightly, strictly observed.

Nonetheless, patient confidentiality is not an absolute right and where the public interest demands, the duty of confidence can be outweighed, just as it can in the general law on confidentiality.[95] In *W v Egdell*[96] the public interest in disclosure of a psychiatric report was said to override any breach of confidence. The report had been obtained in connection with proceedings before a mental health review tribunal, and had been held back by the patient's solicitors as it was not favourable to the patient's case: the doctor had reported that the patient was still dangerous. The public interest was found to override any breach of confidence involved, because those involved in the patient's continuing treatment needed to know the contents of the report. Moreover, a breach of a patient's confidence may be partial rather than total; for instance the disclosure may be of the fact that a treatment was carried out without disclosure of the name of the patient, such that the general public do not know who is referred to but the patient and her relatives do. Where this is all that is disclosed, it is arguable that the public interest may more easily justify the disclosure than where breach of confidence is total. For example, discussion of incidents occurring in day to day medical practice may be necessary to add weight to any general discussion on standards of care; such disclosures may serve the general public interest in the way discussed above, and if this involves a partial breach of confidence, this may be justified.

---

[95] Discussed in Chapter 4 above.   [96] [1990] Ch 359.

LEGAL AND ETHICAL OBLIGATIONS OF CONFIDENTIALITY ON NHS STAFF

The competition between the competing public interests in patient confidence and political speech is played out in the various professional codes and government guidance that govern medical staff. The UKCC and the GMC have professional codes of conduct which refer to both the duty to maintain patient confidence and the duty to uphold the public interest. In addition, the government provided guidance on freedom of speech for NHS staff in 1993, which was updated in 1999 in the light of the PIDA. In 2000, the Commission for Health Improvement produced a model whistleblowing policy. These various documents operate in addition to the usual employment duties of trust and confidence owed by staff to their employers, and so govern the freedom of speech of NHS staff.

UKCC Code of Professional Conduct[97]

The Code of Professional Conduct covers all nursing, midwifery and health visiting staff in the UK. Breach of the Code could lead to loss of registration with the UKCC, which in turn could lead to loss of employment as NHS employers require staff to be registered with their respective governing body.[98] The Code sets out the standards expected in relation to professional practice and covers issues such as the need to work co-operatively with others, to maintain professional competence, and to respect the dignity of patients. On confidentiality, the Code states that staff must 'protect all confidential information concerning patients and clients obtained in the course of professional practice and make disclosures only with consent, where required by the order of a court or where you can justify disclosure in the wider public interest' (Clause 10); and 'report to an appropriate person or authority any circumstances in which safe and appropriate care for patients and clients cannot be provided' (Clause 12).

Several matters are worth noting in relation to these clauses. Most obvious is the reference in Clause 10 to the public interest, something that many individual employment contracts lack. The importance of protecting patient confidence is clear in the clause, but the possibility of the public interest overriding that confidence is acknowledged and provided for. Significantly, the clause also states that the individual nurse is to be the judge of the public interest in relation to such information. The designation of the nurse as the judge of the public interest may be helpful in whistleblowing cases. The nurse who breaches confidence in the genuine belief that the public interest is served by the disclosure can be confident that she is not in breach of the UKCC Code. She may also be able to argue that this part of the UKCC Code is incorporated into her contract of employment, and can be used to resolve any ambiguity in the contract

---

[97] The third edition of the UKCC Code of Professional Conduct was published in 1992.
[98] For example, the UKCC for nursing staff, and the General Medical Council for doctors.

over who may authorise disclosure and, perhaps, what may lawfully be disclosed.

A second point that is made clear from the Code and from explanatory notes that accompany it is the extent to which nurses are expected by their professional body to raise concerns and not to tolerate low standards of care. This is made clear in Clause 12. Additionally, the 1996 UKCC *Guidelines for professional practice* make clear that matters such as the standards of care offered by the NHS and concerns about the practical implications of shortages of resources are the legitimate concern of nursing staff, and should not be ignored. The suggestion from the UKCC Code and its guidelines is that raising concerns, or blowing the whistle, about standards of care in the NHS may serve the public interest, and may therefore give rise to a legitimate restriction on the duty of patient confidentiality.

The GMC Code

In its guidance for doctors 'Confidentiality: Protecting and Providing Information',[99] the GMC is more restrictive in its definition of the public interest than the UKCC. The GMC puts primacy on the duty of confidence owed to patients whilst discussing circumstances in which confidential information can be disclosed, such as where there is patient consent or where disclosure is ordered by a court. The GMC also includes a duty to disclose in the general public interest but, unlike in the UKCC Code, the GMC Code provides a definition of the term. It provides that information may be disclosed in the public interest where 'the benefits to an individual or society of the disclosure outweigh the public interest and the patient's interest in keeping the information confidential'.[100] The emphasis in the Code seems to be more on the duty not to make disclosures than in pointing out the occasions on which it might serve the public interest to disclose information. The Code makes very clear that breaches of confidence harm not only the individual patient, but also the overall relationship of trust between doctors and patients.[101] It also states that, although the courts are the ultimate arbiter on where the public interest lies, the doctor who makes the disclosure is also answerable to the GMC if complaints are received.[102] The implication seems to be that the GMC may take a different view of the need to maintain confidentiality from that of the courts.

Where a doctor needs to blow the whistle on malpractice at work, it may well be that any confidential information disclosed in the process would be covered by the public interest definition allowed in the GMC guidance, although clearly individual confidence should only be breached if there is no other way of raising the concern. If a doctor revealed confidential

---

[99] General Medical Council, London 2000.
[100] 'Confidentiality: Protecting and Providing Information', GMC 2000, para 18.
[101] Ibid., para 19.
[102] Ibid., para 20.

information in the course of more general discussion, it is likely that the guidance would be breached, as there is no suggestion in the Code that raising a matter of concern about general standards of care would be covered by the guidance. This is not to say that doctors will never be allowed to raise such concerns, but, to accord with the guidance, they would need to be raised without breaching an individual's confidence, by ensuring that no patient details are divulged.

Guidance for Staff on Relations with the Public and the Media

Guidance was published in June 1993, by the NHS Management Executive,[103] and circulated to all managers in the NHS, setting out the principles that should be applied in dealing with those who wish to raise concerns at work. Although it is not legally binding, and does not replace contractual duties or local procedures, it does state that confidentiality clauses in individual contracts should not conflict with its terms. The guidance confirms that NHS staff have a right and duty to raise matters of concern,[104] that management must create systems that allow that to be done easily,[105] and that the working culture of the NHS should be one of openness where staff are encouraged to contribute their views on all aspects of health care.[106] It also recognises that free expression of views can lead to an improvement in the service.[107] The procedure envisaged by the guidance, by which this aim can be achieved, is an internal one. Staff should raise matters informally with their line manager first. Only if the informal procedure is ineffective should the matter be raised formally through the management line, or through a senior officer designated to hear such matters. Finally, the guidance refers to disclosures to the media, and states that these will give rise to disciplinary action if unjustified.

In some respects the guidance conflicts with the UKCC Code of Conduct governing the behaviour of nursing staff. Clause 3(iv) states that individual members of staff in the NHS have an obligation to safeguard confidential information, 'particularly information about individual patients and clients, which is *under all circumstances* strictly confidential' (emphasis added). Although the circumstances will be rare, it is possible for the public interest to be served by disclosure in extreme cases, a fact that is recognised in common law, in the UKCC Code and to a more limited extent in the GMC Code. Again, Clause 8 provides that 'unauthorised disclosure of personal information about any patient or client will be regarded as a most serious matter which will always warrant disciplinary action. This applies even where a member of staff believes that she is acting in the best interests of a patient or client by disclosing personal information.' This directly contradicts Clause

---

[103] Now the NHS Executive.   [104] Para 3(i).   [105] Para 3(ii).
[106] Para 5.   [107] Para 5.

10 of the UKCC Code which provides that it is for the nurse to decide for herself whether the public interest is served by a disclosure.

The Public Interest Disclosure Act 1998 and NHS Whistleblowing Policies

In August 1999 the NHS Executive published a circular on 'Whistleblowing in the NHS' designed to help NHS trusts implement the PIDA.[108] This was sent to health authorities together with a resource pack containing model whistleblowing procedures and policies, training and promotional materials and details of a free helpline for NHS staff.[109] The circular requires all health authorities to put into place local policies and procedures by which staff can raise concerns. Any policy must designate a senior manager or non-executive director to deal with matters that have to be raised outside the usual management chain, and staff are to be provided with guidance on how to raise concerns about malpractice reasonably and responsibly. The policy must also make clear that concerns will be treated seriously and staff must be guaranteed not to face victimisation for raising the concern. The circular also confirms again that 'gagging' clauses are not to be used. In April 2000, the newly created Commission for Improvement of Health produced a draft policy on whistleblowing for those who work for the NHS directly or under contract to provide care for NHS patients, so that concerns about issues such as clinical malpractice or healthcare system failures can be reported without reprisals.

These more recent policy developments have followed the introduction of the PIDA, which itself creates significant protection for NHS staff who wish to raise issues of concern at work. Given that health and safety of the employee or others is a protected subject matter under the Act, most concerns raised by staff will be covered. The Act does not require imminent danger to health, and so general concerns about levels of funding or mismanagement can be covered as well as more immediate dangers such as disclosures about competence of particular members of staff. Under the PIDA, staff can raise concerns internally, using the procedures that should be set up in accordance with the 1999 NHS Executive circular. Concerns can also be raised with the Department of Health directly, without losing the protection of the Act. Other disclosures, external to the organisation, will need to comply with the provisions of the PIDA by having good reason for being made externally, and by being reasonable.[110] One factor in assessing reasonableness, which may have particular impact on NHS staff, is whether disclosure is made in breach of a duty of confidence

---

[108] 'The Public Interest Disclosure Act 1998: Whistleblowing in the NHS', NHS Executive, HSC 1999/198, 27 August 1999.
[109] This resource pack was produced by Public Concern at Work.
[110] ERA 1996 s 43(g). See Chapter 5 above.

owed by the employer to any other person. Disclosures that breach patient confidentiality will be less likely to be reasonable. However, this is not to say that they will never be reasonable. Courts may take into account the extent of the breach of confidence, as well as whether the public interest is served by disclosure. Where this is the case, external disclosure may be reasonable.

The Adequacy of Protection for Freedom of Speech in the NHS

As with other sectors, those who engage in whistleblowing speech, raising concerns about illegality or irregularity at work, are likely to be protected against any reprisals from employers. For nursing staff, the UKCC Code of Conduct imposes an obligation to raise such concerns; for all staff, the guidance envisages such concerns being raised; and the public interest exception to the implied duty of confidence will override any express term to the contrary in upholding the right of the employee to disclose such wrongdoing. For serious cases, all these sources of obligation on the employee allow for external disclosure. As in the case of local government staff, those who work for the NHS enjoy, at a policy level, a high degree of protection if they blow the whistle on wrongdoing or other public interest concerns.

Again, as with those in local government, the reality on the ground may feel somewhat different. Dr Stephen Bolsin's difficulty in continuing to work for the NHS, after he had raised his concerns about mortality rates at the Bristol Royal Infirmary, occurred despite the introduction in 1993 of the NHS *Guidance to Staff* which encourages the raising of concerns. Similarly, in November 2000, an external review of the cardiac services at the Oxford Radcliffe NHS Trust highlighted a number of serious inadequacies in the Oxford Cardiac Services. Alongside grave concerns about clinical practice was a concern about the lack of whistleblowing procedures. It was pointed out that a draft policy was introduced in September 1998 but had never been implemented.[111] If staff in the NHS are to feel safe to raise public interest concerns and blow the whistle on malpractice, it is incumbent on those with responsibility for the various policies to ensure that they work as strongly in practice as they appear on paper.

Despite the practical difficulties that they may experience, NHS staff enjoy a significant measure of protection for their freedom of speech in relation to whistleblowing speech, both under legislation such as the PIDA, and under the various codes of practice and NHS policies. Much more limited is the protection for more generalised freedom of speech. Where NHS staff wish to engage in other types of speech, such as political speech or general comment, they have no special protection, despite, or perhaps because of, the potential political importance of their speech. The concerns of NHS staff which do not relate to wrongdoing typically involve issues such as funding levels, staffing

---

[111] Report of the External Review into Oxford Cardiac Services (NHS Executive, 2000).

levels, managerial support, etc.[112] Any accusations arguably amount to no more than 'mismanagement' and as such may not be covered by the PIDA, and may not justify any breach of confidence involved in their disclosure.[113] Although the NHS Executive's Guidance and Circulars recognise that contributions from staff to any debate on the NHS can help improve the service, those wishing to raise such concerns will not find encouragement in the emphasis in these publications on internal reporting, especially since effective debate requires a degree of publicity. Those wishing to participate in any public debate on standards of care in the NHS will need to take great care not to disclose any confidential information, as the public interest defence may not apply in such cases. This is likely to be the case until the general public interest in informed political debate is recognised by the courts. Until this happens, the right to freedom of speech for those who work within the NHS will continue to be inadequately protected, and the lack of a clear voice for those who work within this huge and politically sensitive organisation will continue to impoverish our democratic process.

CONCLUSION

This review of the protection of speech in key areas of the public sector indicates that whistleblowers are well protected. Each area, the civil service, local government and the NHS, now have in place good internal processes by which matters of concern about wrongdoing at work can be raised. In part this is a response to the recommendations in various reports of the Nolan Committee on Standards in Public Life that procedures be set up in these areas. Added to these internal procedures and codes of practice is the Public Interest Disclosure Act 1998, providing strong whistleblower protection.

It is in relation to more general speech, and political speech in particular, where the PIDA does not apply, that the protection is weaker. In none of the sectors is legal recognition given to the positive role in the political and democratic process played by the exercise of free speech. In Chapter 2 it was suggested that staff in the public sector can play a strong role in upholding democracy by their participation in public debate on matters of public importance, and that their political speech should be given protection against work based sanctions. Clearly this always needs to be subject to the needs of a politically impartial public service, the need for confidentiality for local and national government in the formulation of policy, and the need for the efficient delivery of public services. However, the almost total ban on participation in public debate by many public servants suggests that the

---

[112] See *Whistleblow*, Report on the Work of the RCN Whistleblow Scheme (1992) Royal College of Nursing, London.
[113] See *British Steel Corporation v Granada* [1981] AC 1097.

balance between these interests is not correctly set. Without advocating complete freedom, staff could be granted improved freedom of political expression without unduly upsetting the democratic process. Indeed, it is quite arguable that such increased political freedom for staff could result in its improvement.

7

Conclusions: A Right to Freedom of Speech at Work?

Freedom of speech is acknowledged to be a fundamental human right in all international human rights documents. The philosophical basis for its protection is well established, the freedom to speak, write, and discuss freely being fundamental to individual development, autonomy and human dignity. The political importance of free speech is also recognised as being an essential foundation of democratic society, 'one of the basic conditions for its progress and for the development of every man'.[1] Yet, within most human rights documents, the right to freedom of expression remains a statement of principle, albeit one of fundamental importance. The focus of this book has been to explore the practical scope of that right in one particular context, the world of work.

The examination of the right to freedom of expression within the work sphere involves an attempt to resolve an inherent conflict between the interests of the employee speaker and those of the employer and the enterprise for whom the employee works. To an extent, the tension between these competing rights can begin to be resolved by considering a third set of interests, those of the public in hearing what is said.

The rights of the employee to speak are based on the concept that freedom of expression is fundamental to the development and maintenance of individual autonomy and human dignity. For those interests to be fully protected, individuals need to be able to exercise the right to free speech in any sphere in which they operate. The workplace is a particularly important sphere in which individuals need the right to speak freely: a large amount of time is spent at work, and in many cases, individuals' identities can become expressed via their status at work. The workplace can become not only a place to earn a living, but a social space too, and so restrictions on employees' rights at work can be felt strongly. Thus, protection is required at work, because removing the right to free speech from employees will have a significant impact upon the exercise of their human rights. This additional aspect of the role of work in individual lives is reflected in the increasing legal recognition for individual dignity at work. As Collins has suggested, rights not to be discriminated against on grounds of gender or race, limits on working time, and

---

[1] *Handyside v UK* (1981) 1 EHRR 737.

other individual employee rights can be regarded as aspects of the need to protect dignity and autonomy at work.[2] It is suggested that a right to freedom of expression should be added to this list.

The counter argument to this is that protection for free speech in the context of work is unnecessary, because individuals retain their autonomy and dignity via their freedom to leave employment. The speaker is not prevented from speaking, as she can leave her job and then speak. This argument is often accepted by courts;[3] however, its force is weakened by the fact that most employees are dependent on their jobs for financial security, as well as for the fulfilment of individual autonomy and dignity. Freedom to leave employment may exist in legal theory but it is not experienced as a freedom in practice, and it does not begin to protect employees' rights to free speech adequately.

Set against the powerful interests in protecting employee free speech are equally powerful interests of the employer in restricting it. At times, employee speech will cause harm to the employing enterprise, such as financial loss or damage to its reputation. Alternatively, an employer may wish to prevent employees from exercising the right to free speech to prevent disruption at work from other staff who are upset by what is said, or to protect confidential or other sensitive information from reaching a potentially hostile public. In such cases, the employer will have a legitimate interest in restricting speech. Interests of the employer that are legitimate for these purposes include the avoidance of harm to the employer's economic interests; the protection of the employer's managerial prerogative over staff; the maintenance of the employer's own autonomy; and the preservation of employee confidence and loyalty.

These interests are not only personal interests of the employer. A public interest dimension is also involved. The employer is not the only party with an interest in good management and the efficient running of the business. Good management and efficient businesses may serve the employer's private interest in generating a profit, but they also lead to high levels of employment and a strong economy, the encouragement of which is clearly a matter of public interest. There is also a public interest in ensuring the best delivery of public services, both those provided by the public sector and those provided by private firms. Where the exercise of free speech endangers effective service delivery it can be argued that the public interest would be served by imposing some restrictions upon it.

The tension between these competing interests, some public and some private, can be difficult to resolve. Where an individual is prevented from speaking at all, it may be argued that the fundamental right to freedom of

---

[2] See discussion in Chapter 2 and H. Collins, *Justice in Dismissal* (1992) Clarendon Press, Oxford, at 16.

[3] See *Stedman v UK* (1997) 23 EHRR CD 168 and *Ahmad v UK* (1981) 4 EHRR 126.

expression overrides other interests. But where the employee is free to leave employment, he or she ultimately retains freedom of speech, albeit at a very high price in practice. Where the individual's expression is not completely prohibited, but only restricted, the arguments become more complex. A key issue in resolving the conflict between the employers' and employees' interests then becomes the question of the audience interests in hearing what the employee says. This leads to a differentiation between different types of speech, and the different reasons for its protection. The reasons for protecting free speech within the workplace, and the extent of any protection that should be created, vary according to the type and function of the speech.

Four different types of speech have been identified as needing protection within the workplace: whistleblowing; political speech; principled dissent; and general comment. One corollary of basing the right to free speech at work on the interests of those who hear the speech rather than on the rights of the speaker is that, in determining the scope of the right, the focus shifts more obviously to the content of speech. The autonomy of the speaker can be served by protecting any type of speech; true, false, serious or trivial. The interests of the audience are only really served by speech that is worth listening to. As a result, the extent to which free speech deserves protection is closely tied to the type and function of the speech itself.

WHISTLEBLOWING

Whistleblowing speech involves the disclosure of wrongdoing or malpractice that is taking place at work. Examples of the costs of restricting such speech were given in Chapter 1. Failure to listen to the concerns of staff relating to health and safety and other public interest matters have led to huge loss of life, serious injury, and financial loss.[4] The overriding interests served by protecting whistleblowing speech are the audience and public interests in hearing what the speaker has to say. Providing whistleblowers with legal protection should encourage more staff to raise concerns about health and safety, financial irregularity or other wrongdoing. Protection should be provided to employees not so much because the speech upholds the dignity of the speaker, but because it could uncover illegality or protect life and limb.

A number of other factors also suggest that workplace protection is appropriate. Whistleblowing speech relates to work and so protection against work based sanctions is legitimate. In cases where the speech relates to wrongdoing by the employer, or to wrongdoing condoned by the employer, it is right to provide protection at work. Counter arguments exist in favour of

[4] See the Public Inquiry into the Piper Alpha Disaster, November 1990, HMSO Cm 131; Investigation into the Clapham Junction Railway Accident, November 1989, HMSO Cm 820; Court Inquiry on the Capsize of the Herald of Free Enterprise, Department of Transport, Ct No 8074, 1987 HMSO; Inquiry into the Supervision of The Bank of Credit and Commerce International, 2 October 1992, HMSO.

restricting free speech in such cases, but they seem weak when set against the arguments for protection. For example, any argument based on the fact that employers need freedom to manage the enterprise without outside interference is thoroughly undermined when the employing organisation is trying to cover up its own wrongdoing by punishing the employee.

The arguments in favour of strong work based protection for this type of speech are overwhelming. They have recently been accepted and protection provided in the form of the Public Interest Disclosure Act 1998. The PIDA effectively creates a right to free speech at work on certain public interest matters. It is underpinned by the remedy of automatic unfair dismissal and unlimited compensation if the right is infringed. The rights created by the PIDA are extensive: the Act covers workers, not just employees, is exercisable without a minimum period of employment and there is no requirement that the employee be correct about her suspicion of wrongdoing. It applies to a very wide range of subject matters, including health and safety concerns, concerns about financial irregularity, environmental damage or criminal conduct. The protection provided by the PIDA covers cases where the employee exercises the right to free speech by disclosing wrongdoing to the employer. In such cases, there are no good reasons based on the employer's competing interests to deny protection to the employee.

However, the PIDA will only protect employees who use the correct procedures to raise the relevant concern. The main limitation on protection is that disclosures must in the first instance be made internally within the organisation, or to a prescribed outside body such as a regulator. External disclosure is only protected where there is good reason for reporting outside the organisation. Given that the purpose of protection is that the wrongdoings reported can be put right, this limitation balances the competing interests of employer and employee proportionately. As long as the employee exercises the right to free speech by disclosing information to a body enabled to deal with any wrongdoing, strong protection is given. If disclosure goes outside the organisation, for example to the media, then protection is unlikely, unless it is decided by a court that the media were best placed to prevent the reported wrongdoing from occurring. The emphasis on reporting to those who can take action confirms that the basis for protection under the PIDA is to protect the public interest in preventing wrongdoing or disaster, rather than protecting the autonomy rights of the employee.

Given the overwhelming moral argument for protecting whistleblowers at work, it is perhaps surprising that protection has only recently been introduced. However, there does now at last seem to be general acceptance of the need to protect whistleblowing speech at work. Incidents such as the explosion on the Piper Alpha oil rig and the capsize of the *Herald of Free Enterprise*, together with some high profile cases in the NHS, have confirmed in the view of the public that those who blow the whistle are not spoilsports or disloyal employees, but may instead be protectors of the public against malpractice and wrongdoing. The PIDA, together with the reports of the Nolan Committee on Standards in Public Life, has led to the introduction of internal whistleblowing procedures into many workplaces, such as NHS trusts, local government and universities. The practical difficulties that employees may face in bringing and proving their case should not detract from the fact that there is now very strong legal protection for a right to blow the whistle on wrongdoing at work.

POLITICAL SPEECH

More problematic is the position in relation to political speech. Arguments in favour of providing workplace protection for political speech are more likely to be predicated on the autonomy rights of the speaker: the ability to hold political opinions and to express those views clearly forming part of the right to free speech based on human dignity. To these personal interests can be added strong public or audience interests in allowing freedom of political speech. The protection of such speech supports the human dignity of the audience because their beliefs are developed by listening to the ideas and opinions of others.[5] The right to take part in the political process thus serves the personal autonomy goals of both the speaker and the audience.

The democratic process requires full and free participation in public debate, and employees wishing to take part in that public debate should ideally be protected from work based penalties imposed for doing so. However, any right to freedom of political speech is bound to be more circumscribed than the right to blow the whistle on wrongdoing at work as protected by the PIDA. One of the reasons for this is that the employing enterprise will not have forfeited its right to protect its interests by reason of its own wrongdoing. Other reasons for restricting workplace protection for employees' political speech include the employer's own autonomy, the interest in efficient management and the employer's interest in the good reputation of the enterprise.

The private interests of the enterprise could be harmed by political speech in a number of different ways. Depending on the status of the employee, political speech by staff could be taken to include a statement of the employer's position on the subject. The employer's autonomy interest would then be served by signalling his disagreement with the view expressed via dismissal or disciplinary measures taken against the speaker. Alternatively, political speech by the employee could interfere with the smooth running of an organisation. For example, if other staff are offended by the political views expressed, this could result in damage to working relationships. Any publicity generated by the employee's entry into public debate on matters of political significance may also need to be managed by the employer. Moreover,

---

[5] T. Scanlon, 'A Theory of Freedom of Expression' in R. M. Dworkin (ed), *The Philosophy of Law* (1977) Oxford University Press, Oxford.

discussions of a political nature may involve inherent criticism of the employer. For example, if an employee criticises current education policy, making reference to practice in the school in which she works, the employer may well feel the need to defend the implementation of the policy, even if it does not defend the government that introduced it.

As already stated, the interest in the smooth running of businesses and other enterprises is not merely a private employer interest, but has a public dimension. The sectors of employment with arguably the greatest party political importance are the public sector and public services. The delivery of public services via public or private sector organisations is a matter of intense political debate, and so public discussion about many aspects of public service delivery could legitimately be classed as political speech. While this creates strong reasons for protecting the speech, it is also fair to say that the delivery of these services is unlikely to be helped if they are over-politicised by staff working for them. It is therefore the case that a right to free political speech for staff will necessarily be circumscribed to a degree, particularly if the speech interferes too much with the employer's ability to deliver its services effectively.

Nonetheless, despite the fact that there may be both private, and to a more limited extent public, interests in restricting the protection at work of political speech, the important public interest in protecting political speech should in many cases prevail over those interests. Free discussion about how government policies are working, or about how a public utility is being run, can help the public participate knowledgeably in the political process. It can also serve as a form of accountability on the state and government agencies. Political speech is distinctively important: as is consistently recognised in the jurisprudence of the ECHR[6] it deserves significant protection within the workplace in order to prevent employers or the state from deciding what types of speech should be allowed.

Current legal protection for political speech is fairly minimal and falls short both of the international standards set by the ILO in its protection against discrimination on grounds of political opinion in Convention No 111, and of the ideal level required by the strong public interest in this type of speech. Unless wrongdoing is disclosed, the legal protection for employees available under the PIDA does not apply. Instead, the employee is dependent on the general protection against unfair dismissal. As currently interpreted, dismissals are fair unless they are outside the range of reasonable employer responses to the conduct involved. It is quite likely that some reasonable employers would dismiss employees for voicing political views, especially if the views expressed draw on workplace experiences, cause embarrassment to

---

[6] 'Freedom of expression constitutes one of the essential foundations of [a "democratic society"], one of the basic conditions for its progress and for the development of every man.' *Handyside v UK* (1981) 1 EHRR 737.

the employer or generate adverse publicity. This means that the legislation provides employees with very little freedom of political speech. In addition, specific limits are placed on the right of local government and civil service staff to engage in political speech.[7]

PRINCIPLED DISSENT

Principled dissent, as a type of speech, lies on the borders between political speech and general comment. One of the difficulties in framing a clear right to free political speech is in determining when speech should be classified as political, and this category covers that border line. The arguments in favour of protecting principled dissent merge, to an extent, with those for protecting political speech, and are based on the audience's right to hear what is said by the dissenter. At times the speech may be quasi-political, such as public debate on the standards of service in the public sector, and other politically sensitive issues. Examples include teachers speaking in public about the impact on schools of changes in education policy, and NHS staff participating in debate on standards of care in NHS trust hospitals. In both cases, such speech can be classed as either principled dissent or political speech, as the speech relates to issues that are politically important. As with pure political speech, discussion of these matters by those who have first hand experience of them enables the public to obtain sufficient information to participate fully in the democratic process.

As in the case of political speech, employer and public interests can be harmed by principled dissent. In many cases, the speaker will be criticising the employer's policies or practices. The employer will then have a personal interest in preventing the speech, and minimising any adverse public response. There may be a parallel public interest in reducing any workplace disruption caused by the speech. As with political speech, under current law, principled dissent is granted very little protection against work based sanctions. An employee disciplined or dismissed for engaging in such speech would not be protected by the PIDA and would instead be dependent on the more generalised unfair dismissal law. Again, as with political speech, dismissal would be likely to come within the range of reasonable responses to be expected of an employer, and any dismissal would be likely to be fair.

Such a result, however, fails to take into account the full value of this type of speech. In the same way that political speech can act as an additional form of accountability on the state, so principled dissent can improve employer accountability in more general terms. This is particularly the case where employers seek to influence their reputation with the public by creating a particular image, via advertising, or other publicity. For example, there is a growing trend in some industries, such as the clothing trade, to use social labels as part of the marketing strategy for a brand. Such labels inform the

---

[7] Discussed in detail in Chapter 6.

consumer about the conditions in which the goods are produced, and enable them to exercise choice in what they buy.[8] Consumers can avoid buying clothes produced using child labour, they can buy cleaning products which cause minimal environmental damage, and they can choose to buy fairly traded coffee, non-GM foods and organic vegetables. The use of social labels by businesses is not just a matter of public information: the cost of such products is usually higher, and the aim is to improve market share by appealing to those consumers who care enough about the particular issue to change their buying habits. If an employee believes that a particular label is undeserved, and publicises that view, there will be a cost to the business in terms of harm to its reputation and to any extra profits the label has generated. Alternatively, an employee may choose to publicise the fact that an employer has not signed up to a particular set of standards. In either case, the employer will have an interest in preventing the employee's disclosure. But in both cases there is a public interest in the disclosure of any claims that ethical or environmental standards are not being met. The subject matter of the disclosures may, in some cases, be covered by the PIDA, for example, if they involve breaches of health and safety standards; but where this is not the case the public interest in the information should be recognised. Any speech that involves such matters would not be political but could be termed principled dissent and should enjoy a degree of protection against work based penalties. Allowing employees to speak on such matters is an effective way to hold companies to account.

In some cases before the ECtHR, it has been suggested that the public interest is served by disclosing information that corrects the impression that a company has formed for itself. For example, in *Fayed v UK*[9] the point was made that where information had been used in public by the employer to build a favourable public reputation, they could not complain of moves to demonstrate that the information was false. Similarly, in *Bergens*[10] the ECtHR considered the fact that a favourable image had been presented to the public, giving rise to a corresponding public interest in indicating the falsity of that image where there was clear evidence to that effect. There are undoubtedly both public and private interests in restricting workplace protection for principled dissent, in terms of protecting the employer's autonomy and right to manage the business. But as domestic law currently stands, these interests seem to prevail over the public interests in freedom of expression, even though a much wider set of interests are served by principled dissent, particularly in terms of improved accountability of employers. The general public interest would be better protected if this were to be more widely recognised.

---

[8] J. Hilowitz, 'Social labelling to combat child labour: some considerations' (1997) 136 International Labour Review 215.
[9] (1994) 18 EHRR 393.
[10] *Bergens Tidende v Norway* (2001) 31 EHRR 16.

GENERAL COMMENT

The need for employment protection is less clear cut in the case of general comment made by the employee. The main philosophical basis for protecting such speech is that it upholds the personal autonomy of the speaker. However, this interest can easily be overridden in the employment context by the rights of the employer and the public interest in business efficacy, especially if the speech is liable to cause financial loss or disruption at work. Nonetheless, even where speech is of a purely personal type, it should only be possible for an employer to justify imposing restrictions on speech where the public interest or the interests of the employer are seriously infringed. The mere expression of a personal view should not lead to dismissal. Of course it would be unusual in practice for an employee to be dismissed purely for expressing a personal view, but it is worth noting that such speech is not covered by the PIDA, nor is it likely to be given great protection under the general rules on unfair dismissal, as any dismissal would be judged according to the 'range of reasonable responses' test. Views that might embarrass the employer, such as those expressed by Glen Hoddle about the causes of disability,[11] might lead some reasonable employers to dismiss. If an employee were to be penalised for the exercise of free speech in this way, he or she would find very limited legal protection available.

One particular difficulty for those who engage in the last three categories of speech, political speech, principled dissent, or general comment, is that for the speech to achieve its aim, it needs to be made publicly. Yet this very publicity will militate against the speech being protected. Where speech is made in public, it is more likely to infringe the employer's interests: it is more likely to cause economic loss and damage to the reputation of the enterprise; and it is liable to breach the duty of trust and confidence owed by employees to their employers, and thus to result in the employee being in breach of contract. Speech made in public is also more likely to lead to inefficiency in the running of the business if the employer has to deal with adverse publicity created by the speech, and any disruption to the workforce it may cause. Even if the speech includes reference to a matter covered by the PIDA, protection is more difficult to obtain where it is made externally. In the absence of the protection provided by unfair dismissal law or the PIDA, there is no reason, in the law as it currently stands, to prevent work based sanctions from being imposed for speech that is made in public. The legal position would be improved and the public interest better served if there could be greater recognition of the role of employee free speech in increasing accountability and supporting the democratic process.

---

[11] See the discussion in Chapter 1, and *The Guardian*, 30 January 1999 and 3 February 1999, and *The Observer*, 31 January 1999.

CONCLUSION

The legal protection for the right to free speech at work is limited to protection of the right to blow the whistle on wrongdoing or malpractice at work. The more general right to freedom of expression, as defined in the main international human rights documents, does not survive entry to the workplace, and is not adequately protected against work based sanctions. The position seems to be, rather, that the employee's right to free speech is protected via his freedom to leave his employment.

FUTURE DEVELOPMENTS

In Chapter 2, it was suggested that the optimal protection for freedom of speech at work would be provided by the creation of a specific right to protection against work based sanctions for the exercise of free speech. Such a right would address the tension between the public interest in protecting free speech and the public and private interests served by allowing employers freedom to manage their businesses by the creation of exceptions to the right where restrictions on speech would be proportionate. Proportionality would be determined by considering factors such as the subject matter of the speech, any loss caused to the employer, and whether the speech was made in public.

Although the creation of a broader right to free speech may be desirable to provide better protection for political and other speech, it is extremely unlikely to be introduced. This is especially the case after the introduction of the PIDA, which has removed the moral imperative that did exist for some action to be taken to protect employees against reprisals for work based speech. Instead, if there is to be increased protection for these other forms of speech it will need to evolve over time. There are three spheres in which better free speech protection could potentially develop. First is the interpretation of the PIDA by the courts, particularly in relation to the reasonableness of external disclosures. The second is the public interest exception to the duty of trust and confidence owed by employees to employers, which could reflect a broader understanding of the concept of public interest. The third area in which the law could develop better protection for free speech at work is in the test of reasonableness in the rules on unfair dismissal. In all three areas the impetus for positive developments for freedom of speech would be most likely to come from the Human Rights Act 1998, which enables current law to be interpreted so as to be compatible with the ECHR.

The HRA 1998 requires that legislation be interpreted to comply with the ECHR, Article 10 of which guarantees the right to freedom of expression. The scope of the right is limited by the restrictions in Article 10(2), and the protection for work based speech provided by Article 10 is not absolute.[12]

---

[12] See Chapter 3.

Restrictions have been allowed on speech, in particular for employees such as judges or government employees,[13] or where the speech has been made more publicly than necessary.[14] Nonetheless, in a number of areas the ECHR jurisprudence on freedom of speech has been identified as being wider than domestic law. The ECtHR puts greater emphasis on the importance of political speech,[15] and recognises a wider range of issues as being matters of public interest, such as the behaviour of prominent business people.[16] The ECtHR also recognises, perhaps more than our domestic courts, the need for the press and other media to act as watchdogs, to watch out for and report wrongdoing.[17]

INTERPRETING THE PIDA TO COMPLY WITH THE ECHR

The right to blow the whistle at work provided by the PIDA is fairly extensive, and there are few areas in which recourse to the jurisprudence of the ECHR to aid interpretation would be needed. The subject matters which are protected are set out clearly in the Act, and internal disclosures of information relating to these subject areas are given almost automatic protection. This leaves the question of whether an external disclosure is reasonable as the main area of the PIDA which is open to interpretation by the courts. The determination of whether external disclosure is reasonable needs to be made in line with the case law of the ECHR. The protection available to freedom of speech under the ECHR, and the requirement for any restriction to be proportionate to its aim, should be taken into account by domestic courts in deciding the question of reasonableness. For example, if a disclosure has political overtones a court might take into account the ECHR requirements for special protection for political speech, and find that a disclosure made to the media is reasonable, as long as an attempt had first been made to raise a matter internally, in accordance with the requirements of the PIDA.

DEVELOPING THE CONCEPT OF THE PUBLIC INTEREST TO REFLECT THE RIGHT TO FREE SPEECH

The subject matter of the speech is the major factor in determining the scope of the concept of the public interest, and thus the scope of the contract of employment. Domestic case law suggests that there must usually be an element of wrongdoing or danger disclosed by the speaker before the public interest is said to be served by a disclosure. Political significance is not sufficient.[18] Now that domestic law has to be interpreted to comply with the ECHR, with its emphasis on the importance of freedom of political speech for the

---

[13] *E v Switzerland* (1984) 38 D&R, *B v UK* (1986) 45 D&R 41.
[14] *Morrisens v Belgium* (1988) D&R 56.   [15] *Castells v Spain* (1992) 13 EHRR 445.
[16] *Fressoz and Roire v France* (2001) 31 EHRR 1; *Fayed v UK* (1994) 18 EHRR 393.
[17] *Thorgierson v Iceland* (1992) 14 EHRR 843, para 63; *Barthold v Germany* (1985) 7 EHRR 383, para 58; *Jersild v Denmark* (1995) 19 EHRR 1, para 31.
[18] *British Steel Corporation v Granada Television* [1981] AC 1097.

democratic process, it should be easier to argue for a broadening of the understanding of the public interest in protecting speech with a political dimension.

Reference to ECHR case law may also lead to a change in attitude in domestic courts towards public disclosure, particularly via the media. The emphasis on internal disclosures in the case law on confidentiality and the public interest does not cause difficulty to those who blow the whistle on wrongdoing, as concerns can be reported internally or to a regulatory body, unless serious and urgent, in which case external disclosure is accepted. More difficulty is faced by staff who voice political opinions, or principled dissent about work related issues. If their speech is to have any value, it needs to be made publicly, and yet this very publicity can militate against a finding that the speech serves the public interest. It may be helpful in such cases to refer to the recognition by the ECtHR of the significance of the role of the media in supporting freedom of speech.[19]

Determining where the public interest lies in any particular case of employee speech largely turns on the interaction between the subject matter and the channel of communication. The slight difference in emphasis by the ECtHR on both these issues, particularly when it comes to political speech, could lead to a broader understanding of the concept of the public interest in domestic courts, once the decisions of the ECtHR are taken into account in developing the common law.

DEVELOPING THE LAW ON UNFAIR DISMISSAL TO COMPLY WITH THE ECHR

In cases not covered by the PIDA, the question of whether a dismissal for exercising the right to free speech is fair should also be assessed with reference to the jurisprudence of the ECHR.[20] There are a number of changes that would need to be made for the law on unfair dismissal to comply with the standards set by the ECHR, with its greater emphasis on press freedom and the public interest in protecting political speech. First, the current standard against which dismissals are judged, that of the range of reasonable employer responses, would need to change, as it leaves very little scope for the case law of the ECHR to influence the standard of fairness applied by tribunals. Changing the standard of fairness from the 'range of reasonable responses' test would be simple, especially given the duty under the HRA on tribunals and courts to interpret legislation *as far as possible* to comply with the ECHR.[21] The traditional interpretation of the test of fairness is not the only

---

[19] *Thorgierson v Iceland* (1992) 14 EHRR 843, para 63; *Barthold v Germany* (1985) 7 EHRR 383, para 58; *Jersild v Denmark* (1995) 19 EHRR 1, para 31.

[20] Courts and tribunals are bound by the HRA 1998 s 6 as public authorities; courts and tribunals should take account of the jurisprudence of the ECtHR and the Commission in interpreting domestic law, s 2.

[21] HRA 1998 s 3(1).

possible interpretation of the test in ERA 1996 s 98(4). The statute merely requires that the tribunal decide if it was fair or not to dismiss for the reason given, having regard to equity and the substantial merits of the case; it does not set down that the standard should be that of a reasonable employer. Compliance with the ECHR would therefore not require a declaration of incompatibility, just that the test of fairness be interpreted more generously.

The Court of Appeal in *Post Office v Foley, HSBC Bank (formerly Midland Bank) v Madden*[22] makes clear that no change to the test is in contemplation. However, the cases did not involve human rights issues and did not refer to the HRA 1998. It might therefore be open to an employee who is dismissed for exercising the right to free speech to argue that in cases involving fundamental human rights, the Employment Rights Act 1996 should be interpreted to comply with the ECHR, and that the range of reasonable responses test should not be applied. Instead the tribunal should assess the fairness of dismissal giving proper weight to the right to free speech, rather than by reference to employer standards. A reinterpretation of the test of fairness, in the light of the jurisprudence of the ECHR, could significantly enhance the ability of the law on unfair dismissal to protect freedom of speech.

A move away from the 'range of reasonable responses' test would mean that the fairness of dismissals could be assessed taking into account the wider public interest in the speech as well as issues such as the legitimacy of the aim of the employer in dismissing the employee and the proportionality of the employer's response.[23] As suggested in Chapter 5, this would enable tribunals to play a greater role in setting standards for the review of dismissals, a role which is surely appropriate in cases involving the basic human rights of employees. The ECHR sets international standards for the protection of human rights, and these should be protected even if some reasonable employers would prefer it otherwise. As it currently operates, the 'range of reasonable responses' test allows the standard of protection to be lowered to reflect the prevailing level of protection for human rights at work in the business and industrial community. Instead, tribunals should be allowed to set good standards of protection, taking into account the competing public interests in business efficiency and freedom of expression. Of course, even if tribunals are afforded this greater freedom to set the standard of fairness in human rights cases, it will only aid employees dismissed for exercising the right to free speech to the extent that it is recognised that there is a public interest in protecting both political speech and principled dissent.

CONCLUSION

There are a number of prerequisites to any of the developments suggested above being made. First, domestic courts will need to accept that the ECHR

---

[22] [2000] IRLR 827 CA.
[23] See further, H. Collins, K. Ewing and A. McColgan, *Labour Law* (2001) Hart Publishing, Oxford, at 575.

applies to the employment relationship. This may be easier in relation to public sector employers than private sector, although it is quite arguable that under the HRA the Convention can be applied to both.[24] In any event, the case law of the ECHR itself has been uncertain on this issue. At times the ECtHR has relied on the freedom to leave employment to safeguard the employee's human rights,[25] and on other occasions has recognised that the threat of dismissal can act as a significant chill on freedom of expression.[26] Similar uncertainty has been seen in the decisions on whether employees can contract out of their right to free speech at work by signing confidentiality clauses.[27] If the right to free speech is to be given improved protection in domestic law, courts and tribunals will need to accept both that the ECHR applies to the employment relationship and that employees cannot contract out of the rights it contains.

Secondly, the potential for employee speech to serve the public interest needs to gain wider acceptance. This requires a recognition of the contribution that free speech can make to discovering truth, preserving autonomy, improving accountability and upholding democracy. Throughout this book, the argument has been made that employees can play an important role in monitoring the impact of government policies, with their first hand experience of putting them into effect, and their speech can act as a form of accountability on the state. Although this argument does not apply directly to private or commercial information, such information can also enrich public debate on issues of public importance. This is particularly the case where speech relates to the large corporations which are so powerful in our society. It is quite arguable that the accountability that freedom of expression provides for the state should be extended to parts of the private sector. This is not to argue for unfettered freedom of speech for employees, but merely makes the point that the public interest in allowing free speech needs to be given proper weight when set against the employer's right to dismiss. Unless these arguments are accepted by the courts, increased reference to the ECHR and changes in the tests applied by employment tribunals in assessing fairness will not lead to greater protection for freedom of speech at work.

The final prerequisite to changes in the law is a greater recognition of the need to protect autonomy in the workplace. There are two contradictory moves in this regard in contemporary employment law. Pulling in one direction are the unfair dismissal cases. The effect of the recent restatement of the 'range of reasonable responses' test[28] has been to reassert the power of managerial prerogative in the employment relationship. Pulling in the other

---

[24] See Chapter 3.

[25] *Ahmad v UK* (1981) 4 EHRR 126; *Stedman v UK* (1997) 23 EHRR CD 168.

[26] *Van Der Heijden v the Netherlands* (1985) D&R 101; *X v Germany* 9228/80 (1983) 5 EHRR 471; *Vogt v Germany* (1996) 21 EHRR 205.

[27] *Rommelfanger v FDR* (1989) 62 D&R 151.

[28] *Post Office v Foley, HSBC Bank (formerly Midland Bank) v Madden* [2000] IRLR 827 CA.

direction is the case *Malik v BCCI SA*[29] and those that have followed it,[30] in which the responsibility of the employer for the employee has been expanded in the guise of the duty of mutual trust and confidence. These cases suggest greater recognition of the whole person of the employee, with a future career or retirement ahead, and with a reputation that may be injured. These cases suggest a trend towards greater recognition in employment law of employee autonomy.

Currently these competing trends in favour of recognising employer prerogative and recognising employee autonomy have not been cast in direct conflict with each other, as they arise in different contexts, the former in the context of the fairness of dismissal, the latter in determining the scope of the contract of employment. However, as reflections of a general approach to the employment relationship, they do seem to be following divergent paths, and only time will tell which will prevail. If, as has been suggested, the duty of mutual trust and confidence is interpreted, in accordance with the Human Rights Act, to include a duty on the part of employers to comply with the European Convention on Human Rights[31] it may be that the recognition of employee autonomy will gain ascendancy. If that is the case, there may be grounds for cautious optimism that a wider understanding of the public interest in providing greater protection for the freedom of speech of employees will, in time, be recognised in our courts.

---

[29] [1997] IRLR 462.
[30] For example, *TSB Bank PLC v Harris* [2000] IRLR 157 on the duty to provide a fair reference for an employee.
[31] B. Hepple, 'Human Rights and Employment Law' (8 June 1998) Amicus Curiae, at 19–23.

Bibliography

Alcock, A., *A History of the ILO* (1971) Macmillan, London

Aleinikoff, T., 'Constitutional Law in the Age of Balancing' (1987) 96 Yale LJ 943

Baker, Edwin, C., *Human Liberty and Freedom of Speech* (1989) Oxford University Press, Oxford

Barendt, E., *Freedom of Speech* (1985) Clarendon Press, Oxford

Birkinshaw, P., *Freedom Of Information: The Law, the Practice and the Ideal* (2001) Butterworths, London

Blades, L., 'Employment At Will vs. Individual Freedom: On Limiting the Abusive Exercise of Employer Power' (1967) Columbia Law Review 1404

Blumberg, P., 'Corporate Responsibility and the Employee's Duty of Loyalty and Obedience: A Preliminary Inquiry' (1971) 24 Oklahoma Law Review 279

Bowers, J. and Clarke, A., 'Unfair Dismissal and Managerial Prerogative: A Study of "Other Substantial Reason"' (1981) 10 ILJ 4

Bowers, J., Mitchell, J. and Lewis, J., *Whistleblowing: The New Law* (1999) Sweet and Maxwell, London

Browne-Wilkinson, N., 'The Infiltration of a Bill of Rights' (1992) PL 397

Carter-Ruck, P., *Peter Carter-Ruck on Libel and Slander* (4th edn, 1992) Butterworths, London

Clapham, A., *Human Rights in the Private Sphere* (1993) Oxford University Press, Oxford

Clapham, A., 'The Privatisation of Human Rights' (1995) EHRLR 20

Clayton, G. and Pitt, G., 'Dress Codes and Freedom of Expression' (1997) EHRLR 54

Collins, H., Ewing, K. and McColgan, A., *Labour Law* (2001) Hart Publishing, Oxford

Collins, H., *Justice in Dismissal* (1992) Clarendon Press, Oxford

Collins, H., 'Market Power, Bureaucratic Power and the Contract of Employment' (1986) 15 ILJ 1

Cornford, T., 'The Freedom of Information Act 2000: Genuine or Sham?' (2001) 3 Web JCLI

Court Inquiry, Department of Transport, Ct No 8074, 1987 HMSO

Craig, P., 'Public Law and Control over Private Power' in Taggart, M. (ed), *The Province of Administrative Law* (1997) Hart Publishing, Oxford

Cripps, Y., *Legal Implications of Disclosure in the Public Interest* (2nd edn, 1994) Sweet & Maxwell, London

Cross, R., *Statutory Interpretation* (3rd edn, 1995) Butterworths, London

Davies, P. and Freedland, M., *Labour Legislation and Public Policy* (1993) Clarendon Press, Oxford

Davies, P. and Freedland, M., 'The Impact of Public Law on Labour Law 1972–1997' (1997) ILJ 311

Deakin, S. and Morris, G., *Labour Law* (2001) Butterworths, London

Dicey, A., *Introduction to the Law of the Constitution* (10th edn, 1959) Macmillan, London

Dickens, L., Jones, M., Weekes, B. and Hart, M., *Dismissed: A Study of Unfair Dismissal and the Industrial Tribunal System* (1985) Blackwell, Oxford

Dworkin, R., *Taking Rights Seriously* (1977) Duckworth Press, London

Elias, P., 'Fairness in Unfair Dismissal: Trends and Tensions' (1981) 10 ILJ 201 at 213

Emerson, T., *The System of Freedom of Expression* (1970) Random House, New York

Epstein, R., 'In defense of the contract at will' (1984) 51 University of Chicago LR 947

Ewing, K. (ed), *Human Rights at Work* (2000) Institute of Employment Rights, London

Ewing, K., 'The Human Rights Act and Parliamentary Democracy' (1999) 62 MLR 79

Feldman, D., *Civil Liberties and Human Rights in England and Wales* (1993) Oxford University Press, Oxford

First Report of the Committee on Standards in Public Life, 1995, HMSO Cm 2850 I-II

Fiss, O., *Liberalism Divided: Freedom of Speech and the Many Uses of State Power* (1996) Westview Press, Boulder, Colorado; Oxford

Flanders, A., 'The Tradition of Voluntarism' (1974) 12 British Journal of Industrial Relations 352

Fredman, S. and Lee, S., 'Natural Justice for Employees: The Unacceptable Faith of Proceduralism' (1986) 15 ILJ 15

Fredman, S. and Morris, G., *The State as Employer: Labour Law in the Public Services* (1989) Mansell, London

Ganz, G., 'The Depoliticisation Of Local Authorities: The Local Government And Housing Act 1989 Part I' (1988) PL 225

Gearty, C., 'The Human Rights Act 1998: An Overview' in K. Ewing (ed), *Human Rights at Work* (2000) Institute of Employment Rights, London

Glick, C., 'Free Speech, the Private Employee and State Constitutions' (1982) 91 Yale LJ 522

Gobert, J. and Punch, M., 'Whistleblowers, the Public Interest and the Public Interest Disclosure Act' (2000) 63 MLR 25

Government Response to the First Report of the Committee on Standards in Public Life, 1995, HMSO Cm 2931

Grief, N., 'The Domestic Impact of the European Convention on Human Rights as Mediated Through Community Law' (1991) PL 555

Harris, D., O'Boyle, M. and Warbrick, C., *The Law of the European Convention on Human Rights* (1995) Butterworths, London

Hepple, B., 'Human Rights and Employment Law', Amicus Curiae (8 June 1998) 19

Hilowitz, J., 'Social labelling to combat child labour: some considerations' (1997) 136 International Labour Review 215

Hooper, D., *Official Secrets; Use and Abuse of the Act* (1988) Coronet, London

Hunt, M., 'The "Horizontal Effect" of the Human Rights Act' (1998) PL 423

Hunt, M., 'The Human Rights Act and Legal Culture: The Judiciary and the Legal Profession' (1999) JLS 86

Hunt, M., *Using Human Rights Law in English Courts* (1997) Hart Publishing, Oxford

IDS Employment Supplement 72, *Employee Competition and Confidentiality*, Incomes Data Services Ltd, December 1994

Inquiry into the Supervision of The Bank of Credit and Commerce International, 2 October 1992, HMSO, 198

Investigation into the Clapham Junction Railway Accident, November 1989, HMSO Cm 820

Jones, T., 'The Devaluation of Human Rights Under the European Convention' (1995) PL 430

Lavender, N., 'The Problem of the Margin of Appreciation' (1997) EHRLR 380

Leary, V. A., 'The Paradox of Workers' Rights as Human Rights', in L. A. Compa and S. F. Diamond, *Human Rights, Labor Rights and International Trade* (1996) University of Pennsylvania Press, Pennsylvania

Lennane, K., ' "Whistleblowing": a health issue' (1993) 307 *BMJ* 667

Lester, A., 'Universality versus Subsidiarity: A Reply' (1998) EHRLR 73

Lewis, D. (ed), *Whistleblowing at Work* (2001) Athlone Press, London

Lewis, D., 'The Public Interest Disclosure Act 1998' (1998) 27 ILJ 325

Lewis, D., 'Whistleblowing at Work: On What Principles Should Legislation Be Based?' (2001) 30 ILJ 169

Lindsay, J., 'The Implied Term of Trust and Confidence' (2001) ILJ 1

McColgan, A., 'Article 10 and the right to freedom of expression: workers ungagged?', in K. Ewing (ed), *Human Rights at Work* (2000) Institute of Employment Rights, London

Mahoney, P., 'Universality versus Subsidiarity in the Strasbourg Case Law on Free Speech: Explaining Some Recent Judgments' (1997) EHRLR 364

Marshall, G., 'Interpreting Interpretation in the Human Rights Bill' (1998) PL 167

Meiklejohn, A., *Free Speech and its Relation to Self Government* (1972) Kennikat Press, New York

Miceli, M. and Near, J., *Blowing the Whistle: The Organisational and Legal Implications for Companies and Employees* (1992) Lexington Books; Maxwell Macmillan International, New York and Oxford

Mill, J. S., 'On Liberty' in S. Collini (ed), *On Liberty and Other Writings* (1989) Cambridge University Press, Cambridge

Milton, J., *Areopagitica and other prose works* (1927) Dent and Sons, London

Morris, G., 'Political Activities of Public Servants and Freedom of Expression' in I. Loveland, *Importing the First Amendment* (1998) Hart Publishing, Oxford

Morris, G. and Fredman, S., 'Public or Private? State Employees and Judicial Review' (1991) 107 LQR 298

Morris, G. and Fredman, S., 'The Costs of Exclusivity' (1994) PL 69

Morris, G., 'Fundamental Rights: Exclusion by Agreement?' (2001) ILJ 49

Morris, G., 'The Human Rights Act and the Public/Private Divide in Employment Law' (1998) ILJ 293

Morris, G., 'The political activities of local government workers and the European Convention on Human Rights' (1999) PL 211

Napier, B., 'AIDS, Discrimination and Employment Law' (1989) 18 ILJ 84

O'Donnell, T., 'The Margin of Appreciation Doctrine: Standard in the Jurisprudence of the European Court of Human Rights' (1982) Human Rights Quarterly 474

Oliver, D., 'Common Values in Public and Private Law and the Public/Private Divide' (1997) PL 630

Oliver, D., 'The Human Rights Act and Public Law/Private Law Divides' (2000) EHRLR 343

Palmer, S., 'Tightening the Secrecy Law: The Official Secrets Act 1989' (1990) PL 243

Palmer, S., 'Human Rights: Implications for Labour Law' (2000) CLJ 168

Palmer, S., 'In the Interests of the State: The Government's Proposals for reforming Section 2 of the Official Secrets Act 1911' (1988) PL 523

Pasman, N., 'The Public Interest Exception to the Employment at Will Doctrine: From crime victims to whistleblowers, will the real public policy please stand up?' (1993) 70 University of Detroit Mercy LR 559

Pitt, G., *Employment Law* (1997) Sweet & Maxwell, London

Ponting, C., *The Right to Know: The Inside Story of the Belgrano Affair* (1985) Phere, London

Public Concern at Work, *Local Government: Blowing the whistle on fraud and corruption*, London, 1994

Raz, J., *The Morality of Freedom* (1986) Clarendon Press, Oxford

Report of the Committee of Inquiry into Complaints about Ashworth Special Hospital, August 1992, HMSO Cm 2028-1

Rimmington, S., *Open Secret* (2001) Hutchinson, London

Rongine, N., 'Toward a coherent legal response to the public policy dilemma posed by whistleblowing' (1985) 23 American Business Law Journal 281

Royal College of Nursing, *Whistleblow*, Report on the Work of the RCN Whistleblow Scheme (1992) London

Scanlon, T., 'A Theory of Freedom of Expression' in R. M. Dworkin (ed), *The Philosophy of Law* (1977) Oxford University Press, Oxford

Schauer, F., *Free Speech: A Philosophical Enquiry* (1982) Cambridge University Press, Cambridge

Simpson, A. W. B., *Human Rights and the End of Empire* (2001) Oxford University Press, Oxford

Sims, V., 'Is Employment a Fiduciary Relationship?' (2001) ILJ 101

Singh, R., *The Future of Human Rights in the United Kingdom* (1997) Hart Publishing, Oxford

The Public Inquiry into the Piper Alpha Disaster, November 1990, HMSO Cm 131

Thomas, R., *Espionage and Secrecy: The Official Secrets Acts 1911–1989 of the United Kingdom* (1991) Routledge, London

Tushnet, M., 'Anti-Formalism in Recent Constitutional Theory' (1985) 83 Michigan LR 1502

US General Accounting Office, *Whistleblower Protection: Determining whether reprisal occurred remains difficult*, October 1992

Van Dijk, P. and van Hoof, G., *Theory and Practice of the European Convention on Human Rights* (2nd edn, 1990) Kluwer, the Netherlands

Watt, R., 'HIV, Discrimination, Unfair Dismissal and Pressure to Dismiss' (1992) 21 ILJ 280

Wedderburn, W., *Labour Law and Freedom* (1995) Lawrence and Wishart, London

Wells, C., *Corporations and Criminal Liability* (1993) Oxford University Press, Oxford

Woolf, H., 'Public Law—Private Law: Why the Divide?' (1986) PL 220

Yourow, H., *The Margin of Appreciation Doctrine in the Dynamics of European Human Rights Jurisprudence* (1996) Kluwer Law International, The Hague; London

Index